Martyrdom in the Modern Middle East

Sasha Dehghani – Silvia Horsch (Eds.)

EX ORIENTE LUX

REZEPTIONEN UND EXEGESEN ALS TRADITIONSKRITIK

herausgegeben
von

Eli Bar-Chen   Almut Sh. Bruckstein   Navid Kermani
Angelika Neuwirth   Andreas Pflitsch   Martin Tamcke

Schriftenreihe des Projekts
„Islamische und jüdische Hermeneutik als Kulturkritik /
Islamic and Jewish Hermeneutics as Cultural Critique",
Arbeitskreis Moderne und Islam am Wissenschaftskolleg zu Berlin

BAND 14

ERGON VERLAG

Martyrdom in the Modern Middle East

Sasha Dehghani – Silvia Horsch (Eds.)

ERGON VERLAG

Die Drucklegung dieses Bandes wurde vom Bundesministerium für Bildung und Forschung unter dem Förderkennzeichen 01UG0712 unterstützt, die Verantwortung für die Inhalte tragen die Autoren.

Bibliografische Information der Deutschen Nationalbibliothek
Die Deutsche Nationalbibliothek verzeichnet diese Publikation in der
Deutschen Nationalbibliografie; detaillierte bibliografische Daten sind
im Internet über http://dnb.d-nb.de abrufbar.

Bibliographic information published by the Deutsche Nationalbibliothek
The Deutsche Nationalbibliothek lists this publication in the
Deutsche Nationalbibliografie; detailed bibliographic data
are available in the Internet at http://dnb.dnb.de.

ISBN 978-3-95650-030-5
ISSN 1863-9348

Content

Introduction

Part of the significance of the figure of the martyr in the Middle East is without doubt its long tradition. Not only can it be traced back to the early days of Islam, but it developed out of interaction with older religious and cultural traditions. Martyrdom belongs to the terms and concepts of religion in general, especially the monotheist religions and here in particular Christianity. The Greek term "martys", taken from the judicial sphere and used in the sense of "blood witness", was coined during the persecution of the Christians in the second century CE. In Islamic history – at least with regard to majority Sunni Islam – readiness to engage in combat became more essential than readiness to suffer due to the different historical situation and subsequent development, beginning with the emigration of the early Muslim community to Medina. For this reason the most influential *shahīd* (again a term denominating the witness in the judicial sphere) became the figure of the fallen fighter, even though anybody dying an untimely death, whether from natural disasters or epidemic diseases, as well as victims of violence, is also considered a martyr. Whereas in Sunni Islam a fully-fledged martyr cult did not develop before the onset of modernity, the case is different with Shiite Islam, in which Ḥusayn's martyrdom is the pivotal theme.

The respective religious scholars and authorities provide more or less normative definitions as to who is to be regarded as a martyr. But as history has shown, not only the veneration and commemoration of martyrs fails to hold to the line laid out by religious authorities; rather, martyrdom is a highly contested field within the respective religions as well. The historicity of normative concepts is furthermore linked to the competitive position vis-à-vis other religions. As paradigmatic examples for others, the place assigned to the martyrs is the very center of their communities; for that however, they also act in the border areas running between different religions and cultures. As such, martyr figures are not only agents of demarcation but at the same time of entanglement and mediation. This mediation occurs not only synchronously between different religious and cultural traditions but also diachronically between different eras which are, supposedly at least, to be clearly delimited from one another. The hybrid figure of the martyr calls into question the demarcations between pre-modern and modern as well as those between religion and the secular.

The prominent place the martyr occupies in conflicts of modern times is often described as a "recurrence of martyrs", and perceived as a "backslide" into a pre-modern way of thinking. However, not only have the historical and political circumstances changed due to the modern developments of industrialisation, colonialism and nation-state building, but with the advent of mass media and new techniques of image production the media conditions for the 'making of martyrs' have also altered. Hence, the inclusion of traditional cultic, legal or narrative elements into current discourses on martyrdom can be described more aptly as adaptations or re-stagings. Rhetoric and iconographic forms derived from the religious tradition are re-envisioned or gain a modified function in the respective contexts.

These developments and transformations of the concept, the historic manifestations and the cultural specifics of the martyr figure, lie in the field of interest of cultural studies. In research on martyrdom from this perspective there are no "true" or "false" martyrs but events regarded as martyrdom and individuals seen by their respective communities as martyrs insofar as they are accorded some kind of commemoration or veneration that relates to their death as having taken place for a cause – irrespective of whether it is religious cause. Martyrdom is a powerful concept in part because it can bestow meaning upon a violent and unnatural death. Sometimes there are people who consider themselves martyrs prior to their deaths and who take particular discursive actions designed to prompt their posthumous veneration. Martyrdom can thus be described as a cultural practice and pattern of interpretation, which belongs to the sphere of religion but cannot be fully understood in exclusively religious terms. The role of religion is even more sophisticated in modernity, where we have pointedly secular communities and movements in which martyr figures nonetheless play an important role. Religion, however, not only keeps ready at hand concepts, images and ritual forms on which the martyr cult draws, but at the same offers a critique of 'illegitimate' martyrdom which can be used – at least potentially – to keep the phenomenon of martyrdom in check.

The present volume assembles the revised presentations given at the workshop "Traditions of Martyrdom in the Modern Middle East" as well as some additional contributions. It brings together contributions from different academic perspectives (religious and Islamic studies, literary and theatre studies, theology, sociology and history) on modern manifestations of martyrdom in diverse Middle Eastern religious traditions, including Islam, Christianity and the Bahā'ī Faith. The latter is considered in some detail since it is often underrepresented in comparative studies on the monotheistic religions. The workshop was conducted at the Center for Literary and Cultural Studies (Berlin) in cooperation with the Free University Berlin in October 2011 and was part of the research project "Figurations of the Martyr in Near Eastern and European Literature" sponsored by the German Research Foundation (DFG), a project conducted under the direction of Sigrid Weigel (Center for Literary and Cultural Studies) and Angelika Neuwirth (Free University Berlin) since 2005. We would like to thank our colleagues at the Center for Literary and Cultural Studies for their inspiration, which informed a variety of aspects, and the participants for their readiness to contribute to the workshop and the volume. We also wish to express our appreciation to the Center for Literary and Cultural Studies for providing the funds for the publication of this volume. Furthermore, we owe gratitude to Paul Bowman for proofreading the English, Sarah Anne Rennick for proofreading the article by Alice Bombardier, Jean Sinico for proofreading the last article, as well as Shahin Misbah for providing the transcription of some Iran-related articles of this volume.

The transliteration of Arabic and Persian terms and names is based on the system for Arabic of the Deutsche Morgenländische Gesellschaft (DMG), with a number of changes due to the English usage of Arabic words (th, j, kh, dh, sh, and gh instead of ṯ, ǧ, ḥ, ḏ, š, and ġ). The four additional Persian letters are transliterated according to the system for Persian of the DMG. Word endings (such as *tāʾ marbūṭa* or the *nisba* ending) of Arabic terms used within an Iranian context, have been transliterated according to the guidelines of the International Journal of Middle Eastern Studies (IJMES). Moreover the Arabic article is not assimilated. Names of present prominent figures, authors, artists, organisations and well-known places are in most cases not transliterated, but rendered as they appear in English (or French) bibliographical references and literature. The same applies to terms which are lexicalised in the English language (like Imam, sharia, jihad, Koran, Shiite etc.). A certain inconsistency was unavoidable however, but we trust that this will not bother the patient expert who in any case knows the Arabic and Persian form. Dates are in many cases supplied in both forms, the first being the Hijri year and the second the Christian or Common Era year. Where only one date is given it is according the Common Era.

I. Martyrdom in the Bahāʾī Faith

The Bahāʾī Faith is in itself inextricably linked to modernity as Sasha Dehghani shows in his contribution. Not only did it develop in the modern age, but it responds in its teachings to some of the major questions of modernity such as the claims of science, world peace and women's rights. Whereas a host of transformative elements results from these links to modernity, among them the abolishment of military jihad, elements of continuity can be found in the concept of martyrdom which has its prototype in early Christianity and mystical Islam.

From mystical Islam stems the ideal of servanthood, which is preferred over a concept of martyrdom that includes physical death. Per-Olof Åkerdahl discusses the aspect of servanthood and also considers the ideological motivations for the persecution of the Bahāʾīs in different socio-historical circumstances.

Moojan Momen concentrates on the time after the Islamic Revolution in Iran and discusses two opposed models of martyrdom, that of the ruling elite and that of the Bahāʾī community. He shows that the Bahāʾī martyrdom narrative is closer to the traditional Shiite martyrdom narrative, whereas the modern Shiite martyrdom narrative, designed to keep alive the revolutionary spirit, departs in significant ways from Shiite tradition.

II. *Witnessing and Sacrifice:*
Theological and Philosophical Implications of Martyrdom

Angelika Neuwirth's contribution considers paradigmatic differences between Sunni and Shiite Islam apparent in their respective – elaborated or missing – narratives of sacrifice. In Sunni Islam only a rudimentary sacrificial paradigm developed because of its de-mythologizing tendency; this changed, however, in the 20th century, especially in Palestine, where in reaction to the loss of land a modern myth of martyrdom was created drawing from different religious traditions, nationalist culture and mystic love poetry.

The concept of witnessing is at the centre of Joachim Negel's theological considerations. In the face of the hybrid phenomena addressed as martyrdom, he presents normative criteria for the Christian concept of witnessing and considers a modern incident of martyrdom where he finds these criteria manifested in an ideal way. Inquiring into the existential dimension, he argues for an irreducible meaning of witnessing: the reasons for the readiness for death coincide with the reasons for life.

The question of what it is worth dying for is addressed from a different perspective by Faisal Devji, who starts from the intriguing observation that both Muslim extremists and Ghandi argue that they love death more than life. While they refer, of course, to antithetic actions, the underlying concepts of sacrifice share a critique of the modern concept of humanity and human rights. Whereas the element of murder lends the sacrificial act an instrumental quality, it is not a means to some end but an act of sovereignty in itself in the case of nonviolent suffering promoted by Ghandi.

III. *Visual Representations: Ritual, the Arts and New Media*

Ta'ziyih is the 400-year-old ritualised theatrical performance commemorating the martyrdom of Ḥusayn and his family in Iran, practised until today. Maryam Palizban elucidates the features of *ta'ziyih*, the mythological traditions and rituals it draws on and focuses on the distinctive performative processes which affect not only the protagonists but also the audience during the re-enactment of a historical martyrdom.

Alice Bombardier shows how the blending of modern revolutionary Shiite ideology and the old mystical notion of the Perfect Man affects the work of revolutionary Iranian painters as well as their self-conception as artists. In paintings praising martyrdom from the 1980s a parallel is drawn between the process of martyrdom and the spiritual ascent to the model of the Perfect Man.

The Jihadist martyr cult flourishing in contemporary media is the topic of Silvia Horsch's contribution. She focuses on how the two dimensions of salvation, personal and collective, which are central in the thought 'Abdallāh 'Azzām, the main ideologue of Jihadism, are addressed and put into images. Not only these visual elements, but indeed the Jihadist martyr concept itself, can be described as an amalgamation of classical Islamic traditions and modern discourses.

IV. Political Action and Ideological Discourse

The notion of martyrdom in Islam underwent a number of changes in modernity, as Farhad Khosrokhavar explicates in his contribution. It was turned into a means for generating revolutionary (mass) mobilisation, which has often been violent, but it has also occurred in a nonviolent fashion. The 'Arab spring' was accompanied by numerous incidents of nonviolent martyrdom, which he analyses according to different paradigms.

Lisa Franke considers the dimension of gender in martyrdom with regard to the figure of the "self-sacrificer" (*istishhādī*) or "suicide bomber". She analyses how the female *istishhādiyyāt* of the Second Intifada are integrated into the Palestinian discourse on martyrdom, in which ways its distinctive religious and nationalist elements are applied to them and whether the gender relations in society are affected.

Silvia Horsch considers the global circulation and transformation of two extreme martyrdom practices – self-immolation and suicide bombing – and the accompanying discourse about them as well as the nonviolent martyrs of the Iranian (2009) and Arab (2010/2011) uprisings. Here the focus lies on the relation of religious and secular aspects in the practices and the accompanying discourses, which is a complex one inasmuch martyr figures tend to question the distinction drawn between the secular and the religious.

Sasha Dehghani / Silvia Horsch

I.
Continuity and Transformation:
Martyrdom in the Bahā'ī Faith

The Birth of a Monotheistic Religion in Modernity

On Jihad and Martyrdom in the Bahā'ī Faith

Sasha Dehghani (Berlin)

I. Religion, Modernity and Violence

1. Weber and Goldziher: a classification of the Bahā'ī Faith

At the beginning of the 1920s Marianne Weber edited *Wirtschaft und Gesellschaft*, a posthumously published compilation of research materials written by her husband Max Weber (d. 1920), one of the founding figures of German sociology. In a brief remark at the beginning of this work we learn how he viewed the Bahā'ī Faith. Weber writes: "By harmonising religion with Modernity and reclaiming its place in the modern world, the Baha'i Faith and the Salafiyya intend to infuse a disenchanted world with a new spirit. In their visions of a future world order based on divine principles, they dream of a return from society (*Gesellschaft*) to community (*Gemeinschaft*)."[1]

Weber's statement is multilayered and lends itself to the discussion of two different points with respect to the Bahā'ī Faith. The first relates to Weber's enumeration of the Bahā'ī Faith alongside the Muslim Salafiyya, a comparison which requires consideration of an accurate classification of the Bahā'ī Faith. The second concerns the relationship of the Bahā'ī Faith to Modernity, the context within which the subject of monotheism and violence will be looked at.

Weber's lumping of the Bahā'ī Faith with the Salafiyya would be seriously misleading unless read in light of Ignaz Goldziher's *Vorlesungen über den Islam*, Weber's main source on developments then taking place in the Islamic world.[2] Goldziher' *Vorlesungen*, which were published in 1910, included a relatively detailed account of the Muslim Salafiyya, strongly focusing on the Wahhābiyya movement formed in the late 18th century on the Arabian Peninsula, as well as some information on the Bahā'ī Faith. During Goldziher's lifetime the Sunni Salafiyya movement had become famous due to the Islamic reformer Muḥammad ʿAbduh (1905) and his friend and teacher Jamāl al-Dīn al-Afghānī (1897), both of whom believed that the Koranic revelation was to be considered

---

[1] English translation cited in Oliver Scharbrodt, *Islam and the Baha'i Faith: A Comparative Study of Muḥammad ʿAbduh and ʿAbdu-l-Baha ʿAbbas*, London 2008, 175. Scharbrodt refers to Max Weber, *Wirtschaft und Gesellschaft*, vol. 1, second edition, Tübingen 1925, 21ff.

[2] Hans Kippenberg's afterword to Max Weber, *Wirtschaft und Gesellschaft. Religiöse Gemeinschaften*, Tübingen 2005, 178.

the main source for the happiness of civilisation in every age of humanity.[3] Furthermore, al-Kawākibī (1902), another proponent of the Salafiyya, had integrated particular teachings of the Wahhābiyya into the Egyptian Salafiyya ideology,[4] thereby adding to its publicity. Thus a reader of Weber's comment, who is aware that "Salafiyya" here either refers to ʿAbduh and Afghānī or to the pietistic Wahhābiyya movement, could be tempted to classify the Bahā'ī Faith as just another contemporary Islamic reformist movement. Reading Weber's statement in light of Goldziher's *Vorlesungen* however helps to correct such a view.

While the reformation of the Islamic world could be regarded as one goal of the Bahā'ī Faith, its chief objective went far beyond that of a Muslim reformist enterprise. The messianic renewal claimed and envisaged by the central figures of the Bahā'ī Faith transcended Islam and was universal in nature. Consequently, the prophetic claim of Bahā'u'llāh (d. 1892), the central founding figure of the Bahā'ī Faith — as well as the claim of his herald, the Bāb (d. 1850), and the role of his eldest son and authorised interpreter ʿAbdu'l-Bahā (d. 1921) — differed immensely from the *ijtihād* of an Egyptian al-Azhar scholar or the conspiring mindset of a pan-Islamic Iranian activist. It left the confines of Islamic doctrine based on the belief of the finality of Muhammad's prophethood and led to the foundation of a new world religion, as Goldziher had discerned in his *Vorlesungen* when he wrote that Bahā'u'llāh had laid down the "design for a new world religion."[5]

Moreover, unlike Weber, Goldziher accentuated another key difference between the Salafiyya and the Bahā'ī Faith. Whereas the Islamic reformers yearned for a return to the classical order of their pious ancestors *(al-salaf al-ṣāliḥ)*, the Bahā'ī religion offered the idea of a progressively advancing human civilisation. To reach the state of a Golden Age the Salafists looked to the past, while the Bahā'ī vision was oriented on the future.[6] For the Bahā'ī Faith, the concept of a Golden Age included the construction of a world order in the future — as Weber correctly noted — understood in terms of a world civilisation representing the fruit of a new monotheistic revelation,[7] a concept that would have been inconceivable for a classical Muslim reformist movement.

Indeed, the extent to which the differences between the Bahā'ī Faith and the Muslim Salafiyya outweighed their similarities became glaringly clear in 1925,

---

[3]   Whereas in his *Vorlesungen* Goldziher dealt with ʿAbduh in a rather superficial way, in his later work, *Richtungen der Islamischen Koranauslegung*, he analyzed ʿAbduh's teachings in greater detail; see Ignaz Goldziher, *Richtungen der Islamischen Koranauslegung: An der Universität Upsala gehaltene Olaus-Petri-Vorlesungen*, Leiden 1920, 344.

[4]   See Reinhardt Schulze, *A Modern History of the Islamic World*, London 2002, 24ff. Albert Hourani, *Arabic Thought in the Liberal Age*, Oxford 1962, chapters 5-7.

[5]   In German: "[...] schritt Beha zur Entwerfung einer Weltreligion". See Ignaz Goldziher, *Vorlesungen über den Islam*, Heidelberg 1925, 276.

[6]   Ibid. 271.

[7]   For the concept of a Golden Age in Bahā'ī writings, see Ali Nakhjavani, *Towards World Order*, Acuto 2004, chapter 1.

when Egyptian Muftis issued a historical *fatwa* stating that "the Bahā'ī religion is a new religion standing on its own" (*dīn jadīd qā'im bi-dhātihi*) with "beliefs, principles and laws" (*aqā'id wa uṣūl wa aḥkām*) differing entirely from those of the Islamic religion. Furthermore: "In the same way as you do not call a Buddhist, a Brahman or a Christian a Muslim and vice versa, you do not call a Bahā'ī a Muslim and vice versa."[8] Hence, Bahā'īs and Muslim clerics agreed on the independent nature of the Bahā'ī religion[9], and, up to a certain extent, Goldziher's *Vorlesungen* were in line with this classification. Nevertheless, Western academic scholars contemporary to Weber and Goldziher continued to interpret the Bahā'īs as a new Muslim reformist group or a new division of Twelver Shiism for some years. It was only after the experience of the Third Reich —during which the Nazi government dissolved the German Bahā'ī community — that leading German theologians and professors of religious studies, such as Friedrich Heiler, Helmut Glasenapp and Gerhard Rosenkranz, finally emphasised the independence of the Bahā'ī Faith from its Islamic mother religion.[10]

2. The matryoshka *effect*

The second notable aspect of Weber's statement is the positioning of the Bahā'ī Faith in the context of Modernity. But since Weber did not give a substantive explanation of why the Bahā'ī Faith should be seen as a religion in harmony with Modernity, intending to infuse a new spirit into a "disenchanted world", we must move a century forward to the German historian Jürgen Osterhammel. In his impressive study on 19th-century global history, *Die Verwandlung der Welt* (*The Transformation of the World*), Osterhammel presents the 'derivation' missing in Weber's work.

Osterhammel maintains that the Bahā'ī Faith should be regarded as one of the rare modern religious creations that have lasted to our day.[11] He speaks of Bahā'u'llāh as one of the great "lateral thinkers" (*Querdenker*) of his time, who went far beyond the patterns of thought common to his age,[12] and attributes a spirit of Modernity to the religion of Bahā'u'llāh because of its main principles.

---

[8] Extracts of the original text are cited in Shoghi Effendi, *Tawqī'āt-i Mubārakih (1927-1939)*, Tehran 1973, 16. I would like to thank Dr. Omid Ghaemmaghami for bringing this letter to my attention.

[9] See also Johanna Pink, "Deriding Revealed Religions? Baha'is in Egypt", in: *ISIM Newsletter*, 10/2002, 30.

[10] Fereydun Vahman, "Baha'ismus", in: *Theologische Realenzyklopädie*, ed. by Gerhard Krause et al., Berlin 1980, Bd. 5, 130f. Also Udo Schaefer, *Die missverstandene Religion*, Hofheim 1968, 20f.

[11] Osterhammel writes: "...eine der wenigen religiösen Neuschöpfungen des 19. Jahrhunderts, die Bestand hat." See Jürgen Osterhammel, *Die Verwandlung der Welt. Eine Geschichte des 19. Jahrhunderts*, Munich 2009, 1271.

[12] Ibid.

According to him, the following teachings of the Bahā'ī Faith can be designated as modern:[13]

- acceptance of a constitutional state and parliamentary democracy;
- promotion of women's rights;
- rejection of religious nationalism;
- concern for the idea of world peace;
- annulment of the doctrine of Holy War; and
- open-mindedness toward science[14]

Osterhammel's brief reference to the Bahā'ī Faith is significant, and not simply because he connects the Bahā'ī religion to the complex phenomenon of Modernity. Much more important, especially for an examination of the Bahā'ī understanding of martyrdom and *jihad*, is the fact that his portrayal conveys more than just an impression of the nonviolent and peaceful spirit animating the young monotheistic religion. In addition, a glimpse at some of the above-mentioned principles calls into question the assumption, advocated by some antireligious public intellectuals, that the phenomenon of religious monotheism is necessarily violent and intolerant. The evolutionary biologist Richard Dawkins, the neuroscientist Sam Harris and the late journalist Christopher Hitchens have asserted, time and again, that violence and monotheism are inextricably wedded, indeed, that violence must be seen as a quasi-genetic constituent of all monotheistic religions.

In this context a word about the method of such anti-monotheistic authors seems necessary. These writers often tend to focus on one specific religion and epoch instead of undertaking the extensive and careful research required to adequately address the general phenomenon of religious monotheism. The subject of religion and monotheism is treated like a Russian *matryoshka* — the well-known set of wooden dolls of decreasing size nesting one inside the other. The first and largest doll is usually the focus of an observer's attention, while all the others nesting inside are presumed to be miniature replicas of the first. Similarly, the entire phenomenon of monotheism is judged by the impression of one — in many instances the first — monotheistic religion, while all the other subsequent religions are examined in a cursory way. Such a methodological approach leads to more than just a distorted view of monotheism; it also results in a fixation on the epoch of Early Antiquity, thereby ignoring the possibility that post-Antiquity monotheism might be more than just another echo of an *Urszene*.

Such a *matryoshka* effect can be observed, for example, in Dawkins's *The God Delusion*, which for the most part speaks of all monotheistic religions but predominantly refers to the Bible. His preoccupation with this source is evident when he quotes the American novelist Gore Vidal: "The great unmentionable evil

---

[13]   Ibid, 1271f.
[14]   According to Osterhammel, this final principle is possibly the most important criterion for religious modernity. See ibid, 1272.

at the center of our culture is monotheism. From a barbaric Bronze Age text known as the Old Testament, three anti-human religions have evolved – Judaism, Christianity and Islam [...]".[15] And again, only a few lines later, Dawkins admits: "For most of my purposes, all three Abrahamic religions can be treated as indistinguishable. Unless otherwise stated, I shall have Christianity mostly in mind, but only because it is the version with which I happen to be most familiar."[16]

Of course, the presumed connection between monotheism and Antiquity, on the one hand, and monotheism and violence, on the other, is not new. Sigmund Freud's *Der Mann Moses und der Monotheismus (Moses and Monotheism)*, for instance, works along similar lines. In his search for the true origins of monotheism, Freud applied his psychoanalytical tools to unearth the truth hidden in the Hebrew Bible,[17] interpreting the post-Jewish monotheism of Christianity and Islam as a miniature repetition of a bygone and repressed past. To him, messianic Christianity and Christ's martyrdom were to be read in terms of a return of the "violent end" of Moses,[18] who was allegedly killed by the Jewish people[19] guided by Yahweh, "a rude, narrow-minded local god, violent and bloodthirsty."[20] About Islam, similar to Dawkins, but in a more sophisticated way, Freud writes:

> The author regretfully has to admit that he cannot give more than one sample, that he has not the expert knowledge necessary to complete the investigation. This limited knowledge will allow him perhaps to add that the founding of the Mohammedan religion seems to him to be an abbreviated repetition of the Jewish one, in imitation of which it made its appearance. There is reason to believe that the Prophet originally intended to accept the Jewish religion in full for himself and his people.[21]

Freud and Dawkins are just two representatives of a class of scholars whose perception of the object of study is distorted by this *matryoshka* effect.[22] If such generalisations about monotheism and violence are to be formulated, then not only should the historical context of the classical monotheistic religions be examined more carefully.[23] Of even greater importance is that all monotheistic religions need

---

[15] Ibid, 37.

[16] Ibid.

[17] Yosef Hayim Yerushalmi, *Freuds Moses. Endliches und unendliches Judentum*, Frankfurt a. M. 1999, 22f.

[18] Sigmund Freud, *Moses and Monotheism*, Hertfordshire 1939, 59.

[19] Ibid, 139ff.

[20] Ibid, 80. Unsurprisingly the English literature professor Jacqueline Rose has described this treatise as "one of Freud's most violent texts". See Edward Said, *Freud and the Non-European*, London 2002, 75.

[21] Ibid, 148f.

[22] Influenced by Freud, present academics, such as the German Egyptologist Jan Assmann, have located the reality of monotheism in the map of Early Antiquity and labelled it an essentially violent phenomenon. See Jan Assmann, *Die Mosaische Unterscheidung oder der Preis des Monotheismus*, Munich 2003.

[23] The German scholar of religious studies Hans Kippenberg emphasised that the relationship between monotheistic religions and violence should be considered as a "contingent" one. In each case the respective situation and context must be taken into consideration.

to be examined. Treating the origins of monotheism might be an important primary step, but it cannot be the final one. To avoid distortions, it is not only mandatory to study the concept of monotheism as articulated and practiced in Late or Early Antiquity, but also to move forward to the Middle and Modern Ages.

A very different view, for example, is offered by the British historian of religion, Karen Armstrong, who notes in her *History of God:*

> The idea of God formed in one generation by one set of human beings could be meaningless in another. Indeed, the statement 'I believe in God' has no objective meaning as such, but like any other statement it only means something in context, when proclaimed by a particular community. Consequently there is not one unchanging idea continued in the word 'God' but the word contains a whole spectrum of meanings, some of which are contradictory or even mutually exclusive. Had the notion of God not had this flexibility, it would not have survived to become one of the great human ideas.[24]

Although Armstrong might have put too strong an emphasis on the notion of human subjectivity, her understanding reflects a crucial awareness of time and relativity. Up until now, such a differentiated approach to the phenomenon of religion has proven rare, and in general the examination of post-Biblical monotheistic religions leaves much to be desired. While Islam is treated somewhat superficially, a monotheistic religion emerging in times of Modernity, such as the Bahā'ī Faith, is hardly taken into consideration. This neglect, however, can be seen as a natural consequence of a widespread secular scepticism. After all, Modernity's secular heroes passionately questioned the existence of God and the prophet – to Nietzsche God was dead,[25] to Weber the true prophet was regretfully absent,[26] while for Carlyle the absent prophet had been substituted by modern men of letters.[27]

3. The birth pangs of a new religion

Be that as it may, the main purpose of the previous discussion was not to create a naive or pacifistic counter-image of monotheism. A differentiated way of looking at the history of religions would surely acknowledge that the main monotheistic religions which emerged in pre-Modernity are familiar with the phenomenon of violence. But they experience it in different ways and contexts. In some periods they engage in violence, in others they endure violence. It is notable that the latter is to be observed in the emerging period of monotheistic religions. In other

---

See Hans G. Kippenberg, *Gewalt als Gottesdienst. Religionskriege im Zeitalter der Globalisierung,* Bonn 2008, 22.

[24] See Karen Armstrong, *A History of God. From Abraham to the Present: the 4000-year Quest for God,* London 1999, 4f.

[25] "God is dead. God remains dead. And we have killed him." Friedrich Nietzsche, *The Gay Science,* trans. Walter Kaufmann, New York 1974, aphorism 125.

[26] Max Weber, *Wissenschaft als Beruf,* Stuttgart 1995, 40f.

[27] Thomas Carlyle, *On Heroes, Hero-Worship and the Heroic of History,* New York 1906, 149ff.

words, it is during the time of birth and infancy that all monotheistic religions have to endure violence, although this situation changes over the course of time.

Reuven Firestone, a scholar of Jewish and Islamic Studies, observes that new monotheistic religions always emerge in a polemical environment filled with "mimetic tension".[28] The established religion feels threatened by the emergence of the new religion, which preaches that the established religions are failing to meet the spiritual and social needs of the current generation. As a result, the established religion is perceived as attempting to delegitimise the new religion. Firestone writes that established religions can never really countenance the new religion and concludes: "They inevitably attempt to do away with them."[29]

In a similar vein, Bernard Lewis in *Islam and the West* writes about the tense relationship that exists between the main monotheistic traditions.[30] According to him, a major trigger of conflict between these religions is their point of "similarity." The resemblance of their claims and teachings leads to rivalry between them. Another point to be considered, simple yet of great important, is the factor of time. Lewis writes that all monotheistic traditions can, at least to some degree, tolerate their religious predecessors, but the same rule is not valid for their subsequent counterparts or successors.[31] Lewis correctly recognises that Judaism felt threatened by Christianity, while Christianity could integrate parts of Jewish reality but rejected Islam, and Islam, in turn, could tolerate previous religions of the Book (*ahl al-kitāb*), like the Jews, the Christians or Zoroastrians, but not post-Islamic book religions such as the Bahā'ī Faith. Lewis concludes that established religions – or more accurately, their particular religious institutions[32] – fear the new religion and that their fear generates the urge to discriminate and even persecute the new religious community.[33]

At this point the concept of martyrdom comes into play. The newborn religious community, which in the early stage of its history is always in a minority position, has to face up to persecution, and so asks itself how can it deal with the forces of oppression. Since the adherents of monotheistic traditions usually hold the belief that their faith is universally true and valid, the majority of them will not be willing to give up their position. They will accept death rather than deny their belief. The historical examples of pre-*hijra* Meccan Islam[34] and pre-Constan-

---

[28] Reuven Firestone, "The Qur'ān and the Bible. Some Modern Studies of their Relationships", in: *Bible and Qur'ān. Essays in Scriptural Intertextuality*, ed. by John C. Reeves, Atlanta 2003, 2.

[29] Ibid.

[30] Bernard Lewis, *Islam and the West*, Oxford 1993, 5f.

[31] Ibid.

[32] As the German constitutional law scholar Carl Schmitt pointed out, a conflict takes place between instances and not between substances. Cf. Silvia Horsch, *Tod im Kampf. Figurationen des Märtyrers in frühen sunnitischen Schriften*, Berlin 2011, 45.

[33] Lewis, *Islam and the West*, 7.

[34] Explaining the opposition the newborn Islamic religion had to face, the German Islamicist Marco Schöller describes the Koran itself as "a document that shows the struggle of a new

tinian Christianity,[35] as well as the context of the Jewish exodus narrative,[36] demonstrate that all major monotheistic religions have to suffer violence at first. In this context martyrdom should be seen as the consequence of the persecution an emerging religious community suffers during its earliest phase. The case of the Bahā'ī community demonstrates that such a phenomenon is not only confined to historical Antiquity or the Middle Ages but also exists in the Modern era.

II. The Bahā'ī Faith: A Case of Nonviolent Monotheism

1. From weapons of war to instruments of peace

Lewis's analysis ends with the emergence of the Bahā'ī Faith, a religion — as Osterhammel has indicated — with a serious concern for the idea of world peace. Certainly, hardly any other subject could provide a more appropriate lens through which to examine the attitude toward violence within the Bahā'ī Faith than its concepts of martyrdom and *jihad*. Since these two concepts, in turn, will be better understood when explained in light of the historical birth process of the Bahā'ī religion, it is necessary to undertake a brief summary of its history, focusing on the different types of reactions to the persecution which the heralding movement of the Bahā'ī Faith had to suffer.

The Bāb, who was a forerunner to Bahā'u'llāh, claimed in 1260/1844 to be a prophetic figure fulfilling the messianic expectation of (Twelver Shiite) Islam. Within a short period many people accepted his claim, among them a number of Iranian Shiite clerics, who had been tutored in Iraq by the two founders of the

---

faith coming into existence" and interprets the career of Muḥammad as being "very much the story of a man who eventually defeated all odds when shaping the first community of believers." See Marco Schöller, "Opposition to Muḥammad", in: *Encyclopaedia of the Qur'ān*, ed. by Jane Dammen McAuliffe et al., Leiden 2003, Vol. 3, 576. The late Egyptian Muslim philosopher Abu Zaid states that because of the persecution that Muḥammad and his Meccan community had to endure, the Koran refers to the early Muslims as "the downtrodden" *(al-mustaḍʿafūn)*, see Nasr Hamed Abu Zaid, "Oppression", in *Encyclopaedia of the Qur'ān*, Vol. 3, 583.

[35] Historian Patrick Collinson emphasises that persecution and martyrdom should be seen as the two main contrapuntal themes of early Christian church history. The persecution of the early Christians was therefore closely linked to the concept of human rights, since the most fundamental human right, the right to live, was endangered. See Patrick Collinson, "Religion und Menschenrechte: Die Rolle des Protestantismus", in: *Menschenrechte in der Geschichte* ed. by Oliver Hutten, Frankfurt 1988, 36f.

[36] The Pharaonic oppression, which Moses and the Jewish people had to overcome through their exodus to the Holy Land, has entered into the collective consciousness of humanity in such a paradigmatic way that it has not only been of importance to all post-Mosaic founders of monotheistic religions but also, as we may assume on the basis of the political theorist Michael Walzer's study *Exodus and Revolution*, the whole of modern revolutionary political philosophy, which in one way or another is modelled on the figure of Mosaic redemption and the deliverance of the Hebrew people from the Egyptian tyrant. See Michael Walzer, *Exodus and Revolution*, New York 1985, chapter 1.

Shaykhī School – Shaykh Aḥmad al-Aḥsāʾī and Siyyid Kāẓim al-Rashtī. The Bābī community grew rapidly and its growth, in turn, caused the enmity of some influential ʿulamāʾ, who eventually instigated the Persian Shah, Nāṣir al-Dīn Qājār (d. 1896), to attempt to eradicate this new religious movement from the pages of Iranian history. In less than a decade thousands of Bābīs had been killed, including the Bāb, who was shot by a large firing squad in Tabrīz, in the seventh year of his ministry, leaving the movement almost collectively destroyed and virtually erased.

During this first decade of its existence, i.e. between 1844 and 1853, the Bābī community reacted to the persecution of the Iranian government in at least four different ways. Some individuals withstood the pressure of persecution steadfastly and accepted death without defending themselves. Such a passive form of martyrdom took place, for example, in the case of the first Bābī martyr Mullā ʿAlī Basṭāmī, the Bāb himself – whose execution was ordered by the chief Minister Amīr Kabīr (d. 1852) – and his prominent female apostle, Ṭāhirih Qurrat al-ʿAyn, who was strangled to death about two years after the martyrdom of the Bāb. This type of martyrdom was well known to the early Christians, many of whom accepted being killed during pre-Constantinian Roman persecution.[37] But some Bābīs decided to practice dissimulation of their belief, often because they could not withstand the pressure of persecution.[38] Such a practice was endorsed in the culture of Shiite Islam as *taqiyyih*,[39] whereas the early Christian church discouraged this attitude and named those believers who denied their faith in times of persecution *fallen ones* (Lat., *lapsi*).[40] Other Bābīs fought against the army of the Shah and died in a defensive *jihad*.[41] This type of Bābī martyr resembles the Islamic battlefield martyr *(shahīd al-maʿraka)* of the Muhammadan era in Medina or the Shiite martyrs of Karbalāʾ in 680.[42] And there was also a small number of individuals who actively used violence without being in a defensive situation,

---

[37] For the concept of martyrdom in early Christianity, see Glen Bowersock, *Martyrdom and Rome*, Cambridge 1995.

[38] The secretary of the Bāb, Siyyid Ḥusayn Kātib, practiced dissimulation at the time when the Bāb was martyred in Tabrīz in July 1850, but later he accepted to be killed for his belief, see ʿAlī Muḥammad Fayzī, *Ḥaḍrat-i Nuqtih-yi Ūlā*, Hofheim 1994, 332ff.

[39] On the practice of *taqiyyih* in Shiite Islam, see Ethan Kohlberg, *Belief and Law in Imami Shiism*, Hampshire 1991, chapter 3.

[40] See Friedhelm Winkelman, *Geschichte des frühen Christentums*, München 2005, 96.

[41] Many of the apostles of the Bāb, including Quddūs and Mullā Ḥusayn, died during an armed conflict while defending themselves against the royal army, which far outnumbered them. Cf. Siyamak Zabihi-Moghadam, "The Bābī-State conflict in Māzandarān," in: *Studies in Modern Religions, Religious Movements and the Bābī-Bahāʾī Faiths*, ed. by Moshe Sharon, Leiden 2004, 179ff. In the writings of the Bāb the subject of *jihad* is quite complex. Whereas in his early and central *Tafsīr* on the Sura of Joseph the doctrine of *jihad* seems to be of relative importance, in his later and no less central *Persian Bayān*, the same term hardly even appears. In any case, although it is difficult to conclude that the Bāb had explicitly forbidden the doctrine of *jihad*, Saiedi argues that he "effectively eliminated it". Nader Saiedi, *Gate of the Heart: Understanding the Writings of the Bāb*, Waterloo 2009, 368.

[42] On the concept of martyrdom in early Islam, see David Cook, *Martyrdom in Islam*, Cambridge 2007.

with the awareness that their actions would lead to their death. This occurred after the martyrdom of the Bāb, when a group of Bābīs wanted to take revenge for the death of the Bāb and attempted to assassinate the Shah in 1852. The failed plot led not only to their immediate execution, but also to the unjustified killing of a very large number of Bābis who had not been involved. To some Western contemporaries this deed bore similarities to the methods of the Ismāʿilite assassins in medieval Islam.[43]

Bahā'u'llāh, who in the time of the Bāb was seen as a prominent figure in the Bābī movement and later founded the independent Bahā'ī religion with laws differing not only from Shiism but also from the Bābī religion itself,[44] strongly criticised those Bābīs who attempted to assassinate the Shah in his *Epistle to the Son of the Wolf*.[45] The first part of the *Epistle* suggests that Bahā'u'llāh not only condemned the instances of violence on the part of members of the contemporary Bābī community, but also went a step further and reinterpreted the concept of *jihad* in favour of a solely ethical and spiritual struggle. Through this *Epistle*, written in 1891 one year before his death, we can reconstruct Bahā'u'llāh's attitude towards those Bābīs who tried to assassinate the Shah:

> Day and night, while confined in that dungeon, We meditated upon the deeds, the condition, and the conduct of the Bābīs, wondering what could have led a people so high-minded, so noble, and of such intelligence, to perpetrate such an audacious and outrageous act against the person of His Majesty. This Wronged One, thereupon, decided to arise, after His release from prison, and undertake, with the utmost vigour, the task of regenerating this people. (...) We exhorted all men, and particularly this people, through Our wise counsels and loving admonitions, and forbade them to engage in sedition, quarrels, disputes and conflict. As a result of this, and by the grace of God, waywardness and folly were changed into piety and understanding, and weapons converted into instruments of peace *(badal gasht silāḥ bi-iṣlāḥ)*.[46]

Bahā'u'llāh then explains his vision of converting weapons of war into instruments of peace — a formulation bringing to mind Isaiah's vision of the *eschaton*, when the nations shall gather on the holy mountain of God and "beat their swords into ploughshares and spears into pruning hooks" (2:4) — to Shaykh Bāqir Najafi, a hostile Shiite cleric of Iṣfahān to whom the treatise was addressed. Bahā'u'llāh cites passages from his earlier writings to prove that the Bābīs' assassination attempt was antagonistic to the main values of the Bahā'ī Faith and stood in no connection to himself:

> This Wronged One enjoineth on you honesty and piety [...]. Through them man is exalted, and the door of security is unlocked before the face of all creation. Happy the

---

43 After the attempt on the life of the Shah, Lady Sheil, the wife of a British Ambassador to Persia, compared the Bābīs to Ḥasan Ṣabbāḥ; cf. Moojan Momen, *The Bābī and Bahā'ī Religions. 1844-1944 Some Contemporary Western Accounts*, Oxford 1981, 9.
44 See Bahā'u'lláh, *The Kitáb-i-Aqdas*, Mona Vale, 1993.
45 See Bahá'u'lláh, *Epistle to the Son of the Wolf*, Wilmette 1988.
46 Ibid, 21.

man that cleaveth fast unto them, and recognizeth their virtue, and woe betide him that denieth their station. [...] O peoples of the earth! Haste ye to do the pleasure of God, and war ye valiantly *(jāhidū ḥaqq al-jihād)*, as it behooveth you to war, for the sake of proclaiming His resistless and immovable Cause.[47]

Bahā'u'llāh states: "We have decreed that war shall be waged in the path of God *(qadarnā al-jihād fī sabīl allāh)* with the armies of wisdom and utterance, and of a goodly character and praiseworthy deeds *(bi-junūd al-ḥikmat wa'l-bayān wa bi'l-akhlāq wa'l-aʿmāl)*". "Revile ye not one another," he continues,

We, verily, have come to unite and weld together all that dwell on earth [...] In the Book of God, the Mighty, the Great, ye have been forbidden to engage in contention and conflict. Lay fast hold on whatever will profit you, and profit the peoples of the world. [...] Beware lest ye shed the blood of any one. Unsheathe the sword of your tongue *(sayf al-lisān)* from the scabbard of utterance *(ʿan ghamd al-bayān)*, for therewith ye can conquer the citadels of men's hearts. We have abolished the law to wage holy war *(rafʿanā ḥukm al-qatl)* against each other. God's mercy hath, verily, encompassed all created things [...] Every cause needeth a helper *(nāṣir)*. In this Revelation the hosts which can render it victorious *(junūd-i manṣūrih)* are the hosts of praiseworthy deeds and upright character. The leader and commander *(qā'id wa sardār)* of these hosts hath ever been the fear of God [...].[48]

We can see how the term *jihad* appears in the writings of Bahā'u'llāh: the entire passage is infused with pre-modern warfare imagery, the sword, the scabbard, the shield, the citadel, the hosts of an army that fights for victory *(naṣr/nuṣrat)*.[49] Yet none of these terms is employed to encourage a militant *jihad* or a real holy war. Instead, they symbolise the willingness of a believer to struggle through an ethical and spiritual fight. In Bahā'u'llāh's *Epistle* the concept of *jihad* is intentionally divorced from its aspect of militancy and physical fighting, that is, the doctrine of *jihad* is separated from the notion of *qitāl* as found in the Koran and entirely transformed into a nonviolent and spiritual concept.[50]

2. The annulment of militant jihad and the sword

This transformation can be seen as the necessary consequence of the annulment of militant *jihad* — a principle that Bahā'u'llāh had explicitly abrogated a few years earlier in his *Lawḥ-i Bishārāt* (Glad Tidings). There Bahā'u'llāh writes that "the law of holy war hath been blotted out *(maḥw-i ḥukm-i jihād)* from the

---

[47] Ibid.

[48] Ibid, 22ff.

[49] For the importance of the notion of victory *(naṣr/nuṣrat)* in the writings of Bahā'u'llāh, see Nader Saiedi, *Logos and Civilization. Spirit, History, and Order in the Writings of Bahá'u'lláh*, Bethesda 2000, 243.

[50] For the Koranic connection of *jihad* to *qitāl* and the difference between these two terms, see Tariq Ramadan, *The Messenger. The Meanings of the Life of Muhammad*, Oxford 2007, 97f. See also Bassam Tibi, *Der Wahre Imam. Der Islam von Mohammed bis zur Gegenwart*, Munich 1996, 93ff.

Book."[51] This abrogation[52] in itself should be seen as the amplification of an earlier statement that Bahā'u'llāh proclaimed during the time of his residency in 1863 in the garden of Riḍwān in Baghdad. It is reported that during the days of his disclosure to some of his companions of his claim to be the one foretold by the Bāb, he announced three main principles of the new religion to the Bahā'ī community, the first of them being that "the use of the sword is abolished in this revelation" *(sayf dar īn ẓuhūr murtafiʿ ast)*.[53] Hence, in the Bahā'ī writings the physical sword can be read as a synonym for religiously motivated militant *jihad*.

Commenting on the detrimental effects of the physical sword, ʿAbdu'l-Bahā, in his *The Secret of Divine Civilization*, also emphasised that humanity has entered a modern era wherein salvation of the human race at the point of the sword must be seen as an antiquated idea. He writes that "in this day and age the sword is not a suitable means for promulgating the Faith *(dar īn ʿaṣr sayf wāsiṭih-yi tarwīj nah)*, for it would only fill peoples' hearts with revulsion and terror."[54] Addressed to the radical believers willing to propagate their religious conviction violently, he explains that neither Islam nor Christianity — even though their Holy Scriptures did not explicitly prohibit the exercise of violence — won their main victories through coercion or the sword. "According the Divine Law of Muḥammad," he continues, "it is not permissible to compel the People of the Book to acknowledge and accept the Faith. While it is a sacred obligation devolving on every conscientious believer in the unity of God to guide mankind to the truth, the Traditions 'I am a Prophet by the sword' *(anā nabī bi'l-sayf)* and 'I am commanded to threaten the lives of the people until they say, 'There is none other God but God' referred to the idolaters of the Days of Ignorance, who in their blindness and bestiality had sunk below the level of human beings. A faith born of sword thrusts *(bi-ḍarb-i sayf ḥāṣil)* could hardly be relied upon, and would for any trifling cause revert to error and unbelief. After the ascension of Muḥammad, and His passing to 'the seat of truth, in the presence of the potent

---

[51] Bahá'u'lláh, *Tablets of Bahá'u'lláh Revealed after the Kitáb-i-Aqdas*, Chatham 1978, 21. For the original see Baha'u'llāh, *Majmūʿa min Alwāḥ Ḥaḍrat Baha'u'llāh*, Brussels 1980, 37.

[52] In the Bahā'ī writings the principle is upheld that all major prophets and founders of monotheistic religions function as lawgivers who are permitted to cancel or alter the legal enactments of previous religious dispensations. This can be deduced when ʿAbdu'l-Bahā, for example, states that Jesus *abrogated (naskh nimūd)* the religious law of the Jewish people that had lasted up to his time for about a millennium and half. See 'Abdu'l-Bahá, *Some Answered Questions*, Wilmette 1984, 16. For the original, see ʿAbdu'l-Bahā, *Mufāwidhāt*, Karachi, n.d., 13. This concept is similar to the Islamic understanding which holds that abrogation *(naskh)* can either be "internal", pertaining to one and the same revelation, or "external", implying that the younger monotheistic religion can substitute the laws of the older ones. See John Burton, "Abrogation", in *Encyclopaedia of the Qur'ān*, vol. 1, Leiden 2001, 11-14.

[53] Fāḍil Māzandarānī, *Asrār al-Āthār*, vol. 4, Tehran 1973, 22f. See also Saiedi, *Logos and Civilization*, 242.

[54] ʿAbdu'l-Bahā, *The Secret of Divine Civilization*, Wilmette 1990, 43. ʿAbdu'l-Bahā, *Risālih-yi Madaniyyih*, Hofheim 1984, 51.

King,' the tribes around Medina apostatised from their Faith, turning back to the idolatry of pagan times." Then he turns to the example of early Christianity and states that "after the ascension of Jesus to the Realm of Glory, these few souls stood up with their spiritual qualities and with deeds that were pure and holy, and they arose by the power of God and the life-giving breaths of the Messiah to save all the peoples of the earth. Then all the idolatrous nations as well as the Jews rose up in their might to kill the Divine fire that had been lit in the lamp of Jerusalem (...). Under the fiercest tortures, they did every one of these holy souls to death; with butchers' cleavers, they chopped the pure and undefiled bodies of some of them to pieces and burned them in furnaces, and they stretched some of the followers on the rack and then buried them alive. In spite of this agonizing requital, the Christians continued to teach the Cause of God, and they never drew a sword from its scabbard or even so much as grazed a cheek *(bidūn-i sill-i sayf wa kharāshīdan rūy-i nafsī)*. Then in the end the Faith of Christ encompassed the whole earth (...)." He then concludes:

> It has now by the above irrefutable proofs been fully established that the Faith of God must be propagated through human perfections, through qualities that are excellent and pleasing, and spiritual behavior. As for the sword, it will only produce a man who is outwardly a believer *(bi-ḍarb-i sayf bi-ẓāhir muqbil)*, and inwardly a traitor and apostate.[55]

Such texts undoubtedly had a huge impact on the Bahā'ī community and ultimately how the concept of martyrdom was deeply transformed, especially when compared to the notion of martyrdom as it existed in the first decade of Bābī history or in the history of Twelver Shiism.

3. *The greater martyrdom:* al-shahādat al-kubrā

Of the four above-mentioned reactions of the early Bābī community, only the first — to die a passive and nonviolent death in a situation of persecution — was considered acceptable in the Bahā'ī writings.[56] Nonetheless, Bahā'u'llāh seems to

---

[55] 'Abdu'l-Bahá, *The Secret of Divine Civilization*, 43ff and 51ff.

[56] Through the writings of Bahā'u'llāh and his successors the Bahā'ī community gradually learned to abandon the practice of *taqiyyih*. See for example Bahā'u'llāh's dissuasion of "the fearful who seeketh to dissemble his faith" *(khā'if-i mastūr)* or his praise of Ashraf's mother encouraging her son not to back down because of the threats of the enemies and to offer up his life for the new religion in Bahā'u'llāh, *Muntakhabātī az Āthār-i Ḥaḍrat-i Bahā'u'llāh*, Hofheim 2006, no. 64:4 and no. 69. See also Bahā'u'llāh's emphatic denial of press reports falsely stating that out of fear he had fled from Tehran to Baghdad in order to "conceal" *(pinhān)* himself. Only a few passages later Bahā'u'llāh rebukes Mīrzā Hādī Dawlatābādī, who converted to the Bābī religion yet arbitrarily changed his religious identity whenever he deemed it necessary (*Tablets of Bahá'u'lláh Revealed after the Kitáb-i-Aqdas*, 40-44). Already in the Persian *Hidden Words* we find the general attitude of concealing or dissembling *(mastūr* or *pinhān)* being discouraged by Bahā'u'llāh. See Bahā'u'llāh, *The Hidden Words. Persian-Arabic-English*, Bundoora 2001, nos. 59, 60, 72. Also see 'Abdu'l-Bahá's praise of Siyyid Muṣṭafā Baghdādī, who—in the early years of Bahā'u'llāh's exile in Bagh-

have preferred yet a different type of martyrdom. In one of his letters to an early believer named Kāẓim (possibly Shaykh Kāẓim Samandar), we come across the term "Greater Martyrdom" (*shahādat-i kubrā*): a form of martyrdom not necessarily involving the physical death of the believer for the sake of his religion, but rather demanding that the individual strive to submit one's own will to the higher will of God and dedicate one's life entirely to the service of God's cause and to humanity.[57] Similarly, in another letter Bahā'u'llāh writes that "today the greatest of all deeds is service to the Cause," adding: "martyrdom is not confined to the destruction of life and the shedding of blood. A person enjoying the bounty of life may yet be recorded a martyr in the Book of the Sovereign Lord."[58]

Thus, although passive and nonviolent blood martyrdom (*Blutzeugnis*) is acceptable in the Bahā'ī religion, one might reasonably argue that the nobler form of martyrdom is the living martyrdom of offering up one's self in the path of service.[59] Indeed, during his early years of exile and banishment in Baghdad, Bahā'u'llāh had already alluded to modes of self-sacrifice more commendable than physical death in the path of God. In the last of the Arabic *Hidden Words* he writes:

> O Son of Man! Write all that We have revealed unto thee with the ink of light *(midād al-nūr)* upon the tablet of thy spirit *(ʿala lawḥ al-rūḥ)*. Should this not be in thy power, then make thine ink *(al-midād)* of the essence of thy heart *(min jawhar al-fuʾād)*. If this thou canst not do, then write with that crimson ink *(al-midād al-aḥmar)* that has been shed in My path *(sufika fī sabīlī)*. Sweeter indeed is this to Me than all else, that its light may endure forever.[60]

This passage reveals that physical martyrdom, i.e., to write with the red ink that has been shed in the path of God,[61] is not the only way to bear witness. This *Hidden Word* even suggests that physical martyrdom could be seen as the lowest act of

---

dad—did not try to hide his belief, though many Bābīs preferred to practice *taqiyyih* and *kitmān* (*Tadhkirat al-Wafāʾ*, Hofheim, 2002, 131). Additionally see Shoghi Effendi's letter to the Iranian Bahā'ī community written during the early period of his own ministry, in ʿAbdu'l-Ḥamīd Ishrāq-Khāwarī, *Ganjīnih-yi Ḥudūd wa Aḥkām*, New Delhi, 1980, 456ff. However, one might argue that if *taqiyyih* is conceived along the lines of prudential wisdom (Gr., *phronesis*) rather than as denying one's faith, then such a principle was not discouraged. On the contrary, Bahā'u'llāh repeatedly warns the members of the Bahā'ī community not to disregard the cardinal virtue of wisdom (*ḥikmat*). See Susan Maneck, "Wisdom and dissimulation: The use and meaning of ḥikmat in the Bahā'ī writings and history", in: *Bahá'í Studies Review*, vol. 6, 1996, 11ff.

57 This letter is published in Bahā'u'llāh, *Laʾālī al-Ḥikmat*, vol. 3, Rio de Janeiro 1991, 406ff.

58 Quoted in Janet Khan, *The Heritage of Light: The Spiritual Destiny of America*, Wilmette 2009, 39.

59 For the concept of martyrdom and servitude, see the article of P.O. Akerdahl in this volume.

60 See Bahá'u'lláh, *The Hidden Words*, 48f, 55.

61 The passive form of the Arabic verb *sufika* implies that the shedding of one's own blood is intended, not the shedding of someone else's blood. Thus the Bahā'ī concept of martyrdom differs completely from the type of self-inflicted martyrdom observable in the recent phenomenon of suicide bombers. See Khan, *The Heritage of Light*, 35ff.

bearing witness. According to Bahā'u'llāh, two higher testimonial acts of witness-ing exist, which we can associate with the concept of *al-shahādat al-kubrā*. In this regard it is worth mentioning that a relationship between blood and ink is already familiar from Shiite traditions, for example, the sixth Imam, Ja'far al-Ṣādiq, is re-ported to have said that the ink of the scholars *(midād al-'ulamā')* will outweigh the blood of the martyrs *(dimā' al-shuhadā')* on the Day of Judgment.[62]

In accordance with the three alternatives of written testimonies mentioned in the *Hidden Words*, some decades later, during the earliest years of the ministry of Shoghi Effendi (d. 1957), a short commentary on the multiple aspects of the con-cept of martyrdom was published in the leading international Bahā'ī magazine *Star of the West*. The first aspect described was "to stand bravely and meet death unflinchingly in the path of God, as those wonderful souls have recently done in Persia, without wavering for an instant in constancy nor for a single moment de-nying their faith." The second aspect was "to little by little detach one's heart en-tirely from this world, laying aside, deliberately, all vanities, worldly seductions, and devoting oneself to the vineyard of God in whatever capacity he is fitted to serve, letting action, word and deed become a telling monument, a fitting praise and an everlasting glory for His Holy Name." The third aspect was portrayed as "doing the hardest and most difficult things with such willingness and self-sacrifice that all behold it as your pleasure"; accepting one's lot, be it poverty or wealth, with the same attitude; seeking the company of those who suffer rather than that of the frivolous and pleasure-seeking; dressing simply and plainly such "that your appearance becomes a comfort to the poor and an example to the rich"; accepting "the decree of God" and rejoicing "at the most violent calamities, even when the suffering is beyond endurance" – the fulfilment of the last of these conditions qualified one to become a true martyr.[63]

Although the commentary is a personal opinion and not an authoritative Bahā'ī statement, the threefold concept of martyrdom helps us to reflect on the afore-mentioned *Hidden Word*, and also to understand why the title of "martyr" could be bestowed on Bahā'īs – in the time of Bahā'u'llāh on Eastern believers[64] and in the time of Shoghi Effendi on Westerners[65] – who were not physically killed by ene-mies of the Bahā'ī community and had obviously died a natural death.

---

[62] See Angelika Neuwirth, "Blut und Tinte – Opfer und Schrift", in: *Tinte und Blut. Politik, Erotik und Poetik des Martyriums*, ed. by Andreas Kraß et al., Frankfurt a.M. 2008, 25ff.

[63] See *Star of the West*, vol. 8, Oxford 1978, 377 (vol. 14, January 1924, No. 10).

[64] In the years after the martyrdom in 1869 of Badi', a young Bahā'ī who was killed after he personally delivered a letter of Bahā'u'llāh to the Persian Shah, Bahā'u'llāh wrote to an-other Bahā'ī known as Ibn Aṣdaq, who yearned for martyrdom, that he should not actively seek physical martyrdom in the path of God. It would be better to strive for the station of the Greater Martyrdom. Since Ibn Aṣdaq's wish to die for his religion was judged as pure in its motivation, Bahā'u'llāh gave him the title of "martyr, son of a martyr" *(shahīd ibn shahīd)*. See Adib Taherzadeh, *The Revelation of Bahā'u'llāh*, vol. 4, Oxford 2000, 303.

[65] Shoghi Effendi bestowed the title of martyr also upon Bahā'īs of the West. Keith Ransom Kehler was titled "the first martyr" of the American Bahā'ī community. She died in 1933

The Greater Martyrdom in the Bahā'ī Faith may be said to find its religious prototype in early Christianity and in mystical Islam. To be sure, early Christianity was dominated by passive blood martyrdom, a phenomenon that early Christians called "red martyrdom." Nonetheless, they also held a concept of "white martyrdom" imparting the idea of an almost unreservedly ascetic life dedicated to service to Christ and the needs of the Church.[66] Since the submission of one's lower carnal self was intended, the Christians' white martyrdom can be compared to the station of a human soul's annihilation *(fanā')* as we know it from mystical Islam. At the same time, it resembles to some extent the *al-shahādat al-kubrā* of the Bahā'ī writings, a term that in turn evokes the notion of *al-jihād al-akbar (the Greater Jihad)* — Sufi Islam's fight against the lower ego and hence its main tool to achieve the elevated station of *fanā'.*[67]

4. *Munā and the crucifixion of Christ*

With regard to similarities to Christianity, it may be of importance to add that in Bahā'ī scripture the crucifixion of Christ — setting aside his bodily resurrection[68] — is seen as a historical event,[69] whereas the majority of the leading Sunni and Twelver Shiite Koran exegetes do not accept it as such.[70] Therefore the "red martyrdom" of the Bahā'īs not only finds its paradigmatic role model in the martyrdom of the Bāb and the tragedy of Imam Ḥusayn, but also in the sacrificial death of Jesus. Christ's sufferings surely encouraged many Bahā'īs to accept a nonviolent "red martyrdom" in the face of the severe persecutions that afflicted the Bahā'ī community during the late Qājār and Pahlavi eras[71] and which, with the establishment of the Islamic state of Iran,[72] have intensified in varied ways.[73]

---

in Iran (cf. Shoghi Effendi, *Messages to America*, Wilmette 1947, 3). The Canadian Bahā'ī May Maxwell also was seen as a martyr of the Faith. She died in 1940 in Argentina (see ibid, 38). Moreover, the German Bahā'ī Adam Benke can be mentioned, who was named "the first European Bahā'ī martyr." He died in Bulgaria in 1932 (see Shoghi Effendi, *The Light of Divine Guidance*, vol. 1, Hofheim 1982, 263).

[66] See Sasha Dehghani, *Martyrium und Messianismus*, Würzburg 2011, 70f.

[67] Ibid., 8f.

[68] 'Abdu'l-Bahá, *Some Answered Questions*, chapter II: 23.

[69] Ibid, chapter I:6.

[70] Todd Lawson, *The Crucifixion and the Qur'an. A Study in the History of Muslim Thought*, Oxford 2009.

[71] Roy Mottahedeh, *The Mantle of the Prophet. Religion and Politics in Iran*, Oxford 2000, 238ff.

[72] For the situation of the Bahā'īs since the beginning of the Iranian revolution, see the article of Moojan Momen in this volume.

[73] Some people have become victims of the chimera that the Bahā'ī community is nothing else but an invention of Western imperial powers to subvert the Islamic world. Even Bahā'u'llāh's prohibition of religiously motivated violence and militant *jihad* has been interpreted by a few people in terms of subversion: the annulment of *jihad* would only intend the weakening of the *dār al-islām* and support foreign powers, who desire to rule the Islamic world. See for example 'Abd al-Raḥmān al-Gharīb's entry "Al-Qādiyāniyya wa'l-

Fig. 1 Photograph of Munā's bedroom

Appertaining to Christ's example for persecuted Bahā'īs, it is notable that a short time ago a set of photographs appeared on the worldwide web. These pictures show the apartment of the family of a young Iranian woman named Munā Maḥmūdnižād. The then seventeen-year-old Munā was one of more than two hundred Bahā'īs killed for religious reasons during the first years of the Islamic Revolution in Iran.[74] Some of these photographs show that Munā and her family had images of Christ in their apartment.[75] In the photograph of Munā's bedroom below a drawing of the crucified Christ can be seen on her bed (see. fig.1).[76]

Munā and many other Bahā'īs practiced, as did the early Christians, an entirely nonviolent form of religious belief, willing to die but not to kill for their

Bahā'iyya" on Manbar al-Tawḥīd wa'l-Jihād: URL: http://tawhed.ws/r?i=xszmcby4 (retrieved on 05.05.2012).

[74] She was hanged for giving Bahā'ī children classes that were regarded by the Islamic government of Iran as propaganda activities of a "dangerous sectarian movement". For more information about her life, see the webpage: "Omid: A Memorial in Defense of Human Rights" a project of the Abdorrahman Boroumand Foundation, URL: http://www.iran rights.org/english/memorial-case--2990.php, retrieved 15.04.2012.

[75] URL: http://media.photobucket.com/image/mona%20mahmudnizhad/ (photos no. 11-13) (retrieved 15.04.2012).

[76] See ibid, photo no. 11. Mina Yazdani, who knew Munā's family personally, informed me that the Maḥmūdnižād family had these images of Christ in their home because to Munā's father the unity of religions was one of the essential principles of the Bahā'ī Faith and he made no distinction between Bahā'u'llāh and the divine messengers of the past.

religion. However, in view of Lewis's analysis and with reference to a thought-provoking statement of Christoph Bürgel, a professor emeritus of Islamic Studies from Switzerland, one could argue that the nonviolent character of the Bahā'ī religion is due to its own historical stage of early childhood. Bürgel states that while the peaceful character of the Bahā'ī Faith is admirable, its real attitude towards violence can only be manifested when the Bahā'ī community leaves the stage of being an oppressed minority and finds itself in a majority position.[77] Should such a day arrive it is assumed that the Bahā'ī community will have learned the lessons of religious history, as abundantly reinforced within its own scriptures, and will not follow the example of post-Constantinian Christianity or post-Ṣafawīd Shiism, both religious confessions which — after becoming majorities and subsequently state religions — turned from nonviolent and oppressed to violent and oppressing religious cultures.

---

[77] See Christoph Bürgel, "Die Bahā'ī-Religion und der Friedensgedanke", in: *Iran im 19. Jahrhundert und die Entstehung der Bahā'ī Religion*, ed. by Christoph Bürgel et al., Olms 1998, 30f.

Martyrdom and Servanthood
in the Bābī and Bahā'ī Faiths

A Struggle to Defend a Cosmic Order

Per-Olof Åkerdahl (Gävle)

I. *The Bābī and Bahā'ī Concepts of Martyrdom and Its Relations to Other Religions*

For a long time martyrdom has been included within the general study of each of the Abrahamitic religions. It has particularly been treated as a central subject within the study of Shia Islam, Church history, and the Bahā'ī Faith. The importance for Shia Islam stems from the central importance of Imam Ḥusayn and 'Āshūrā'. In Church history the study of martyrdom is connected to the period of persecution of the early Christians. Martyrdom is also of great importance in the study of the Bahā'ī Faith, due to the persecution of the Bahā'īs in Iran.

The concept of martyrdom has been used in a number of religions – including the Bahā'ī Faith – in such a way, that I would like to refer to the study of martyr ideals in different religions as comparative martyr studies. My point is that in order to understand how this concept was taken up in different situations in the history of religion, it is not enough to study it in isolation within a single religion. While the idea of martyrdom has been developed within different religions, a process of exchange between these religions always existed, leading to sufficient similarities between these concepts to discuss their development in a comparative context. One such example is the Bahā'ī Faith, where the idea of martyrdom has its roots in Shia Islam in Iran, but has taken a unique direction in the specific Bābī and Bahā'ī context.

In Judaism, Christianity and Islam the idea of martyrdom was developed over centuries. In Islam two separate martyr ideas emerged: a general idea of the martyr and a concept specific to Shia Islam. Though distinct in its development, the idea of martyrdom in the Bahā'ī Faith is so strongly rooted in Shia Islam that it is basically – in the first instance at least – the same idea. This can to some extent be seen as a parallel to the way the Tamil Tigers started to use the concept of martyrdom. The Christian concept of martyrdom was adopted by the Tamil Tigers in Sri Lanka, influenced by the presence of the British colonial system, a background recently illuminated by Peter Schalk.[1] Other ideas have circulated which reveal parallels, referring to similar phenomenon though certainly not

---

[1] Peter Schalk, *Cavilum valvom. Auch im Angesicht des Todes werden wir leben*, Dortmund 2006, 180-181.

rooted in a firm concept of martyrdom. Prominent among these is the Japanese idea of the kamikaze in the Second World War, which was rooted in the Shinto religion and Japanese history.

During the waves of persecution beginning in the 1840s of first the Bābīs and later the Bahā'īs in Iran, a great number were killed for their religious beliefs and subsequently named martyrs. They choose not to deny their faith and had to pay for this with their lives; but this does not mean that martyrdom is an ideal in the Bahā'ī Faith. The believers are not encouraged to actively search for martyrdom. Rather it recognises their willingness not to deny their religious beliefs, even if the price to be paid for this steadfastness is their own life. In 1932 Shoghi Effendi, the Guardian of the Bahā'ī Faith between 1921 and 1957, wrote the following to a believer:

> The Cause at present does not need Martyrs who would die for the Faith, but servants who desire to teach and establish the Cause throughout the world. To live to teach in the present day is like being martyred in those early days. It is the spirit that moves us that counts, not the act through which that spirit expresses itself, and that spirit is to serve the Cause of God with our heart and soul.[2]

Here Shoghi Effendi is explaining that the Bahā'ī Faith had no need for martyrdom at the time. He certainly does not rule out that there could be need for martyrs again in the Bahā'ī Faith; the guiding ideal, though, was servanthood and not martyrdom. This shift of ideal was not new in the Bahā'ī Faith however. Bahā'u'llāh had expressed it almost 80 years earlier in one of the most famous and appreciated tablets of the Bahā'īs, the *Tablet of Aḥmad*.

The background to this shift of ideal is related to the general development of the Bābī and Bahā'ī Faiths. In the Bābī and Bahā'ī Faiths the situation shifted over time, also depending on the situation facing the leadership of the time: it shifted from the time of the Bāb, to Bahā'u'llāh, to ʿAbdu'l-Bahā, to Shoghi Effendi and, from 1963, to the Universal House of Justice. It is, however, important to realise that a central authority was in place at practically all times. This has proven to be of great importance for the recognition of believers that were killed for their faith as martyrs.

The naming of martyrs has always been strongly related to the spiritual leader of the time in these two Faiths, for it is only God who knows who really is a martyr and it is God, according to beliefs of the Bahā'ī Faith, who raised the leader. In the period after the execution of the Bāb in July 1850 and the declaration of Bahā'u'llāh in April 1863, the leadership of the Bābī community might not have been very clear to many, particularly when seen from a theoretical point of view; but there seems to be little reason to believe that Bahā'u'llāh was not seen as the leading figure in the community by the majority of the Bābīs.[3]

---

2   Shoghi Effendi, *Compilation of Compilations*, vol. 2, Mona Vale 1991, 5.
3   For a more detailed description on the question of the succession to the Bāb see Hasan M. Balyuzi, *Edward Granville Browne and the Bahā'ī Faith*, Oxford 1970, 87.

The number of recognised Bābī martyrs during this period was very large, as Shoghi Effendi later showed in *God Passes By* and other writings. Bahā'u'llāh also refers to this in the *Tablet of Ahmad*, which was written at a time when the martyrdom of these Bābīs was still quite fresh in the mind.

After the 1863 declaration of Bahā'u'llāh in Baghdad, he and a relatively small group consisting of his family and a few others were sent to Constantinople (Istanbul) and from there to Adrianople (Edirne), leaving behind most of the believers in Baghdad. After some time one of the believers, Mīrzā Ahmad Yazdī, longed so much to see Bahā'u'llāh that he decided to follow him. When he reached Constantinople he received a tablet from Bahā'u'llāh that had been revealed in Adrianople, and is known today as the *Tablet of Ahmad*. Upon reading this tablet carefully, he realised that he should not continue his search for Bahā'u'llāh but should instead go to Iran and teach the Bābīs living there that Bahā'u'llāh was the 'Promised One' predicted in the Bābī Faith. Undertaking this mission he became a key person, and together with some other Bahā'īs initiated the process that saw the majority of the Bābīs of Iran became Bahā'īs.[4]

A part of the *Tablet of Ahmad* is of special interest for the aspect of martyrdom. Seen in terms of general conceptions of martyrdom, two sentences are entirely unexpected considering the high esteem given to martyrdom in the Middle East[5]:

> Learn well this Tablet, O Ahmad. Chant it during thy days and withhold not thyself there from. For verily, God hath ordained for the one who chants it, the reward of a hundred Martyrs and a service in both worlds.[6]

The statement that the one who chants it has a reward of a hundred martyrs and a service in both worlds indicates the change of an ideal: from the ideal of martyrdom so common in the Middle East to the ideal of the faithful servant. According to this ideal, not only can the station of the servant be compared to the station of one martyr, but it can be compared to the station of a hundred martyrs. During the first decade of the Bābī Faith the persecution had been brutally severe, with many dying and subsequently hailed as martyrs among the Bābīs. The ideals of martyrdom inherited from Shia Islam, where Imam Husayn was the primal martyr and the believers were encouraged to follow in his footsteps, had dominated the minds of the Bābīs. Now Bahā'u'llāh set about changing this, encouraging service instead.

---

4   H. Richard Gurinsky, *Learn Well This Tablet*, Oxford 2000, 8.

5   In 1997 I had a short discussion about these lines with the late Jan Bergman, a professor of comparative religion. We both agreed that seen from the aspect of general martyr studies, this was more or less impossible to understand and that Bahā'u'llāh must have had something very special in mind when writing these lines. My suggestion for a solution presented here goes back to very this brief discussion. I am extremely grateful to him for pointing out this problem to me and his suggestion to look at it from the background of the martyr studies project that was being conducted at the University of Uppsala at that time.

6   *Bahá'í Prayers*, Wilmette 1982, 212.

The ideal of servanthood has been central to the Bahā'ī Faith. Whenever the death of a Bahā'ī deserved to be called martyrdom, he or she was called a martyr, but it is the ideal of servanthood that was always given priority and preferred. As there is no form of priesthood in the Bahā'ī Faith, neither hereditary nor based on a theological education and followed by an ordination, the ideal of servanthood is the sole basis for the individual's active participation in any part of the Bahā'ī administration. The Bahā'ī administration is thus based on this ideal in terms of membership in local and national Assemblies as well as the Universal House of Justice. It is also the basis for the institutions of the Counsellor, the Auxiliary Board members and their assistants. Another aspect of servanthood in the Bahā'ī Faith is teaching, both in organised classes for children and adults as well as the act of teaching in the sense of spreading information of the Bahā'ī Faith and kindling interest to know more.

II. Parallels to Christian Martyr Concepts

It is correct to say that to be a martyr in Christianity is to be a witness, as the word *martys* means "to witness". The word was used in the sense that a person who was suspected to be a Christian, refusing to pay homage to the statue of the emperor, was taken to a court, where they had to bear witness or testify to their belief in Christianity. Once it was clear that the person was a Christian they were killed in ways described as gruesome and cruel. This situation changed in the year 311 with the publication of the Edict of Tolerance, which accepted all religions in the Roman Empire as approved religions, including Christianity. From that time on, the number of martyrs ceased to increase by any substantial number. Nonetheless, martyrs continued to be hailed in different ways, especially among the common believers, which meant that the church had to accept this situation. A step in this direction was taken when in 608 Pope Boniface IV asked for and gained approval from the Emperor to use the heathen temple of the Pantheon in Rome as a Catholic church dedicated to "Virgin Mary and all the Martyrs". A further step in this direction came when the Catholic Church started to officially name saints in 993. The first to be named a saint was the bishop Ulrich of Augsburg. By naming saints, the Church had officially left behind the earlier ideal of martyr, accepting instead an ideal of servanthood, whereby persons other than martyrs could become saints.

In the Christian context the concept of martyrdom was used according to the principle of sheep going to slaughter, meaning that the martyrs had not tried to resist their martyrdom. To the Christians Jesus Christ was the primal martyr and he was the one to set the pattern of how to face martyrdom. The path he took showed this principle. To the Bābīs it was natural to follow the existing pattern in Shia Islam, which was to meet the persecutions with sword in hand, the pattern set by Imam Ḥusayn. With the martyrdom of the Bāb however, a new pattern was set. At his martyrdom he desisted from any kind of resistance, accepting his martyrdom in complete submission. In this way his martyrdom was a parallel to the martyrdom of Jesus Christ. Was this one of the aspects Shoghi Effendi was actually referring to in *God Passes By*? Even if not, there can be no doubt that he saw this parallel as central and of great importance, an aspect that was well worth the effort for a student of comparative religion to engage in for a deeper study.

> The passion of Jesus Christ, and indeed His whole public ministry, alone offer a parallel to the Mission and death of the Bāb, a parallel which no student of comparative religion can fail to perceive or ignore: in the youthfulness and meekness of the Inaugurator of the Bābī Dispensation; in the extreme brevity and turbulence of His public ministry; in the dramatic swiftness with which that ministry moved towards its climax; in the apostolic order He instituted and the primacy He conferred on one of its members; in the boldness of His challenge to the time-honoured conventions, rites and laws which had been woven into the fabric of the religion He Himself had been born into; in the role which an officially recognised and firmly entrenched religious hierarchy played as chief instigators of the outrages which He was made to suffer; in the indignities heaped upon Him; in the suddenness of His arrest; in the interrogation to which He was subjected; in the derision poured, and the scourging inflicted, upon Him; in the public affront He faced; and finally, in His ignominious suspension before the gaze of a hostile multitude – in all these we cannot fail to discern a remarkable similarity to the distinguishing features of the career of Jesus Christ.[7]

III. The Bahā'ī Community in ʿIshqābād – An Example of Servanthood

The concept of martyrdom was born in Judaism and Islam from theological concepts and in Christianity from a historical situation – the crucifixion of Jesus Christ. The same applies to the martyrdom of Imam Ḥusayn on the Karbala plain in 680 CE in Shia Islam. Once a concept of martyrdom has been set out and established, it becomes imperative to then defend, for it is a key component in the cosmic order of that group. There are thus a number of historical situations where defending this concept has led to religious persecution, with the persecution of the Iranian Bahā'īs one example from modern history. The background to this persecution is that in Shia Islam there is the expectation that Imam Mahdī, the twelfth Imam, will return, while the very foundation of the Bābī and Bahā'ī Faiths is that this expectation was fulfilled with the emergence of the Bāb. This was not accepted by the Shia ʿulamā', who lead and guide the Shia community in the name of Imam Mahdī. Their station in society rests on this expectation and the trust of the people that when Imam Mahdī returns the ʿulamā' will accept his sovereignty. The Bahā'ī community is therefore seen as a threat to the Shia ʿulamā', albeit not a political or military threat, for the Bahā'īs have neither the means nor the ideological motivation for this. The threat is rather on a level of principles. If these expectations have been fulfilled, the basis

---

7   Shoghi Effendi, *God Passes By*, Wilmette 1982, 56f.

for the rule of the *ʿulamāʾ* would disappear and so the persecution becomes a defence of the cosmic order of Shia Islam as seen by the Shia *ʿulamāʾ*. They maintain that his return will come from the hidden place where he has been since his disappearance and that he will come in the flesh. Many have, however, accepted the Bābī and Bahāʾī viewpoints and the Bahāʾī community has grown in size over time, with the result that the persecution has continued.

I have used and explained this idea of defending a cosmic order in my *Bahāʾī Identity and the Concept of Martyrdom*. In my discussion on the persecution of the Bābīs and the Bahāʾīs in Iran I came to the conclusion that although the persecution was often described as very aggressive, the persecutors saw it as an act of defence, one they had to undertake because it fell within their responsibility. To them, the existence of these two religions was itself an attack on a cosmic order that existed within Shia Islam, where Imam Mahdī was the central figure and the Shia *ʿulamāʾ* were his representatives and the protectors of this cosmic order.

As far as the Bahāʾī community in ʿIshqābād, Turkmenistan, is concerned, it was built by Iranian Bahāʾīs who had moved to the new city of ʿIshqābād at the end of the 19th century. Hassan Balyuzi has described the background of this migration as follows: "Persian Bahāʾīs, harassed in their native land, were attracted to ʿIshqābād, as were others of their countrymen."[8] Seen from this perspective, the migration becomes results from the defence of the cosmic order of Shia Islam. It can also be seen as a wish to become servants in the Bahāʾī Faith in accordance to the writings of Bahāʾuʾllāh. Perhaps though, the background can be seen as a combination of these two factors.

The persecutions in Iran made life very problematic for the Iranian Bahāʾīs and thus those who moved to the newly founded city of ʿIshqābād had reason to believe that life would be safer there. This hope was put to a test when a Bahāʾī in ʿIshqābād was murdered by two assassins from Iran in September 1889. If the murder had taken place in Iran, then there was a good chance that they would have gone unpunished; but as this was in Russia, a reasonably well-functioning judicial system pursued the case. Eventually, the two murderers were condemned to death, but the Bahāʾī community pleaded that they should not be executed. As a result they were sent instead to Siberia together with six others implicated in the plot.[9]

If this incident is seen as defending a cosmic order, this must be considered a part of the defence undertaken in the name of Shia Islam in Iran, expanded into Turkmenistan. It is not possible to say today if this undertaking was actually meant to test the plausibility of expanding defence to a neighbouring country at the time of its conception; what is clear though, is that it has meanwhile become an efficient test. There seems to be nothing written about any more attempts by

---

[8]   Hasan M. Balyuzi, *ʿAbduʾl-Bahá – The Centre of the Covenant of Bahāʾuʾllāh*, Oxford 1971, 108.

[9]   Ibid., 108-109.

the enemies of Bahā'ī to murder Bahā'īs in 'Ishqābād or to arrange any other form of persecution. The situation had changed though, and it changed once again for the Bahā'īs in 'Ishqābād when 'Abdu'l-Bahā asked Hājī Mīrzā Muḥammad Taqī, a Bahā'ī in 'Ishqābād, to build the first Bahā'ī temple in the world.[10] The foundation stone was laid in December 1902 and the dome was completed in 1907.[11] Close to this temple schools for boys and girls were built respectively, in accordance with the basic plan for how a Bahā'ī temple should function.[12] Once completed, the whole temple complex soon developed into a centre for the activities of the Bahā'ī community in 'Ishqābād.

With the outbreak of the Russian Revolution in 1917 not very much changed for the Bahā'ī community in general, although it probably brought about major changes to the lives of individual Bahā'īs. Activities continued as before and the temple remained their hub, organised and guided by the Local Spiritual Assembly. However, upon Stalin taking over a well-documented systematic persecution against potential threats and possible adversaries was launched, and its targets included the Bahā'īs of 'Ishqābād. The persecution is described in two books, *Years of Silence – Bahā'īs in the USSR 1938-1946* by Asadullāh 'Alīzād and *Exiles of the City of Love* by Mahīntāj Īzadī. Both books are biographies: the first describes the experiences of the author in Soviet Union, while the latter relates the story of Mrs. Laqā' Shahīdī as told by her daughter. Both were living in 'Ishqābād. The first book features quite a number of pictures of the Bahā'ī temple as well as different groups of members from the Bahā'ī community in 'Ishqābād.

As mentioned, it was not until Stalin took over power that changes impacted the Bahā'ī community in 'Ishqābād. 'Alīzād relates a relevant incident. The authorities closed and sealed off the temple, preventing the Bahā'īs from reading the early morning prayers there.[13] In response they gathered in the gardens around the temple instead to read prayers. The Local Spiritual Assembly asked its chairman to go to Moscow to plead with the government and persuade it to change its decision to close the temple. After many long discussions this proved successful. He was, however, also interrogated and tortured by G.P.U.[14] in 1928 and died as a result of the injuries suffered during torture. The following year the nine members of the Local Spiritual Assembly were arrested and deported to Iran.[15] The problems continued into the next year, but it was not until 6 February, 1938 that a great wave of arrests came. On the first night 80 Bahā'īs were detained, but a greater number of Muslims was also arrested. The common factor was that they were foreigners in the Soviet Union, and foreigners were specifi-

---

[10] Ibid., 109.
[11] Ibid., 110.
[12] Asadu'lláh 'Alízád, *Years of Silence – Bahá'ís in the USSR 1938-1946*, Oxford 1999, 1.
[13] One of the functions of a Bahā'ī temple is to be a place where the Bahā'īs can gather to read prayers at dawn before they start the work for that day.
[14] The name of the secret police in Soviet Union during the years 1922-1934.
[15] 'Alízád, *Years of Silence*, 2-4.

cally targeted in this operation throughout the Soviet Union.[16] Mentioned in both books, it is looked upon as the major catastrophe.[17]

Years of Silence opens with a short history of the Bahā'ī community in 'Ishqā-bād, which ends with the closure of the Bahā'ī temple by the authorities. When the text comes to describing the wave of arrests, the author switches to his own memories and experiences. The majority of the men and some women were sent to Siberia, while many of the women and a few men were sent to Iran. The author knew many members of the Bahā'ī community in 'Ishqābād and got to know others during his time in Siberia. He describes the background of many of these persons and what happened to them. He also writes about the everyday life in prison and some incidents that happened there. The book ends in 1946 when the author was finally released and could travel to Iran.

Exiles of the City of Love starts with a dedication: "Dedicated to those brilliant souls who suffered imprisonment and exile, and to those who bravely laid down their lives during the years of persecution from 1938 to 1946." The book about Laqā' Shahīdī is introduced in the same way as *Years of Silence*, with the difference that the introduction is shorter. The story starts on the day of the wave of arrests, 6 February 1938, when Laqā"s husband, Muḥammad 'Alī Shahīdī is arrested. Laqā' herself was then arrested three months later. Now left alone, the children joined relatives and they managed to travel to Iran. The book continues with Laqā"s prison time in Siberia, describing life there. The book ends when Laqā' is finally set free and is able to travel to Iran, where she is united with her children. Her husband however had passed away during his imprisoned exile in Siberia.

The persecution of the Bahā'īs in 'Ishqābād stemmed from secular motivations under Stalin's rule, but is this the complete motivation? The motivation was that they were foreigners, but my suggestion is that this is not the only reason. The fact that they were believers in a religion was also of importance. Although the wave of arrests carried out on 6 February, 1938, targeted foreigners, they were not the only 'category' affected. Stalin was obviously trying to put into place a 'dictatorship of the proletariat' and there was no room for competing ideologies, neither religious nor secular.

It is possible to see it as an irony of fate that the Bahā'īs of 'Ishqābād had to confront the "defence of the cosmic order" from two directions: first from the Shia 'ulamā' in Iran and a few decades later from the Soviet state under Josef Stalin. During the persecution in the Soviet Union some Bahā'ī were taken to prison camps, while others managed to escape to Iran where the power of the 'ulamā' had been limited under Reza Shah. As for the remainder of the Bahā'ī community in the Soviet Union, they mostly kept the Bahā'ī Faith as their private religion within the family, only practicing in secret so as to avoid punishment. Thus,

---

[16]　Ibid., 52-53.
[17]　Mahíntáj Ízadí, *Exiles of the City of Love*, New Delhi 2006, 5.

generational differences in the practice of religion arose and the Bahā'ī Faith developed into a "grandmother's religion". The first generation practiced it very cautiously, the second generation ignored it and the third generation, which experienced the fall of the Soviet Union, had the possibility to really look into what grandmother actually believed in. I have had the opportunity to meet and interview a handful of these persons. Their accounts have shaped the description given here of the development of the Bahā'ī Faith in the former Soviet Union, especially around 'Ishqābād. The expansion of the Bahā'ī community in what was once the Soviet Union has given the community a boost in the Central Asian Republics. And it is this boost that afforded me the opportunity to meet and interview them.

These interviews were not designed as part of a comprehensive research project. They are the result of meetings with Bahā'īs during my travels in India and the United Arab Emirates, whom I spontaneously interviewed 'on the spot'. Although the pattern of events they describe is largely uniform and coherent, I would like to suggest that a suitable research project be planned and carried out – there is undoubtedly a lot more interesting and important information to be found in Russia and the Central Asian Republics.

The examples of religious persecution discussed in this article covered the Bahā'īs in Iran and the Soviet Union. This persecution is divided into two parts. The first part took place in Iran and was purely religious. This is evident in the fact that persecution was ceased if a Bahā'ī gave in and converted to Islam. The persecution in the Soviet Union however was completely secular in its motivation. What these two parts have in common is that they are motivated by a defence of a cosmic order, whether religious or secular.

Between Karbalā' and Tabrīz

Contested Martyrdom Narratives

Moojan Momen

This article is about the contest presently going on in Iran between two visions of martyrdom: the first vision is that of the ruling elite, who have turned martyrdom into a political weapon to be used actively against their enemies; the second is that held by the Bahā'ī community, which maintains a more traditional view of martyrdom, seeing it as a readiness to die in order to bear witness to one's belief, but only as a last resort. While in the former the martyr is actively trying to get himself/herself martyred as a means of achieving a political aim, for the latter the martyr is the victim of circumstances: confronted by an overwhelming force, martyrdom is seen as the only way out without compromising fundamental beliefs. At the outset we need to keep in mind the dual sense conveyed by the Persian/Arabic word *shahādat*: it means martyrdom both in the sense of witnessing, which is the meaning of the Greek root of the word martyr, and as someone who dies for a cause.

I. Martyrdom in Shiite Iran

Whereas for the religious communities in the West and in most countries of the world, the martyrdom motif or narrative is regarded as a relic of the past, as something that belongs to religious history rather than to the present, in Iran the martyrdom narrative is very much part of the active religious life of the majority of the population. Although the martyrs commemorated were killed some 1300 years ago, the memory is kept alive through numerous rituals in present-day Shiite Iran: ritual recitation of the story of the martyrdoms, ritual dramas re-enacting the martyrdoms, ritual processions in which self-flagellation and other forms of self-injury are carried out, invocations, prayers and numerous other local forms of commemoration. In particular it is the martyrdom of Imam Ḥusayn on the plain of Karbalā' in 680 CE by the forces of the Umayyad caliph Yazīd that raises the emotions of the crowd. Those who caused the martyrdoms of the Shiite Imams are singled out as unjust and evil and are execrated regularly. In this way, the ethos of martyrdom is kept very much at the forefront of the consciousness of the populace.

There has been a considerable shift in this martyrdom narrative however since Iran's 1979 Islamic Revolution, at least in the government-controlled media. It is therefore necessary to describe both the pre-revolutionary and the post-revolutionary narratives. The former narrative involved, in particular, the commemoration of the Imam Ḥusayn travelling from Medina towards al-Kufā in Iraq and being trapped by his enemies, the army of the caliph, at Karbalāʾ and martyred there. The emphasis is very much on the fact that the Imam Ḥusayn already knew what his fate was before he set off on this journey and his attitude is described by the Persian word *"maẓlūmīyat"* – which denotes the patient endurance of tyranny and injustice and a death that bears witnesses to the martyr's sincerity and moral superiority. This narrative fitted well with the experience of Shiites through most of their history as a persecuted minority. It encouraged the Shiites to bear their persecution with fortitude and patience in the knowledge that their cause was the true Islam and that they would be vindicated through the messianic and apocalyptic return of the Hidden Twelfth Imam.

Since the 1979 Revolution, and under the influence of a discourse led by Ayatullah Khomeini, Ali Shariati and others in the preceding years, the Karbalāʾ narrative changed its emphasis, casting Imam Ḥusayn as a person who rose up against injustice, was prepared to fight it and indeed ready to die in battle for this cause.[1] This narrative is epitomised by the word *"qiyām"*, which signifies a rising up against injustice. Inspired by this narrative, Khomeini mobilised the Iranian people to pour into the streets and risk death at the hands of the Shah's security forces, many of them wearing shrouds as symbols of their readiness to die. They chanted "every day is ʿĀshūrāʾ (the day on which Imam Ḥusayn was killed) and every place is Karbalāʾ (the place where Imam Ḥusayn was killed)." This narrative was again used by Khomeini a year later to inspire the people of Iran to join the forces resisting Saddam Husain's invasion of Iran shortly after the Revolution. Wave after wave of untrained child soldiers went to their death in battle against the Iraqis in certainty that this was the route to paradise. This martyrdom narrative enabled Khomeini to continue the war for another six years after all of the territory taken by Saddam Husain had been recaptured, leading to a prolongation of the conflict that was to last ten years in all and result in an estimated 1 to 1.5 million deaths. Khomeini's government was also able to send abroad numerous assassins who were ready to sacrifice themselves to carry out the orders of the government. The martyrdom narrative thus changed from a religious narrative encouraging the Shiites to patiently accept their fate to a political narrative motivating Iranian Shiites to rise up and fight against what the Shiite religious leaders deem to be injustice and tyranny. This change that has occurred in Iran is but one example of a general shift observable in a host of religious communities in many parts of the world: it is part of what may be called the "politicisation of the sacred."[2] The purveyors of this

---

[1] This narrative has always existed potentially in the universe of the Shiite discourse and in the past has occasionally been used when Shiite religious or political leaders have wanted to rouse the masses for some purpose. Before the 1979 Revolution this discourse emerged gradually over several decades. 1979 was when this new martyrdom narrative gained general acceptance and replaced the old narrative, at least in Iranian public discourse.

[2] Apart from Islamism or "political Islam" in both the Sunni and Shiite world, such politicisation of the sacred has occurred – to cite better known examples – as part of Hindu na-

new martyrdom narrative have tended to disparage the old Shiite martyrdom narrative, portraying it as weak and passive. In effect they are saying that there is no need to wait for the *parousia* of the Hidden Twelfth Imam; a just world can be established by human effort and the sacrifice of the martyrs. Of course the old martyrdom narrative lives on among ordinary people, but the state's hegemonic control of the media ensures that it is mainly this second revolutionary narrative that is promulgated in public discourse.[3]

II. Martyrdom in the Bahāʾī Faith

This new revolutionary narrative of martyrdom can be set against the narrative of martyrdom of the Bahāʾī community in Iran, the largest non-Muslim religious minority in the country. This religion was founded by Bahāʾuʾllāh (1817-1892), whose writings form the principal scriptures of the community. The foremost martyr of this community is the predecessor of Bahāʾuʾllāh; called "the Bāb" (1819-1850), he was executed by a firing squad in Tabrīz in July 1850 because of his new teachings. He had in effect proclaimed the end of Islam and the start of a new religious dispensation. He had been tried before a court consisting of the heir apparent and Islamic clerics and had refused to recant. Similarly, a month earlier, seven prominent followers of the Bāb had been arrested in Tehran. Each was offered his life if they recanted but all refused and were executed in public. The history of the Bahāʾī Faith is filled with such stories of martyrdom. In many cases the victims were offered their lives and even inducements such as wealth if they would recant but they refused. In a handful of cases, individuals who have led lives of exceptional self-sacrifice are considered by the Bahāʾī leaders as martyrs even though the person concerned was not actually killed because of their religion. This indicates that the willingness to sacrifice one's life is the important element in the narrative, not any political or social impact the individual has. In a sense then, the Bahāʾī martyrdom narrative is closer to the traditional Shiite martyrdom narrative than either of these is to the modern Shiite martyrdom nar-

---

tionalism in India, Hindu Tamil separatism and the Buddhist Sinhalese response in Sri Lanka, the campaign for Tibetan independence, the campaign against abortion in the USA. It is also to be found among indigenous traditional religious communities seeking to assert their rights; see for example the use of sacred sites in a campaign "to focus attention on the oppression and liberation of the Hawaiian nation", David Chidester and Edward T. Linenthal, "Introduction", in: *American Sacred Space* ed. by David Chidester et al., Bloomington, 1995, 3.

3   For more on the two paradigms of *maẓlūmīyat* and *qīyām*, see Moojan Momen, *An Introduction to Shiʿī Islām: The History and Doctrines of Twelver Shiʿism*, New Haven 1985, 236. Some of the success of former President Ahmadinejad and his supporters may be seen in how he represents a partial reversion to the old narrative, appearing to believe that by creating chaos and inducing an attack on Iran, the advent of the Hidden Imam can be accelerated. However, he also seems to advocate a political martyrdom narrative. He has, in any case, been increasingly sidelined by President Khamenei and his supporters, who cling to the political martyrdom narrative of Khomeini.

rative. Indeed, the closest parallel to the modern Shiite martyrdom narrative is that of the communist martyr from the era of "Heroic Communism" (both types being used for much the same purpose – that of keeping alive a revolutionary fervour once the revolution has succeeded).[4]

At this point we should note that there was certainly the potential in the history of the Bābī and Bahā'ī religions for the second, politicised martyrdom narrative to emerge. Between 1848 and 1853 there was a series of four episodes in which followers of the Bāb were besieged for long periods at various locations around Iran and defended themselves desperately and effectively against the professional soldiers and artillery dispatched. However, their actions were defensive and any tendency to change this to an offensive campaign was held in check by the Bāb and the leading Bābīs. Later in the Bahā'ī religion, when Bahā'u'llāh meditated upon the narrative of the Imam Ḥusayn, he dwelt upon it as a traditional martyrdom narrative rather than an active, politicised one.[5] Moreover, he specifically forbade holy war[6] and seditious and subversive political activity: "Sedition hath never been pleasing unto God, nor were the acts committed in the past by certain foolish ones acceptable in His sight. Know ye that to be killed in the path of His good pleasure is better for you than to kill."[7]The Islamic regime in Iran is at present trying to extinguish the Bahā'ī community in Iran. This is being done on a physical level by killing Bahā'īs, destroying their holy places, levelling their cemeteries and carrying out "ethnic cleansing" of most of the villages and small towns where Bahā'īs live. This targeting also extends to the psychological level: Bahā'īs are deprived of any way of making a livelihood, either in employment or running businesses; access to education is denied to young Bahā'īs; the constant arresting and re-arresting of Bahā'īs leads to psychological stress (since each instance of arrest could result in execution) and an inability to generate income; and finally, a black propaganda seeks to cast the Bahā'īs as not being intrinsically Iranian (claiming that most Bahā'īs are of Jewish ancestry), as the enemies of Iran (accusing Bahā'īs of spying for foreign powers such as America, Britain and Israel), as the enemies of Islam (asserting that the Bahā'ī Faith was created by Russia and Britain in order to weaken Islam), as participants in the worst excesses of the previous regime (secret police, torture, corruption), and as perpetrators of the worst immoral and criminal actions (killing opponents, bribery and corruption, promiscuity and incest).[8] The Bahā'īs have even been ac-

---

4   I am grateful to Phillip Tussing for this insight.
5   Bahá'u'lláh, *Kitáb-i-Íqán, the Book of Certitude* (trans. Shoghi Effendi, 2nd ed.), Wilmette 1974, 123-130. Bahá'u'lláh, *The Summons of the Lord of Hosts: Tablets of Bahá'u'lláh*, Haifa 2002, 204-207.
6   For example, Bahá'u'lláh, *Tablets of Bahá'u'lláh revealed after the Kitáb-i-Aqdas*, Haifa 1978, 21.
7   Bahá'u'lláh, *Summons of the Lord of Hosts*, 110. See also Bahá'u'lláh, *Gleanings from the Writings of Bahá'u'lláh*, Wilmette 1983, 56-8, 94, 129, 203; ʿAbdu'l-Bahá, *Selections from the Writings of ʿAbdu'l-Bahá*, Haifa 1978, 234-236.
8   On the human rights violations against the Bahā'īs in Iran, see Nazila Ghanea, *Human Rights, the U.N. and the Bahá'ís in Iran*, Oxford 2002; Christopher Buck, "Islam and Minori-

cused of ritual murder (resurrecting the myth of the "blood libel").[9] The intense atmosphere produced by this black propaganda leaves no room for the Bahā'īs, or indeed more moderate Iranians, to counter it publicly in any format published within Iran (and the state has been successful in blocking the access of most Iranians to sources of information from outside the country). This creates an ethos conducive to the fabrication of bizarre conspiracy theories which can be put forward with no danger of any sane voices objecting.[10] This black propaganda has two purposes: its primary purpose is to pressure Iranian Bahā'īs to abandon their religion and adopt Islam; its second, even more sinister objective is to prepare the minds of the populace for acts of genocide against the Bahā'ī community should the first aim fail.[11]

The response of the Iranian Bahā'ī community to this persecution has not been to take the pathway of traumatised, passive victimhood (concentrating on blaming the oppressor, insisting upon just punishment of the oppressor and adequate reparations).[12] Their response has been described as "constructive resilience": the Bahā'īs have taken a nonviolent and non-adversarial stance that involves responding to the persecution by actively trying to build unity and social cohesion through bringing together all of the progressive and peaceful elements in society in order to advance an agenda of social reform through direct neighbourhood action.[13] The word "resilience" also denotes the stance the Iranian

---

ties: The Case of the Bahá'ís", in: *Studies in Contemporary Islam* 5 (2003): 1-2:83-106; Mohamad Tavakoli-Targhi, "Anti-Baha'ism and Islamism in Iran", in: *The Baha'is of Iran*, ed. by Dominic Brookshaw et al., London 2008, 200-231; and Reza Afshari, "The Discourse and Practice of Human Rights Violation of Iranian Baha'is in the Islamic Republic of Iran," in: ibid., 232-277.

[9] See for example, http://rajanews.com/Detail.asp?id=50762 (retrieved 12.04.2012).

[10] For example, the Iranian government media recently (September 2011) tried to persuade Iranians that the BBC is run by Bahā'īs (this after the BBC Persian service had broadcast a programme on Khamenei that the Iranian authorities did not like), URL http://www.youtube.com/watch?v=sowcL97Fouo (retrieved 12.04.2012) and http://www.youtube.com/watch?v=MP4ITa-mucw (retrieved 12.04.2012).

[11] The steps taken by the Iranian regime could be compared with those taken by the Nazi regime in Germany against the Jews, a parallel that shows that the Iranian government has gone through all of the preparatory steps for committing genocide against the Bahā'ī community. See Moojan Momen, "The Babi and Baha'i community of Iran: a case of "suspended genocide"?", in: *Journal of Genocide Research* 7/2 (June 2005): 221–241; Friedrich W. Affolter, "The Specter of Ideological Genocide: The Bahá'ís of Iran", in: *War Crimes, Genocide, and Crimes Against Humanity* 1:1 (2005), 59-89; Bill Frelick, "Iranian Bahá'ís and Genocide Early Warning", in: *Social Science Record* 24:2 (1987), 35–37.

[12] See for example Robert Meister, "Human Rights and the Politics of Victimhood", in: *Ethics and International Affairs* 16 (2002), 91-108; Rhoda E. Howard-Hassmann, "Getting to Reparations: Japanese Americans and African Americans", in: *Social Forces* 83 (2004), 823-840. I am grateful to Nazila Ghanea for the latter reference.

[13] Michael Karlberg, "Constructive Resilience: The Bahá'í Response to Oppression", in: *Peace and Change* 35:2 (2010), 222-257. A particular instance of this constructive engagement in social programmes in Iran is the efforts made by 54 young Bahā'īs in collaboration with young Muslims to bring literacy and empowerment to deprived areas around Shiraz, an

Bahā'īs have been asked to take by the Bahā'ī leadership in the course of 160 years of persecution described above. This stance is not one that involves any opposition to or subversion of the government or even recourse to any of the traditional pathways of political protest (strikes, street demonstrations, etc.); instead, it is determined resistance to all the pressure exerted to deny their religion or compromise its teachings. As the present head of the Bahā'ī Faith, an elected council called the Universal House of Justice, has written: "The proper response to oppression is neither to succumb in resignation nor to take on the characteristics of the oppressor. The victim of oppression can transcend it through an inner strength that shields the soul from bitterness and hatred and which sustains consistent, principled action."[14]

III. Martyrdom as a Setting of Boundaries

This article will focus on the theme of martyrdom, leaving aside questions of human rights violations and potential genocide (although in fact these form a spectrum of religious persecution and much of what is said in this article about martyrdom also holds for the human rights violations). The main topic of consideration is the specific role played by the Bahā'ī martyrs and the contrast between this concept of martyrdom and that being advanced by the religious and political leadership of the Islamic Republic of Iran. These two visions of martyrdom could be called passive and active martyrdom respectively, but the word "passive" is inadequate to describe the stance described above taken by the Iranian Bahā'īs. Thus, in line with the above suggestion, it is perhaps more apt to call these two types resilient and politicised martyrdom. This article suggests that the main function of the Bahā'ī martyrs in the drama being played out in Iran is to lay down boundaries; they seek to use their lives both to assert the validity and worth of their religion and at the same time show up the injustice, and perhaps even the illegitimacy, of their persecutors.[15]

1. The first area in which a boundary is set by the Bahā'ī martyrs concerns the question of what is to be considered a legitimate religion.

The Islamic government has continuously tried to delegitimise the Bahā'ī Faith by setting it outside the boundaries of legitimate religion; by claiming that it is not a religion at all, but a political movement formed and perpetuated by foreign powers – at first Russia and Britain, in more recent years, the United States and Israel. From the Shiite point of view however, legitimisation comes

---

activity for which they were arrested in 2006 and the Bahā'īs convicted, three of them to a term of imprisonment; see http://www.iranpresswatch.org/post/62 (retrieved 14.04.2012).

[14] Letter to the Bahā'īs of Iran, dated 23 June 2009; see http://news.bahai.org/story/720 (retrieved 14.04.2012).

[15] This article owes much to the analysis of martyrdom in David Cook, *Martyrdom in Islam*, Cambridge 2007, esp. 1-6.

from martyrdom. In the official history of Shia Islam, all of its leading figures, the Shiite Imams, are considered to have suffered injustice and tyranny and to have been martyred. Most of the public ritual in Shia Islam consists of a mourning for and a glorification of these martyrdoms, particularly that of the Imam Ḥusayn at Karbalāʾ. Thus, in the ethos of Shia Islam, martyrdom is the guarantor of truth, a sign of legitimacy and a justification of a cause.

By standing firmly against the attempts by the government interrogators and torturers and accepting martyrdom rather than denying their religious faith, the Bahāʾī martyrs are demonstrating the falsity of the government's assertion that the Bahāʾī Faith is just a man-made religion; they are stating publicly that there is something in the Bahāʾī Faith that is worth dying for. They are taking on the government and showing that, by its own religious criterion of truth, the Bahāʾī Faith is true. They may even be casting doubt on the government's veracity and moral status because, just as martyrdom is the guarantor of truth in the culture created by Shia Islam, so causing martyrdom and acting unjustly is evidence of perfidy and unbelief (those figures who martyred the Shiite Imams are regularly execrated in Shiite rituals for their injustice and their betrayal of Islam in causing the martyrdom of the Imams). By submitting meekly to martyrdom within the context of Iranian Shiite culture, the Bahāʾī martyrs are forcing the government to re-enact the Karbalāʾ motif; but whereas in 1979 the Shiite religious establishment was cast on the side of the Imam Ḥusayn, this time they are cast as Yazīd and Shimr, the perpetrators of injustice against the Imam Ḥusayn.

It should be noted that this is not the first time that this drama has been enacted on the Iranian stage. Negar Mottahedeh has observed that the role of the Bābī precursors of the Bahāʾīs in 1848-53 was "to replay, once again, the scenes in Karbalāʾ and to appeal from this position to the injustices inflicted on the people of the Imam. This appeal calls directly on the nation, whose national identity as Shiʿite is constituted as the supporter of the meek Imam (Imam Ḥusayn) against the unjust Caliph."[16]

2. By standing firmly but non-violently against the government, the Bahāʾī martyrs are creating through their deaths a boundary that limits the actions of the persecuting authority.

In its persecutions of the Bahāʾī community, the Iranian government and the Shiite Islamic authorities are aiming to extinguish the Bahāʾī community and obliterate all traces of its culture. Their ultimate method for achieving this goal is genocide, and they are preparing the minds of the populace for this undertaking through a stream of black propaganda. However, their ideal goal would be for the Bahāʾī community to apostatise and become Muslims. This would be the best evidence supporting the truth of their claims that the Bahāʾī Faith is not a

---

[16] Negar Mottahedeh, *Representing the Unrepresentable: Historical Images of National Reform from the Qajars to the Islamic Republic of Iran*, Syracuse 2008, 143.

religion at all but a pseudo-religious movement created by foreign powers to destroy Iran and Islam – because it would show that when pressure was applied, Bahā'īs were not willing to sacrifice themselves for their religion. And so the government has been ruthlessly pursuing a campaign of random imprisonments, confiscation of property and denying the Bahā'īs access to employment, education and the law courts, hoping to demoralise the Bahā'ī community and force desertions.

By making a stand and not giving in to the violence and persecution directed against them, the martyrs are creating a boundary, a boundary that blocks the intrusion of the government's ideology, erecting a barrier against the erosion of the ideals and morale of the Bahā'ī community. By standing up to the government and showing that, despite the pressure and the threats, it cannot bend the will of the martyr, the martyr is effectively saying, "thus far and no further"; drawing a boundary in this way turns their act into a source of inspiration for the whole of the persecuted community, who now actively seek to adopt and help maintain this boundary. By their action the Bahā'ī martyrs thus help to maintain the boundaries of the community, preventing it from being reabsorbed into the majority persecuting community, which is the aim of the persecutors.

3. Through their martyrdom the martyrs are also setting a boundary for the Bahā'ī community, impelling it to maintain its non-adversarial and nonviolent stance.

It is a remarkable fact that, despite the severe persecution, the unwarranted denial of human rights to which the Bahā'ī community has been subjected and also the removal of both its national and local leadership through arrests and executions, there have been no instances of any Bahā'īs breaking from the self-imposed stance of nonviolence and non-adversarial constructive action. In other words: there have been no credible examples of Bahā'īs forming or joining subversive or terrorist groups in the more than three decades since the present round of persecutions began with the Islamic Revolution. Accusations of involvement in terrorism is a regular part of the black propaganda directed at the Bahā'ī community by the Islamic Republic's government but no credible evidence has emerged of any such case and no independent observers have ever reported such a case.[17] Of course, the Iranian government would have been delighted and would have relentlessly publicised any such breach by the Bahā'ī community, for this would justify its attacks on the community.

---

[17]   There are regular attempts by the Iranian authorities to try to link the Bahā'īs to any cases of terrorism that occur in Iran; for example the attempt by officials of the Information Ministry to link the arrest of seven national Bahā'ī leaders to the terrorist bomb blast in Shiraz in April 2008 was initially reported on http://www.qodsdaily.com/news/daily/818.html, but this accusation was clearly spurious and this report can only now be found on the Wayback Internet archive site: http://web.archive.org (retrieved 14.04.2012).

Martyrdom is the epitome of this pathway of non-adversarial resilience that the Iranian Bahāʾī community has chosen. In the absence of a local or national leadership to direct the community, the Bahāʾī martyrs may well have inspired the Bahāʾī community's discipline to maintain this stance.

4. The fourth boundary that the Bahāʾī martyrs have drawn lies in their vision of what is to be achieved through their martyrdom, which contrasts to the martyrdom goals of present-day Iranian Shiite martyrs.

Perhaps nothing highlights the difference between the two sets of Iranian martyrs, Bahāʾī and modern Iranian Shia, more than the testamentary statements made by these martyrs. In the case of the Shiite martyrs these statements are filled with a desire that their death will make a political difference – contributing to the victory of Islam over the tyrannical powers of the West (the "Great Satan"). Also, these statements disclose that, although the people concerned freely and deliberately took a path that would lead to their martyrdom, they were not placed in a situation where they had to make this choice. Their choice was between living a normal religious life and going out to be martyred.[18]

> I have the honour of being a martyr at a time when the signs can be seen throughout the world, and particularly in our country, of the victory of the downtrodden and the obliteration of the arrogant [...].
> To my father and mother and brothers and sisters I send my greetings and I desire that, since like every revolutionary Muslim I have fulfilled my obligations, you should not be distressed; rather know that now every sign of the life of the Revolution is a sign of my continued existence and my nearness to you [...].[19]

In their testamentary statements the Bahāʾī martyrs make no political statements; they reveal no desire for the overthrow of the government or ill-will towards those who have forced them down this path. They testify primarily to their faithfulness to God. The statements reveal that although they have made a choice for martyrdom, this was a choice forced upon them. Their choice was between martyrdom and denying their faith.[20]

> With a sincere heart I seek the good pleasure of God and am prepared for martyrdom. I am free of worry and I consider martyrdom a source of honour for myself and my children . . .I have prayed tens of times that God may grant me to drink of the wine of martyrdom and that my sacrifice may result in other friends' release and return to the warmth and comfort of their homes and families.[21]

---

[18] See a range of these martyrdom testamentary statements in Persian at http://www.shohada. ir/archiv.php?nserv=5 (retrieved 10.09.2011).

[19] Testament of Muḥsin Farshčī, http://www.shohada.ir/newsreader.php?nid=364 (retrieved 10.09.2011).

[20] See a number of these martyrdom testamentary statements in *The Bahāʾī World*, Vol. 18 (1979-1983), Haifa 1986, 284-289.

[21] Testament of Masīḥ Farhangī, ibid. 285.

5. The fifth boundary that the Bahá'í martyrs create is one marking a division in the values held by the government and those of the Bahá'í community. This boundary discloses the government's actions for what they are by juxtaposing them with their opposite.

The Iranian government claims to be based on religious ethics and law and an upholder of the moral order. It claims a divine mandate for its actions. And yet, it has to resort to violence in order to maintain its authority and to force the population to behave and dress in accordance with its norms and stipulations. It has to suppress opposition and carry out brutal acts of violence, rape and torture in order to keep its grip on power. In its campaign against the Bahá'ís the government has killed harmless 80-year-old men and innocent 18 year-old girls. It has killed young women for the "crime" of teaching children's classes and farmers from remote villages on charges of spying for foreign powers.

Through their non-adversarial, nonviolent response, by standing up for the values of truthfulness (refusing to dissimulate their beliefs), trustworthiness (in not seeking to subvert the government), peacefulness (not resorting to violence, even in self-defence), obedience to the government (to any directives the government issues, short of denying their beliefs) and their forbearance and patriotism (by going first through the due legal channels within the country before appealing to international institutions), the Bahá'í martyrs are demonstrating the clear difference between their values and those the government is actually demonstrating in practice. Here the Bahá'í martyrs are following in the footsteps of a long line of distinguished advocates of passive resistance to tyranny, persons such as Mahatma Gandhi and Martin Luther King – except of course that the Bahá'ís do not engage in civil disobedience but rather focus on constructive resilience.

IV. Impact of the Bahá'í Martyrs

The striven-for impact in creating these boundaries is only achievable if they become known – to the other Bahá'ís in Iran and to the Iranian population in general. Hence the active campaign of the world Bahá'í community to publicise the Bahá'í persecutions in Iran is of major importance. While primarily intended to draw the attention of national and international organs to the human rights violations going on in Iran, it is also generating a secondary effect, drawing the attention of Iranians to this matter. There is evidence that the witnessing of the Bahá'í martyrs is having an impact in three important areas.

1. The continuing resilience of the Bahá'ís of Iran. There is good evidence that the morale of the Bahá'ís of Iran continues to be high. While a number of people publically apostatised in the early days of the Revolution, most of them were individuals, born into Bahá'í families, who had already become estranged from the Bahá'í community and were seeking to clarify their position. Since that time the number of apostasies has dropped to a very low level. The witnessing of the

faith by the martyrs does indeed appear to have succeeded in drawing a boundary and preventing erosion of Bahā'ī membership in Iran. As indicated above, the martyrs may well also be contributing to the Bahā'ī community maintaining its stance of constructive resilience.

2. While the Iranian government vilifies the Bahā'ī martyrs as traitors, spies and purveyors of corruption, and is able to clamp down fairly effectively within Iran on any other portrayal of the Bahā'ī martyrs and of the Bahā'īs in general diverging from this line, it is not able to control the flow of information to Iranians outside Iran. Although these are in the main people who fled the Revolution and may thus be expected to be sympathetic to the Bahā'īs suffering in Iran, this was certainly not the case in the years immediately after the 1979 Revolution. Thanks to decades of black propaganda spread by officials and clerics even before the Revolution and the inability of the Bahā'īs to gain any access to the media to counter this, most of the Iranian population, even intellectuals and scholars who might be expected to be more rational and neutral, have often voiced extreme and uninformed views about the Bahā'ī Faith because of their life-long exposure to this black propaganda. Over the last two decades however, a gradual but very radical change is discernible among expatriate Iranians. Where previously even the word "Bahā'ī" was not usually even mentioned or occasionally uttered disparagingly, this has changed into respect and indeed assertions that the Bahā'īs should be guaranteed the same level of rights as all other Iranian citizens. The few still maintaining the discourse of hatred and disparagement are treated as extremists, as relics of the past or agents of the present government, and certainly as not belonging to the Iran of the future. This change is reflected on websites, in the expatriate Iranian media (newspapers and television stations) and at scholarly conferences.[22]

There is also anecdotal evidence of a great change among ordinary citizens in Iran towards the Bahā'ī community. Despite government's attempts at isolating, ostracizing and "othering" the Bahā'īs, prominent Iranian lawyers such as Nobel Peace Prize laureate Shirin Ebadi have stepped forward to defend Bahā'īs facing the death sentence. Furthermore, some of the political parties taking part in the 2009 presidential elections tentatively broached, for the first time in Iran's his-

---

[22] For an example of such change, see the article by the Iranian intellectual Bahram Choubine, "Sacrificing the innocent: Suppression of Baha'is of Iran in 1955", http://www.iranian.com/main/2008/sacrificing-innocent (retrieved 10.04.2012); see also the list of Iranian intellectuals and scholars gathered at a conference in July 2011 at the University of Toronto on: "Intellectual Othering and the Baha'i Question in Iran", which included such persons as Mohamad Tavakoli, Ahmad Karimi-Hakkak, Farzaneh Milani, Homa Katouzian, Mehrangiz Kar, Abd al-Karim Lahidji, Reza Afshari and Ramin Jahanbegloo. There is also the open letter signed by 42 prominent Iranian expatriates (and subsequently over 200 further signatures were added), expressing their dismay and regret at the persecutions that the Iranian Bahā'ī community has suffered over the last 160 years; URL: http://www.iranian.com/main/2009/feb/we-are-ashamed (retrieved 12.04.2012).

tory, the possibility of granting Iran's Bahā'īs full rights of citizenship and religious freedom. During the demonstrations in the streets of Tehran in the summer of 2009, one group was heard to chant "Bahā'ī, Bahā'ī, ḥimāyatat mīkunīm" (Bahā'ī, Bahā'ī, we will protect you).[23] The evidence is too patchy at present to know whether this change represents a major shift in the perceptions of the whole population or only that of small urban pockets of educated middle-class Iranians who are in close contact with Bahā'īs. It is not really known if there has been any change among the urban poor or the rural population. There is, however, also anecdotal evidence of many people in Iran converting to the Bahā'ī Faith, despite the dangers this would entail; as apostates from Islam they would incur the death penalty. Certainly there have been references to such conversions on the websites of individuals close to the central government.[24]

3. The actions of the Bahā'ī martyrs have contributed to the great change in the attitude of the Iranian public towards their own government. Thirty years ago, the government enjoyed widespread support and easily carried referenda on such matters as adopting the Islamic constitution. At the present time however, the government remains in power only by committing a long list of human rights abuses, while demonstrations take place and contempt towards it is widespread. Of course many factors are contributing to this, but the Bahā'ī martyrs must play some part in this reversal of sentiment. Furthermore, the deluge of government media propaganda against the Bahā'īs (far out of proportion to any realistic assessment of a possible threat they might pose) and their attempts to whip up moral panic amongst the people by claiming that the Bahā'īs are posing a threat to Iran's societal and religious values, may well be an indicator that the actual panic is within government circles over the potential of the Bahā'īs to inflict great moral and religious damage on the government in the minds of the public.[25]

---

[23] See the video at http://www.youtube.com/watch?v=YtU9FMsP1pQ (retrieved 12.10.2011). I am grateful to Adib Masumyan for this reference.

[24] See for example the article by Rasul Jafariyan at http://www.khabaronline.ir/detail/161539 and interview with Ḥujjatu'l-Islām Sayyid Ḥusayn ʿAlī Mūsawīzādih at http://www.farsnews.com/newstext.php?nn=13900724001154 (retrieved 15.04.2012); see also http://www.iqna.ir/fa/news_detail.php?ProdID=627381 (retrieved 15.04.2012). I am grateful to Erfan Sabeti and Omid Ghaemmaghami for these references. The author has also met several Iranian refugees who have stated that they have become Bahā'īs in Iran in recent years. Specific details cannot be given since this would compromise the safety of these individuals and their families.

[25] On this government media campaign, see the document published by the Bahā'ī International Community, *Inciting Hatred: Iran's media campaign to demonize Bahá'ís,* at http://www.bic.org/resources/documents/inciting-hatred-book (retrieved 14.04.2012).

V. Conclusion

This article has contrasted two martyrdom narratives. Symbolised by the town of Karbalā', the first has been the predominant narrative in the speeches of Iranian leaders since the Islamic Revolution of 1979 as well as the Iranian media. It can be described as an active or politicised martyrdom where the martyr seeks out death without it being forced upon them, their goal to convey a political message or achieve a political or military aim; it is part of a wider phenomenon: the politicisation of the sacred. The second martyrdom narrative is symbolised by the place name Tabrīz and has been the narrative of the Bahā'ī martyrs in Iran. It can be described as a passive or resilient martyrdom because the victims do not seek out martyrdom but have had a choice forced upon them: between death and denial of their faith. The intention of these martyrs is to be witnesses to the truth of their religious position. While the first seems to have failed in its intent insofar as there is now a general disillusionment in many parts of Iranian society with this narrative and with those who have fostered and proposed it, the second appears to have succeeded in creating a barrier to insulate the Bahā'ī community, if not physically then at least psychologically, from the aggression directed against it.[26]

---

[26] Some of the concepts in this article were presented and discussed on two e-mail lists (Tarikh and Varqa) and I am grateful to those who participated in this since it led to improvements in the article. Some specific changes made as a result are acknowledged in the footnotes. I am also grateful to Negar Mottahedeh and Sasha Dehghani for their comments on this article.

II.
Witnessing and Sacrifice:
Theological and Philosophical
Implications of Martyrdom

Sunni and Shiite Passion Stories Revisited

On the Superseding of Sacrifice and Its Eventual Re-Empowerment

Angelika Neuwirth (Berlin)

In the Western imagination – at least until recent times – the passion story of Christ's violent death on the cross has figured as the original scene, or *Urszene*, of meaningful sacrificial suffering and compassion. Annually conveyed in elaborate liturgies and portrayed in innumerable visual, aural and textual representations – involving a number of concomitant figures such as the weeping women under the cross or the *Mater Dolorosa* –, it has proven to be a very powerful trigger of emotions. Moreover, Jesus Christ has occasionally been perceived as a martyr and thus as the prototype and role model for generations of Christian martyrs, though this view has been subject to some controversy.[1] Far from claiming that the history of martyrdom "begins" with the Christian passion story,[2] I regard the contextualisation of the Islamic passion stories and martyr narratives with this emblematic event – which they mirror in diverse aspects – as particularly challenging. It is difficult to ignore that Sunni and Shiite Islam have approached the two main concepts involved in the Christian passion story and its reception, sacrifice and emotionality, in substantially different ways. Indeed, one may claim that their peculiar exposure to these two concepts in early Islamic history marks a fault line in the religious landscape of Islam, one still awaiting closer investigation. The preliminary observations presented here – analogies to the story of Christ's passion including its Biblical subtext on the one hand, the negotiating and superseding of its theological dimension on the other, are meant to shed some light on the contrasting hermeneutics that govern the self-understanding of the two denominations of Islam, Sunnism and Shiism.

I. Two Myths of Origin, Sunni and Shiite

One of the most striking differences between the two denominations of Islam is the contrasting status assigned not only to the set of issues relating to sacrifice, but more basically to emotionality. Sunni Islam – the majority branch – is re-

---

[1] Jan Willem van Henten, "Jesus als Märtyrer", in: *Grenzgänger der Religionskulturen: Kulturwissenschaftliche Beiträge zu Gegenwart und Geschichte der Märtyrer*, ed. Silvia Horsch et al., Munich 2011, 47-64.

[2] See the discussion by Sigrid Weigel, "Exemplum und Opfer, Blutzeugnis und Schriftzeugnis. Lucretia und Perpetua als Übergangsfiguren in der Kulturgeschichte der Märtyrer", in: *Grenzgänger der Religionskulturen*, 25-45.

nowned for its sobriety: it holds a firm grip over both private and the publicly exhibited emotions. Neither carnivalesque displays of excessive joy nor particularly pathos-laden forms of mourning are admitted. At funerals, females are excluded from the act of burial to avoid possible emotional outbursts. There are no commemorations of historical catastrophes, nor are the anniversaries of the death of memorable figures, be they public or private, marked. The idea of endowing suffering with meaning does not easily conform to the rigorous monism of Sunni Islam – though it did assert itself in the realm of Sufism. The officially accepted forms of public emotional display are thus strikingly sparse – an impression that historical sources seem to affirm for the earliest epochs of Islamic history as well. This low status granted to emotions – according to the most plausible explanation – is a reaction against forms of excessive emotional self-expression displayed in the neighbouring religious cultures, an explanation that is in tune with the new, self-confident and optimistic collective identity of early Islam. And it comes as no real surprise, for since the emergence of the mainstream Sunni branch of Islam – accompanying the establishment of a new world empire – has presented itself as an unprecedented success story.

II. Shiite Martyrdom

By contrast, Shiism presents itself as decidedly pessimistic. Shiite piety is widely dedicated to the mourning of religious heroes who died a violent death.[3] Not only male victims are lamented, there is also a female founding figure – sometimes compared to the Virgin Mary – who suffered a tragic fate. But the main role belongs to her son, Ḥusayn. According to its foundation narrative, Shiism grew out of the experience of an historical catastrophe dating back to the very beginnings of Islam. After Muḥammad's death in 632 prominent members of the community claimed that he had chosen his son-in-law and cousin, ʿAlī b. Abī Ṭālib, as the caliph to rule after him. Ali was, however, repeatedly passed over until he was finally elected in 656. Soon civil strife broke out which culminated in Ali's murder, after a short rule, in 661. His opponent, Muʿāwiya, took power and founded the Umayyad dynasty, which ruled for the following century. Many of the followers of ʿAlī, the *shīʿat ʿAlī*, remained loyal to his name and family however, the closest blood relatives to Muhammad. They encouraged Ḥusayn, one of ʿAlī's sons to re-establish his father's claim. In 680 Ḥusayn started a revolt, claiming the right to the caliphate. It is here that the Shiite passion story is staged: Ḥusayn entered the battle against a large caliphal army near the Iraqi town of Karbalāʾ in 680 with no more than 72 followers and they were soon overwhelmed and massacred by their enemies. The death of ʿAlī's son and

---

[3]   Mahmoud Ayoub, *Redemptive Suffering in Islam*, The Hague 1988.

Muhammad's grandson Ḥusayn is remembered with great mourning until this day. As scholars like Reuven Firestone have observed, it is considered to be the most tragic of a continuing series of martyrdoms experienced by Shiites throughout the generations.[4] Shiites refer to ʿAlī and his sons, as well as their successors, as the rightful leaders by divine legacy. Imams, of Islam; their personas came to be seen as the "rightly guided", or *mahdīs* of the community, bearing a redemptive, indeed messianic aura. The last of his line to have assumed physical existence is believed to gone into occultation but is expected to return in a *parousia*, initiating a glorious age of rightful rule. The events of 680 thus constitute the founding scene of a martyr religion – diametrically opposed to the successful Sunni majority of Islam.

It is obvious that the passion narrative tells a hagiographic story. It is packed with superlatives: the enemy's overpowering number, Ḥusayn's fearlessness, the enemy's excessive cruelty, etc. But yet another element points to its mythic dimension: its date. The Incident of Karbalāʾ, labelled ʿĀshūrāʾ ("tenth day"), coincides exactly with the Jewish 'tenth day' – the tenth of Tishri, Yom Kippur. Yom Kippur, the Day of Atonement, stands for sacrifice; it commemorates Moses' sprinkling of the blood of a sacrificial animal over the community in order to atone for their sins (Exodus 24:8). This momentous, foundational event – which in its Biblical guise involves massive sacrificial bloodshed – is recognised as the typological pre-figuration of Christ's institution of the Eucharist (Mark 14:23). Likewise, it connects into ancient Mesopotamian rituals celebrating the autumnal turn, when the God Tammūz, or Adonis in the Syrian context, dies violently, spilling his blood on the earth and thereby reviving the seasonal cycle. In Judaism the rite of atonement introduced by Moses was successively transformed into an unbloody ritual celebrated annually; though some sprinkling of animal blood may still be involved, it primarily consists of commemorative recitations of texts which extol the capacity of the sacrificial blood to cleanse human beings of guilt. The placing of the Shiite ʿĀshūrāʾ into the context of the Day of Atonement should be regarded as an act of mythopoesis, endowing the narrative with an extremely significant typological redemptive subtext.

Thus, from the very beginning, Shiite Islam subscribes to the paradigm of sacrifice. It adopts the aetiology of the Biblical Yom Kippur, the idea that blood sacrifice will re-establish truth and justice in the community. The self-sacrifice of Ḥusayn in particular – soon followed by similar collective acts – links the story to Christ's vicarious death on the cross. Although Shiite theology did not develop a theological edifice comparable to Christology – as Ḥusayn was never endowed with divinity –, the similarities are striking: self-sacrifice, the awaited *parousia*, the mimesis of the adherents, and even iconic representations recalling

---

[4] Reuven Firestone, "Merit, Mimesis, and Martyrdom: Aspects of Shiʿite Meta-historical Exegesis on Abraham's Sacrifice in Light of Jewish, Christian, and Sunni Muslim Tradition", in: *Journal of the American Academy of Religion* 66/1 (1998), 93-116.

Fig. 1: Icon of a Shiite martyr

Christian precursors, for instance a "Mater Dolorosa" canvas[5] and a poster of an "Ecce Homo" image (fig. 1).[6]

It is unsurprising that the Shiite re-enactment of the Christian passion story presents itself as a martyr narrative. Islam was born into the cultural landscape of Late Antiquity where a Christian cult of martyrs had long prevailed. In contrast, and of course contrary, to this, not only the term "martyr", *shahīd*, but moreover the concept of the martyr itself were excluded from the theology of the Koran: the new type of warrior sacrificing himself for the sake of the community's cause, who would at least in substantial aspects have met the formal preconditions of martyrdom, is deliberately kept apart from the martyr discourse of Christianity.[7] And yet, just a short time after the death of the Prophet, the warrior slain in battle recognised as a martyr was adopted as a powerful role model by the Muslim community at large.[8] But it was Shiism that raised martyrdom to the rank of the very core of its ideology. The vitality of the martyr cult, still alive today in Shiite Islam, would hardly be understandable without a rich centuries-old ritual tradition: the processions of flagellants as well as re-enactments of Ḥusayn's martyrdom in the so-called passion plays, or *taʿziyih*, practiced by the Shiites from early times onward, but officially encouraged and fostered by the authorities since the Ṣafawīd reign in the 16th century.[9] Once a year, in the month of Muharram, i.e.,

---

[5] Kazem Chalipa, "Self Sacrifice", see fig. 4 in the article by Bombardier in this volume.

[6] Cf. Eric Butel, "Martyre et sainteté dans la literature de guerre Iran-Irak (1980-1988)", in: *Saints et héros du Moyen-Orient contemporain*, ed. by C. Mayeur-Jaouen, Paris 2003, 301-318, fig. 28, undated.

[7] Silvia Horsch-Al Saad, *Tod im Kampf: Figurationen des Märtyrers in frühen sunnitischen Schriften*, Würzburg 2011.

[8] Maher Jarrar, "The Martyrdom of Passionate Lovers. Holy War as a Sacred Wedding", in: *Myths, Historical Archetypes and Symbolic Figures in Arabic Literature. Towards a new hermeneutic approach*, ed. by Angelika Neuwirth et al., Beirut 1999, 87-108.

[9] See for the history of the ceremonies Angela Gregorini, *La dolorosa festa: Per un ʾinterpretazione antropologica della taʿziye persiana*, Florence 2004.

the first month of the year, corresponding to the Jewish Tishri, the month of Yom
Kippur, the martyrdom of Ḥusayn is commemorated in an extended feast with
spectacular mass processions of self-flagellants. Furthermore, on each day of the
ten-day festival, a specific episode of Ḥusayn's martyrdom is enacted in a kind of
theatre play, which due to its cathartic impact has been compared to ancient
Greek drama.[10] Both forms of commemoration, which have their roots in very
early Shiite history, have persisted until today, and are observed in Shiite communities not only in Iran but also in other countries and regions, particularly in
south Lebanon.[11] Three elements – the exhibition of blood as a medium of
atonement, the suffering of pain as an *imitatio* of the founder figure, and the verbal commemoration of an *Urszene* – all of them powerful triggers of emotion,
clearly connect the ritual to the Christian passion, which is virtually re-staged.
Due to space constraints we cannot dwell here on the re-actualisation of martyrdom in the Iranian-Iraqi wars, but it should be mentioned that the slogan "Every
day is '*Āshūrā*', every grave is Karbalā'"[12] was powerful enough to witness thousands of young men march into the fatal venture of desperate battle.

III. Koranic Foundations of Sunni Martyrdom

Let us now return to Sunnism, a denomination which, contrary to Shiism, has
shown little interest in the religious practices surrounding traditions, preferring
instead strict adherence to the Koranic text's literal sense. The Koran adamantly
rejects the Bible's ascription of an immanent redeeming power to blood ritual. Although the Koran has preserved the reminiscence of bloody sacrifice, which continues to constitute part of the hajj, the annual great pilgrimage, the idea of sacrifice as such – the shedding of sacrificial blood to atone for guilt – is completely
absent. The Koran goes so far as to eliminate sacrificial meaning even where sacrificial rites continue to be carried out – thus sura 22:36f., discussing the hajj sacrifice, explicitly states: "The flesh and blood of the sacrificial animals will not reach
God, but your piety will reach him." The significance of this verse as a clear
statement against the forms of mythopoesis prevailing in the neighbouring religious cultures can hardly be overestimated.[13] According to Sunni Islam, there is

---

[10]   Navid Kermani, "Katharsis und Verfremdung im schiitischen Passionsspiel", in: *Die Welt des
       Islams* 39 (1999), 31-63.
[11]   Cf. Jalal Toufic, *Ashura: This Blood Spilled in My Veins*, Beirut 2005.
[12]   Hans G. Kippenberg, "Jeder Tag 'Ashura, jedes Grab Kerbela. Zur Ritualisierung der Stra-
       ßenkämpfe im Iran", in: *Religion und Politik im Iran. Mardom nameh – Jahrbuch zur Geschichte
       und Gesellschaft des Mittleren Orients*, ed. by Kurt Greussing, Frankfurt 1981, 217-256, and
       Farhad Khosrokhavar, *L'islamisme et la mort: Le martyre révolutionaire en Iran*, Paris 1995.
[13]   The point has been missed by Walter Burkert, *Homo necans. Interpretationen altgriechischer
       Opferriten und Mythen*, Berlin 1972, 19, who counts Islam among those religious cultures
       still adhering to the concept of sacrifice. His misreading of the Koranic evidence has mis-
       led a number of later scholars.

no mythic power whatsoever involved in the shedding of blood. Sacrifice is thus reduced to an act of mere obedience or – at the most – a mimesis of Abraham, who is – according to the Koranic narrative – the initiator of the Meccan rituals.

This refusal to mythologise bloodshed must be seen in the Late Antiquity context out of which the Koran emerged – a context in which a negative attitude toward animal sacrifice had already manifested. Sunni Islam took the Late Antiquity "end of sacrifice" particularly seriously;[14] not unlike Judaism and Christianity, it replaced sacrifice with liturgical acts. But unlike Judaism, which kept the memory of liturgical sacrifice alive as a core part of its spirituality, and unlike Christianity, which spiritualised sacrifice in the shape of Christ's redemptive suffering, the Koran, and subsequently Sunni Islam, played down sacrifice by framing the act of ritual slaughtering with strikingly low-profile gestures of piety. It thus defied the emotionally dramatic models of both Christianity and Shiism. In the absence of a grand narrative of vicarious suffering, the question arises as to what sources does Sunni Islam draw on in order to endow suffering and violent death with meaning? Looking into this will reveal the remarkable fact that, in spite of its refusal to mythologise, Sunni Islam has not remained devoid of a sacrificial paradigm.

Whereas the Shiite concept of vicarious suffering emerged *against* the spirit of the Koran, so to speak, in Sunni Islam the opposite is true: the roots of Sunni sacrificial hermeneutics are found in the Koran itself. Here a rigorous refusal to adopt a mythic dimension of bloodshed is manifest. Yet, on closer examination, there is one breach in the Koranic paradigm of absolute abstention from mythmaking based on bloodshed – the image of the warrior slain in battle. Unlike the Shiite martyr, this type is virtually dissociated from individual historical personages; there is no Biblical or early Islamic figure to feature as the prototype of what was to become the Sunni martyr. His emergence as an idealised role model is in no way self-evident but surprising – not only in view of orthodox Islam's strict rejection of saints, but also in light of the pronouncedly life-affirming, hedonist pagan culture that preceded Islam. We have to remember that although the heroic death of the hero in pre-Islamic times meant honour and glory for the tribe, it was nonetheless perceived as a taboo – a sacrilege that had to be immediately atoned for by avenging his loss of life.[15] Therefore in the Medinan period, when the Koran summoned believers to fight and risk their lives,[16] the sacrilegious suffering of death had to be re-evaluated; it had to be transformed into a rewarding achievement. There is one short text in the Koran that today still serves as the most evident religious justification for voluntary suffering and death

---

[14] Guy Stroumsa, *Das Ende des Opferkults: Religiöse Mutationen der Spätantike*, Berlin 2011.

[15] Angelika Neuwirth, "From Sacrilege to Sacrifice: Observations on Violent Death on Classical and Modern Arabic Poetry", in: *Martyrdom in Literature: Visions of death and meaningful suffering in Europe and the Middle East from Antiquity to Modernity*, ed. by Friederike Pannewick, Wiesbaden 2004, 259-281.

[16] See for the unwillingness of Muhammad's followers to fight: Koran 2:216, and for the negotiation of "heat on earth" vs. "heat in Hell" Koran 9:81.

(Koran 3:169f.). Indeed, it is a praise of the martyr: "Count not those who have been killed in the way of God as dead, nay, alive with their Lord, provided for, delighting in what God has vouchsafed them of His bounty and rejoicing [...]".[17]

With this Koranic reappraisal of voluntary self-sacrifice acclaiming violent death as a means of achieving closeness to the Divine, the Biblical sacrificial paradigm of blood exchanged for divine favour surreptitiously re-entered the Islamic orbit. Blood, the most disturbing sign of the body's destruction, took on a mythical meaning, transforming violent death into a promise of life. The result was nothing less than the invention of a new ideal: the Sunni martyr.

This however is not yet implied in the Koranic text. On the contrary, it is striking that there is no explicit identification of this figure with the type of the "martyr", *shahīd*, most familiar in the milieu of the Koran, i.e. in Christian tradition. The Koran though, acknowledging a category of martyrs among the historical righteous of monotheist tradition (see 4:69, 39:69, 57:19), evidently avoids the designation "martyr" for the new community's religious heroes. No continuity is intended – the new hero is kept distinct.[18] There is no sanctification of the new hero, the verse does not raise those killed in battle to the rank of saints; there is not even explicit mention of their entering paradise. Yet the paradoxical claim of non-death in a situation of obvious death and the martyr's immediate enjoyment of life in the – undefined – hereafter are both very expressively phrased. The verse does not sound triumphal, but rather appeasing; it is a consolation rather than a propagandistic invitation to give up one's life.

IV. The Sunni Martyr and His "Sacred Wedding" – Cultural and Literary Prototypes

It did not take long, however, until martyrdom emerged as a programmatic practice to vindicate a most intransigent concept of Islam: in the movement of the Khārijiyya.[19] This militant opposition group who waged extended wars against the Umayyads, demanding that not the most powerful pretender but the most pious Muslim should rule as caliph, first appeared on the historical stage as early as 658. Applying a most rigorous interpretation to Koranic moral rulings, they excommunicated all non-adherents of their views from the community of the believers, raising those of their own group killed in battle against the religiously half-hearted Umayyads to the rank of martyrs. The numerous poems transmitted from individual Khārijiyya fighters express an ardent desire for martyrdom, and this is often

---

[17]   The translation is that of Richard Bell (1937).

[18]   Even according to the later juridical categorisation of martyrs, which will raise diverse other victims to the rank of martyrs, the battlefield martyr, *shahīd al-maʿraka*, will remain "the martyr" *par excellence*.

[19]   Tilman Seidensticker, "Martyrdom in Islam", in: *Awrāq: Estudios sobre el mundo arabe e islamico contemporaneo* 19 (1998), 64-76, esp. 65-67.

connected to images of paradise. And yet their extremism, their defiance of the majority's social and political stance, meant that their concept of martyrdom was hardly conducive for emulation.

All the same, martyrdom in a far more comprehensive sense soon became part of the Islamic discourse.[20] Moreover, an elaborate Sunni martyr myth emerged – one that does not so much draw on the Koran which – as we saw – does not advocate voluntary death, but bears a striking resemblance to ancient Oriental mythology. In the oldest Islamic martyr traditions – which date from the 8th/2nd century, from an area in which a Christian martyr cult was prominent – the notion of the battlefield martyr's untimely death soon gained new momentum. In some traditions it was re-interpreted as a union to a divine winged female being – reminiscent of Nike, the ancient Greek goddess of victory.[21] While the close connection between *eros* and *thanatos* which these traditions celebrate apparently harmonises with the Koranic promise that male believers will experience paradise as a place of sensual, indeed erotic, pleasures, the staging of the "wedding of the martyr", *ʿurs al-shahīd* – as the union between an individual warrior and a mythical being – is more reminiscent of an ancient Oriental *hieros gamos*: the wedding of a hero to a goddess, which raises him to the rank of a ruler.

This equation between violent death and sacred wedding proved fruitful time and again. After having been marginalised in collective memory for some time, the *ʿurs al-shahīd* powerfully re-emerged in Modernity, conferring a simultaneously tragic and exhilarating quality on martyrdom. This is particularly evident in the Palestinian celebrations in honour of the martyr, practised until 2002 and which will be discussed in the final section.

Since the mid-1960s, the Palestinian reaction to the 1948 loss of land has included acts of resistance which feature the fighter, *fidāʾī* (literally: "he who gives himself as a ransom"), or *shahīd* (martyr), as the bearer of collective hope. In various poems between 1966 and 1977, Mahmud Darwish, the Palestinian national poet who died in 2009, created the icon of the fighter as a hero who, through his violent death, consummates a mythical marriage, a "marriage of the martyr", *ʿurs al-shahīd*, seemingly reviving the old model of the early Islamic warrior – upon closer inspection however, this was very much new venture. The bride of this hero is not a mythic being but a creation of nationalist culture, the personified homeland. And yet the concept of the martyr's union with an imagined, supernatural beloved remains unintelligible as long as it is merely contextualised with its surrounding nationalist culture. To sound out the psychological dimensions of the Palestinian suffering, Darwish has referred to diverse universal religious symbols that appeared suggestive enough to express the agony of the bereaved, the image

---

[20] Silvia Horsch, "Kampf, Tod und Zeugnis. Sunnitische Märtyrerfigurationen im Feld der Abgrenzung und Aneignung zwischen den Religionskulturen", in: *Grenzgänger der Religionskulturen*, 65-82.
[21] See Jarrar, "The Martyrdom of Passionate Lovers".

of the cross figuring most prominently.[22] In the case of a martyr's voluntary death for the sake of an ideal beloved, he draws however on a core experience pervading Islamic culture, the Sufi tradition. It is no exaggeration to state that transferring the dying fighter's mythic wedding from the religious into the nationalist discourse would be unthinkable in isolation from an extremely powerful poetic genre that had exercised a massive impact on educated society in classical Islam: mystic love poetry, the *ghazal*. Throughout the Islamic world, the *ghazal* tradition has spiritualised the idea of passionate love into an attachment to a divine beloved and further into a kind of sacrificial death.[23] True love for God could only be made manifest in the ultimate form of self-dedication, in voluntary death or self-sacrifice. It is love poetry, the genre of the *ghazal*, whose highly sensual theoerotic imagery is deeply inscribed into classical Islamic culture. Its motto can be gleaned from the 13th-century poet Ibn al-Fāriḍ: *man māta fihi gharāman ʿāsha murtaqiyan/ mā bayna ahli l-hawā fi arfaʿi darajī.*[24] "Whosoever dies in ardour for his sake, lives evermore raised up/ among the people of passion, to the most exalted degree".[25] Even a prophetical saying was discovered to justify passionate unconsummated love: *man ʿashiqa wa-ʿaffa wa-māt/ māta shahīdan*; "Whosoever loves passionately but remains chaste and dies, dies as a martyr".[26] The Hadīth has a long history: in the romantic recollections of early Islamic ʿudhrī, chaste lovers,[27] the saying is introduced to underpin their heroic endurance. It is moreover in the very focus of the mystic *ghazal* where the lover, *ʿāshiq*, can hope to achieve union with the beloved only through extreme efforts in adoration and faithfulness that will never allow him a normal rhythm of life and even will induce him to willingly accept death. A particularly famous case is that of the early mystic al-Ḥallāj (d. 922), who voluntarily accepted death for his passionate love of God. Over the centuries the mystic *ghazal* has exerted its power to counterbalance and often subvert the normative sharia-informed Islamic discourse. Whereas in the case of the mystic *ghazal* no real active killing is involved, the metaphor of a battle or violent fight, if only against the soul's desires, *nafs*, is powerfully present. An activist implication of martyrdom thus remained lurking and was to come to the fore again in times of political crisis. In modern times it has even managed to challenge superimposed foreign power structures.

---

22 Friederike Pannewick, "The Martyred Poet on the Cross in Arabic Poetry: Sacrifice, Victimization or the Other Side of Heroism?" in: *Martyrdom in Literature*, 105-124.

23 Angelika Neuwirth, "Victims Victorious. Violent Death in Classical and Modern Arabic Ghazal", in: *Ghazal as Word Literature I: Transformations of a Literary Genre*, ed. by Thomas Bauer et al., Beirut et al. 2005, 258-280.

24 Ibn al-Fāriḍ, *Dīwān*, Beirut 1903, 72-75.

25 The poem has been translated by Arthur J. Arberry, *The Mystical Poems of Ibn al-Fāriḍ*, Dublin (1956), 27-34.

26 On the so-called *ḥadīth al-ʿishq* see Stefan Leder, *Ibn al-Ǧauzi und seine Kompilation wider die Leidenschaft*, Beirut et al. 1984, 271-276.

27 Renate Jacobi, "The ʿUdhra: Love and Death in the Umayyad Period", in: *Martyrdom in Literature*, 137-148.

V. The Palestinian Martyr as the Redeemer of Collective Memory

In the Palestinian context the classical poet's "martyrdom of love" is theatrically re-staged. It is embedded in a rural wedding ritual – by far the most emotional ritual in Islamic culture. It draws on ancient local traditions in which the bride figures as a representation of mother earth and the groom as a ruler. Numerous panegyric hymns, sung in praise of both the bride's and the groom's physical beauty, celebrate them as ideal symbolic figures – as warrants of new life. The feast culminates in the couple's consummation of the marriage, and the display of the bride's virginal blood, traditionally stained on a bed sheet, which the women of the family receive with ululations. The groom is thus perceived as having performed a bloody sacrifice, the climactic part of his marital *rite de passage*, from which he emerges as an adult and full-fledged member of society. The ceremony thus involves a number of emotionally loaded situations: the delight in the description of the couple's bodies, the climax of the bride's blood being spilled (an event immediately communicated to the public). Taken together, these moments make the wedding feast the most significant collective event in rural society. It was Mahmud Darwish's poetical genius that successfully suggested the substantial congruity of the two *rites de passages*, the wedding and (sacrificial) death, to the collective consciousness, not only of the Palestinian but the Arab public of the 1970s and 1980s. Indeed, martyr celebrations came to fill the vacant place of religious rituals of collective mourning which Sunni Islam does not offer. For a few decades the martyr was received as a redeemer figure who, though militarily mostly ineffective, succeeded in restoring not only Palestinian but Arab collective memory in general.[28]

What does it mean, then, to celebrate the martyr's death as a wedding? The carnivalesque exchange of one *rite de passage* for another, the inversion of loss and defeat into triumph, inspired an elaborate ritual drama enacted by the collective: to dramatise the *fidā'ī*s burial as a wedding, the dead fighter was cast as a bridegroom. His female partner, however, remained symbolic; the martyr's bride was an abstract entity, none other than the imagined homeland – a most ambiguous ensemble.[29] An inverted world emerged. The condolence ceremony was chosen as the setting, in light of the prohibition against women at burials. This

---

[28] It needs to be mentioned however that Darwish himself – though the creator of the poetically founded martyr ideology – soon became aware of its moral ambivalence, see Neuwirth, "Hebrew Bible and Arabic Poetry. Reclaiming Palestine as a Homeland Made of Words: Mahmoud Darwish," in: *Arabic Literature: Postmodern Perspectives*, ed. by Angelika Neuwirth et al., London 2010, 171-196.

[29] This was recognised very early on by Arab intellectuals, see for the case of Emile Habibi, Angelika Neuwirth, "Traditions and Counter-Traditions in the Land of the Bible: Emile Habibi's De-Mythologizing of History", in: *Arabic Literature*, 197-219. For the case of Rashid al-Daif see Angelika Neuwirth, "Lingustic Temptations and Erotic Unveilings: Rashid al-Daif on Language, Love, War, and Martyrdom", in: *ibid.*, 110-133.

ceremony, staged by women rather than men, was transformed from a gathering of mourners into a feast of joy, a wedding ritual. In this ritual the groom is represented by a large portrait of the young man, placed on a seat next to his mother, so as to establish a substitute to the traditional verbal wedding panegyrics which praise the bridegroom's body. The mother is expected to play her traditional role as the groom's mother, i.e. to utter the ululations at the event of his sacrifice; she is cheered by the attendants who sing: "Mother of the martyr, rejoice – all the young men are your sons."[30]

In this ritual the martyr's mother obviously represents the Palestinian collective, to whom "her sons" offer the sacrifice of their own blood. Like a real bridegroom, the dead fighter guarantees the perpetuation of his community – not genealogically, but by upholding their collective honour and identity. This pragmatic gain is, however, only the surface achievement. What is more important is that the martyr, whose body bears fatal wounds, permits the mental wound of the collective body to keep bleeding. There is a strong claim to redemptive suffering here which is publicly acclaimed, not least thanks to a comprehensive corpus of martyr poetry that is avidly promulgated: he thus perpetuates both the collective's victimisation as well as its heroic persistence. This is equally manifest in the martyr's visual representation: the fighter remains iconically present through the publication of his image; reproduced onto posters and fixed on the walls of his camp or neighbourhood, the nationalist martyr's image – that of a physically intact, handsome, sometimes triumphant young man (fig. 2) – became an icon of virile virtues. It does not depict real suffering, as in the case of the Shiite martyr (fig. 1) – who is at least in the Iranian case always shown dead bearing the traces of violence on his body –, but shows triumphal perseverance, as if the young man had been resurrected and given his physical integrity once again.

This complex mythopoesis appears to reflect particularly Palestinian political exigencies: a new revolutionary nationalism seeks to express itself through the myth of earth/mother/bride and fighter. The literary critic Harold Fisch has asked if it would not "perhaps be more correct to reverse the formula? May it not be that political movements are actually generated by the changes in literary mythology, literature preceding history? At the moment when the father image declines and the mother image comes to replace it, we find everywhere the passionate devotion to the land becoming more articulate".[31] What affirms Fisch's hypothesis is the fact that upon Darwish revoking his poetical pact with the martyr figure, the Palestinian martyr ideology as such has since disintegrated. Almost forty years after his invention of the martyr, in a long poem of some hundred pages[32] Darwish lets him-

---

[30] The verse is part of a panegyric that the peers of the dead young men recite on their visit to his mother. I have been present at several such occasions in the Old City of Jerusalem.

[31] Harold Fisch, *Remembering the Future: A Study in Literary Mythology*, Bloomington 1984, 115.

[32] Mahmud Darwish, "Ḥālat Ḥiṣār", in: *Al-Karmil* 70/71 (2002), 7-19.

Fig. 2: Mural of a Sunnite martyr[33]

self be taught by the figure he himself created. 'His martyr' – again no real person but a poetical persona – tells him to retreat and leave him alone. He claims that there is no poetry about martyrdom, "no aesthetic outside my freedom".[34] Still, the poet cannot but speak about the shocking phenomenon of martyrdom which as a manifestation of strife – in As'ad Khairallah's words – "seems to originate somewhere deeper or higher than the human condition and thus to possess the power to make us transcend it".[35] A few verses from *Ḥālat Ḥiṣār* speak for the entire poem in which Darwish bids farewell to the martyr, his poetic creation:

> The martyr besieges me when I live a new day
> He asks me: Where have you been?
> Return the words you gave me as presents
> To the dictionaries,
> Relieve the sleepers from the buzzing echo.
>
> The martyr teaches me: There are no aesthetics outside my freedom
> The martyr explains: I have not searched beyond the distance

---

33   From Elias Sanbar, *Les Palestiniens: La photographie d'une terre et de son peuple de 1839 à nos jours*, Paris 2004, 327, 363.

34   Ibid. Translations of extracts have been published by Amina Elbendary, in *Al-Ahrām Weekly online*, 11-17 April 2002, Issue No. 581. The poem was written in February 2002, during the siege of Ramallah.

35   As'ad Khairallah, "'The wine-cup of death': War as a mystical way", in *Quaderni di Studi Arabi* 8 (1990), 171.

For eternity's virgins, I love life
On Earth, among the pines and figs,
But I had no access to it. I have searched
For it, using every last thing I own: blood in a body of azure

(...)

The martyr warns me: Do not believe the women's ululations
Believe my father when he looks at my picture, crying
Why did you change turns, my son, walking on ahead of me
Me first me first.

V. Conclusion

To return very briefly to our initial question as to the hermeneutic foundations of the various readings of the sacrificial paradigm in Sunni and Shia Islam: the Koran rigorously rejects the Biblical sacrificial paradigm and accordingly does not accept Christ's death on the cross, let alone a veneration of a sacrificial hero. It remains completely silent about the ideal of martyrdom that prevailed in neighbouring Christian belief. Though officially accepting the Koranic message, Shiites chose to cling to the idea of vicarious suffering and death – deeply anchoring it in their foundational narrative and supporting it through strategies of allegorical interpretation of the Koran. In Sunni Islamic societies it was another venue of allegorical thinking, namely mysticism, which kept a counter-narrative alive: the theo-erotic paradigm of passionate love implying the ideal of sacrificial death. It thus needed little more than the substitution of the "Great Other" imagined as God and male by the "Great Other" of nationalism, the homeland and the imagined female, to arrive at the myth of the modern Sunni martyr. We can thus affirm Harold Fisch's assumption that it was not least the literary/philosophical image of a weakened father figure or figure of God in Modernity that paved the way for the establishment of the "modern", Darwishian, sacrificial paradigm, which conversely – with the receding of the grand narratives and perhaps also its incompatibility with Sunni literal readings of the Koran – lost its *raison d'être* and vanished almost completely from the scene. Emotions – emanating from the Biblical paradigm and formerly so efficient in creating a delusive collective coherence – have been extinguished, giving way to more pragmatic endeavours in overcoming the political crisis.

Martyrium als Zeugnis

Zur Frage nach der theologischen und politischen Valenz religiöser Zeugenschaft, dargelegt am Beispiel des Martyriums der Trappistenmönche von Tibhirine/Algerien

Joachim Negel (Münster/Marburg)

I. Verwirrende Märtyrerdiskurse

Religion und Gewalt… Im Rahmen dieser nicht enden-wollenden Debatte ist wohl kaum ein theologischer Schlüsselbegriff so sehr ins Zwielicht geraten wie der des Märtyrers. Ursprünglich Ehrentitel für jene, die um der Bezeugung der Wahrheit Christi willen ihr Leben ließen, erfährt der Begriff derzeit eine semantische Verschiebung, die man geradezu als atemberaubend bezeichnen muss: „Märtyrer – das sind Leute, die andere in die Luft sprengen", so die Aussage hessischer Schüler im Rahmen einer Befragung über die Bedeutung religiöser Grundbegriffe.[1] Mag man sich als christlicher Theologe einstweilen bei der Vorstellung beruhigen, dass für die hier vorgenommene gedankenlose Verknüpfung zweier schlechterdings konträrer Begriffe („Zeuge" und „Mörder") die medial verbreitete Selbsteinschätzung islamistischer Selbstmordattentäter verantwortlich ist,[2] so ist eine solche Selbstberuhigung nicht mehr möglich, wo man dieselbe Verknüpfung (wenngleich natürlich subtiler) bei Kulturtheoretikern wie Peter Sloterdijk[3] oder Jan Assmann findet. Als „zentrales Motiv der jüdischen und christlichen Religion", so Assmann, „tritt uns [das Martyrium] ebenso wie sein aktives Gegenstück, das Töten für Gott, [als] ein Phänomen [entgegen], das nur im Horizont des exklusiven Monotheismus […] denkbar ist." Als „religiös motivierte[r] Totaleinsatz[.] des eigenen Lebens" ist das Martyrium „die letzte Konsequenz eines ‚Eiferns' für jenen Gott, der als der einzige der wahre" ist[4] – man spürt, wie Assmann seine Leser sensibilisieren will für die unterirdisch laufenden Verbindungslinien zwischen der „Bereitschaft, für den eigenen Glauben eher zu sterben, als sich zu Handlungen

---

[1] Mitgeteilt von Dr. Irene Polke, Bischof-Neumann-Schule Königstein/Ts.

[2] Vgl. die entsprechenden, meist über das Internet verbreiteten Belege bei Hans Maier, „Politische Märtyrer? Erweiterungen des Martyrerbegriffs in der Gegenwart", in: *Opfer – Helden – Märtyrer. Das Martyrium als religionspolitologische Herausforderung*, hg. von Józef Niewiadomski et al., Innsbruck 2011, 26f., 29. Gegen die hybride Selbsteinschätzung islamistischer Jihadisten wendet sich der religionsgeschichtliche Beitrag von Hamideh Mohagheghi, „Martyrium aus islamisch-šīʿitischer Perspektive", in: ebd. 181-193.

[3] Peter Sloterdijk, *Gottes Eifer. Vom Kampf der drei Monotheismen*, Frankfurt et al. 2007, 15f., 26f., 40-62 u.ö.

[4] Alle Zitate Jan Assmann, „Monotheismus und die Sprache der Gewalt", in: *Das Gewaltpotential des Monotheismus und der dreieine Gott*, hg. von Peter Walter, Freiburg/Br. 2005, 32, 34.

oder Überzeugungen bereit zu finden, die mit der wahren Religion unvereinbar sind", und jener anderen „Bereitschaft, in bestimmten Konstellationen [...] andere für die eigenen Überzeugungen sterben zu lassen."[5] Nach Assmann haben diese Linien ihren gemeinsamen Fokus in einem exklusiven Wahrheitsbegriff. Dieser erst verleiht die seelische Energie, sowohl das eigene als auch das Leben anderer für die Wahrheit zu opfern. Wo immer daher die Vertreter monotheistischer Religion im emphatischen Sinn des Wortes von Wahrheit sprechen, sei hohe Vorsicht geboten.

Man sieht, dass die Polysemie der Begriffe „Martyrium" bzw. „Märtyrer" für eine erhebliche Kategorienverwirrung sorgt. Die gegenwärtige kulturphilosophische Debatte ist viel zu sehr überformt vom Diskurs über islamistische Selbstmordattentäter, nationalistische Vaterlandsverteidiger und religiös-(auto)erotisch aufgeladene Performances,[6] als dass das, was die exegetischen, historischen und systematischen Fachdisziplinen der christlichen Theologie hierzu zu sagen hätten, Gehör finden könnte. Im Folgenden werde ich deshalb auf den Märtyrer-Begriff weitgehend verzichten; statt dessen werde ich die den profangriechischen Ausdrücken ὁ μάρτυς bzw. μαρτυρεῖν entsprechenden Synonyma „Zeuge" bzw. „Zeugnis ablegen" benutzen; denn um nichts anderes als um eine Selbstpräsenz des Zeugnisses Christi im Zeugnis des Christen geht es, wenn die christliche Theologie von „Martyrium" spricht.

Zunächst dürfte es sinnvoll sein, Kriterien für den christlichen Zeugnisbegriff festzulegen; die einschlägigen Quellen sind hier neben dem Neuen Testament die frühchristlichen Märtyrerakten. Sodann wird zu fragen sein, inwieweit diese Kriterien heuristischen Wert im Blick auf das Gespräch zwischen den Kulturwissenschaften und der Theologie haben: Könnte die Theologie zur Lösung der beklagten Begriffsverwirrung einen klärenden Beitrag leisten? An einem Beispiel aus dem algerischen Bürgerkrieg der 1990er Jahre, dem Schicksal der Trappistenmönche von Tibhirine, sei die Möglichkeit eines solchen Beitrags eingehend dargestellt und analysiert. In einem letzten Schritt soll dann wenigstens knapp der Frage nachgegangen werden, welche politische und ethische Bedeutung dem Phänomen existentieller Zeugenschaft in einer sowohl postreligiösen als auch postsäkularen Gesellschaft zukommt und was die Gründe dafür sein mögen, dass der aktuelle kulturphilosophische Diskurs so sehr von Argumenten dominiert wird, die der aus Sicht des Theologen zu beklagenden Begriffsverwirrung eher beisteuern, statt ihr abzuhelfen.

---

[5] Jan Assmann, *Die mosaische Unterscheidung – oder Der Preis des Monotheismus*, München et al. 2003, 34.

[6] Stellvertretend sei hier nur der gelehrte Essay von Sigrid Weigel genannt, der in den von ihr herausgegebenen Sammelband *Märtyrer-Porträts. Von Opfertod, Blutzeugen und Heiligen Kriegern* (München 2007) einführt (ebd. 11-37).

II. Kriterien christlicher Zeugenschaft

Recht besehen, gibt es christlich nur einen einzigen Märtyrer: Jesus von Nazareth, der den Titel des „treuen und zuverlässigen Zeugen" (ὁ μάρτυς ὁ πιστὸς καὶ ἀληθινός) – nämlich der Liebe Gottes – trägt (Offb 1, 5; 3, 14) und von dem es heißt, er habe „vor Pontius Pilatus das herrliche Zeugnis abgelegt" (1Tim 6, 13). Christliche Zeugenschaft hat sich ausschließlich an Jesus zu orientieren, an seiner Reich-Gottes-Botschaft, die im Feindesliebegebot ihre steilste Aufgipfelung findet (vgl. Mt 5, 38-48 par) – eine Haltung, die der Evangelist Lukas in Jesu Kreuzeswort „Vater vergib ihnen, denn sie wissen nicht, was sie tun" erfüllt sieht (Lk 23, 34), weshalb im zweiten Teil des lukanischen Doppelwerkes, in der Apostelgeschichte, der Diakon und „Protomärtyrer" Stephanus ganz nach der Figur Christi beschrieben wird (Apg 7, 54-60). Dem Lynchmord an Stephanus geht eine stilisierte Verteidigungsrede des Stephanus vor dem Hohen Rat der Juden voraus, die eine einzige Bekenntnisrede zu Christus ist (Apg 7, 1-53) und ihrerseits wieder der Verteidigungsrede Jesu vor Pilatus ähnelt (vgl. Mt 27, 1f.11-26; Mk 15, 1-15; Lk 23, 1-5.13-25; Joh 18, 28-40; 19, 9-12). Das theologische Kriterium, was als christliche Zeugenschaft zu gelten hat, leitet sich ausschließlich von diesen Zusammenhängen her. Das profangriechische „μαρτυρεῖν" (vor Gericht Zeugnis ablegen)[7] wurde sehr früh mit dem Zeugnis Jesu vor dem Hohen Rat und vor dem römischen Statthalter Pontius Pilatus gleichgesetzt. Sich diesem Zeugnis lebensdramatisch anzugleichen, als Knecht Christi nichts anderes zu tun als der Meister (vgl. Mt 10, 24f.; Joh 15, 20), ist der Kern dessen, was die frühchristliche Tradition „Martyrium" nennt: gewaltlose Standhaftigkeit des christlichen Bekenners, wenn es sein muss bis in den Tod: das sog. „Blutzeugnis".

Mit den „Acta Martyrii Polycarpi", dem Bericht über die Zeugenschaft des 86 Jahre alten Bischofs Polykarp von Smyrna (hingerichtet ca. 160 n. Chr.), deren Grundlage wohl die amtlichen Protokolle der vernehmenden Behörde sind und die zum Zweck der erbaulichen Lektüre narrativ-apologetisch stilisiert und mit Einleitung und Schluss versehen wurden, ist dann nicht nur eine neue Textgattung erfunden, sondern auch die spezifische Bedeutung dessen festgelegt worden, was bis heute als „Martyrium" im christlichen Sinne zu gelten hat.[8] Im Wesentlichen lassen sich vier Kriterien unterscheiden:

(1) Als erstes ist da die „Gnade des Martyriums" zu nennen. Christliche Zeugenschaft „usque ad effusionem sanguinis" darf nicht selbst inszeniert, provoziert oder gar aus eigener Initiative gewählt werden. Die „Gnade des Martyriums" beinhaltet zwar die Bereitschaft zum Lebenszeugnis, aber nur in äußerster

---

[7] Vgl. Norbert Brox, *Zeuge und Märtyrer. Untersuchungen zur frühchristlichen Zeugnis-Terminologie*, München 1961, 17f.

[8] Vgl. Bernhard Kriegbaum, „Märtyrer – das christliche Heiligkeitsideal der frühen Kirche", in: *Opfer – Helden – Märtyrer*, 35-49.

Notlage. Es ist Gott selber, der aussucht, wen er als seinen Bekenner haben will und wen nicht.[9]

(2) Das zweite Kriterium liegt in der Leidensgemeinschaft mit Jesus, weshalb die frühchristlichen Märtyrerakten, insbesondere die des Polykarp von Smyrna, die grundsätzliche Gewaltlosigkeit christlicher Zeugenschaft herausstreichen (vgl. Mt 26, 51-54; Mk 14, 47; Joh 18, 10f.): Polykarp wendet nicht nur keine Gewalt an, sondern bewirtet noch die Soldaten, die kommen, um ihn zu verhaften.[10]

(3) Das dritte Kriterium ist das des öffentlichen Bekenntnisses: „*Christianus sum*"[11], so lautet die stereotype Antwort der angeklagten Christen auf die ihnen vorgelegten Fragen nach Herkunft, Stand und Religion. Man sieht: Der Grund der Anklage liegt im Bekenntnis. Angeklagt ist die Identität des Angeklagten, die dieser nur aufrechterhalten kann unter Hintansetzung seines Lebens. Polykarp will nur das tun dürfen, was er, der jetzt 86-Jährige immer getan hat: Christus dienen.[12]

(4) Als viertes Kriterium streichen die frühchristlichen Märtyrerakten die den Bekennern von Gott geschenkte Souveränität gegenüber jenen heraus, die nicht anders als gewaltsam gegen die Wehrlosen vorgehen können[13] – erneut ist hier das Beispiel Jesu stilbildend, erinnert sei an die Haltung Jesu im Garten Gethsemani (Joh 18, 4-11), die sich fortsetzt im Verhör vor Pilatus (18, 33-39; 19, 9-12). In der Dialektik von Macht und Ohnmacht ist der Zeuge Christi nur scheinbar ohnmächtig (vgl. Lk 21, 14f. parr). Seine seelische Kraft wächst dem Zeugen Christi aus dem Wissen zu, dass – wie schon bei Jesus – Gottes Stärke sich in die Hohlform menschlicher Schwäche ergießt, um diese ganz mit ihr zu erfüllen: „Denn das Törichte an Gott ist weiser als die Menschen, und das Schwache an Gott ist stärker als die Menschen" (1Kor 1, 25), schreibt der Apostel Paulus, weshalb gilt: „Deswegen bejahe ich meine Ohnmacht, alle Mißhandlungen und Nöte, Verfolgungen und Ängste, die ich für Christus ertrage; denn wenn ich schwach bin, bin ich stark." (2Kor 12, 10) So wird deutlich, dass das Zeugnis des Christen nicht auf seine eigene menschliche Leistung zurückzuführen ist, sondern auf das Wirken des Heiligen Geistes.

---

[9] Zu den frühesten, sich im Brief der Gemeinde von Smyrna findenden kirchlichen Äußerungen, die das „Martyrium gemäß dem Evangelium" vom eigenwilligen Drang zum Martyrium abzugrenzen versuchen, vgl. Gerd Buschmann, *Das Martyrium des Polykarp*, Göttingen 1998. Zum Ganzen auch Christel Butterweck, *„Martyriumssucht" in der Alten Kirche? Studien zur Darstellung und Deutung frühchristlicher Martyrien*, Tübingen 1995.

[10] Mart. Pol. 7, 2f. – Dasselbe Motiv findet sich in den Akten über das Martyrium des Cyprian von Karthago. Cyprian lässt seinem Scharfrichter, bevor dieser zur Tat schreitet, 25 Goldstücke aushändigen (Act. Procons. Cypr. 5).

[11] Mart. Polyc. 10, 1; Mart. Just. 4; Mart. Carp. 1; 3; Mart. Scil. 9; 10; 13; Mart. Apoll. 1f.; Act. Perp. 3, 2; 6, 6; Act. Pion. 7; 8; 9; 16; 18; Act. Procons. Cypr. 1.

[12] Mart. Polyc. 9.

[13] Mart. Polyc. 2; 8-12; 14; Mart. Just. 5; Mart. Carp. 4f.; Act. Perp. 18-21; Act. Pion. 6-10; 15f.; 18-21; Act. Procons. Cypr. 3-5.

Nun klang allerdings schon an, dass die frühchristlichen Märtyrerakten stilisierte Texte sind. So sehr die Ereignisse, von denen sie berichten, ein historisches Fundament in der Sache haben, so deutlich ist auch, dass sie dem Genre religiöser Erbauungsliteratur angehören, der Gemeinde beim liturgischen Jahresgedächtnis der Märtyrer vorgetragen, ihr historischer Faktengehalt also theologisch überformt ist. Das muss an sich noch kein Einwand gegen ihre Glaubwürdigkeit sein, artikuliert sich in solchen Texten doch vor allem die Selbstwahrnehmung einer soziologisch präzise beschreibbaren Gruppe.[14] Problematisch werden solche Texte hingegen dort, wo die theologische Stilisierung eine Wirkungsgeschichte in Gang setzt, die alles andere als unschuldig ist. So ist es nicht zuletzt der deutliche Antijudaismus der Acta Polycarpi, der dem heutigen Leser zu denken gibt.[15] Ferner befremdet der in den Märtyrerakten massiv herausgestrichene Heroismus der Protagonisten – wohl ein Erbe der frühjüdischen Makkabäertradition und des antiken Stoizismus, das im frühen Christentum bisweilen seltsame Früchte trug. Schließlich ist die nicht selten moralistische Signatur jener Texte, die die Umwelt dualistisch in Gut und Böse einteilt, wenig geeignet, der Frage zur Klärung zu verhelfen, wie man das komplexe Phänomen „christliche Zeugenschaft" aus heutiger Sicht zu bewerten habe.

Will man hierauf eine substantielle Antwort hören, so scheint es sinnvoll, zunächst in Abstand zu den genannten Texten zu treten und an einem aktuellen Beispiel zu klären, was „Martyrium" im christlichen Sinne meint. Ich greife hierzu auf einen Text zurück, der in den Weihnachtstagen des Jahres 1993 entstanden ist und unter dem Titel *Das Testament der Mönche von Tibhirine* weltweit für Aufsehen gesorgt hat. Der Text lässt sich als eine Art existentialtheologische Summe christlicher Zeugenschaft lesen. Insofern scheint er mir außerordentlich geeignet, Kriterien für einen Begriff christlichen Martyriums bereitzustellen, die dazu beitragen können, der eingangs beklagten Begriffsverwirrung abzuhelfen. Schauen wir uns den Text und die konkreten Zusammenhänge, in denen er situiert ist, etwas genauer an.

III. Das Zeugnis der Mönche von Tibhirine

Am 29. Mai 1996 erschien auf der Titelseite der französischen Tageszeitung *La Croix* ein Text, der weit über Frankreich und die katholische Welt hinaus Menschen unterschiedlichster Herkunft, Weltanschauung und Religion bewegte. Der Text war überschrieben mit dem Satz „Wenn ein Lebewohl ansteht...", und als erklärenden Untertitel hatten die Herausgeber von *La Croix* hinzugefügt: „Das Tes-

---

14 Vgl. Theofried Baumeister, „Zeugnisse der Mentalität und Glaubenswelt einer vergangenen Epoche. Hagiographische Literatur und Heiligenverehrung in der Alten Kirche", in: *Kriminalisierung des Christentums? Karlheinz Deschners Kirchengeschichte auf dem Prüfstand*, hg. von Hans Reinhard Seeliger, Freiburg/Br. et al. 1993, 267-278.

15 Die Juden sind an der Errichtung des Scheiterhaufens, auf welchem Polykarp hingerichtet wird, besonders eifrig beteiligt. (Mart. Polyc. 13. Vgl. auch ebd. 17; Act. Pion. 4, 2-20; 13f.)

tament von Pater Christian de Chergé".[16] Wer war dieser Mann, dessen Leben und Sterben solches Aufsehen erregte?

Colmar und Algerien, dann Paris und Algerien, schließlich Rom und Algerien sind die Lebensstationen von Christian de Chergé.[17] Als zweitältester Sohn einer französischen Offiziersfamilie im elsässischen Colmar geboren, verbringt Christian de Chergé seine Kindheit in Algier, Constantine und Oran. In dieser frühen Zeit der kindliche, im Stillen gefasste Entschluss, Priester zu werden – auch und wohl nicht zuletzt beeinflusst von der tiefen Frömmigkeit algerischer Muslime: „Ich stand wie angewurzelt und wusste nicht den Blick abzuwenden von jenen Männern, die, das Gesicht zur Erde geneigt, schweigend im Gebet verharrten."[18] Heimgekehrt nach Frankreich, tritt Christian im Alter von 19 Jahren ins Pariser Séminaire des Carmes ein. Nach Abschluss des dreijährigen Philosophiezyklus Unterbrechung der Studien: der Militärdienst ist abzuleisten. Im Frühjahr 1960 findet er sich in Algerien wieder; die zum französischen Mutterland gehörende Kolonie kämpft um ihre Unabhängigkeit. In diese Zeit fällt ein Ereignis, das seinem Leben eine entscheidende Wende geben wird: Christian befreundet sich mit einem Muslim, Muḥammad, Vater einer zwölfköpfigen Familie, der als Feldhüter für die französischen Behörden arbeitet, zugleich aber Sympathien für die antikolonialistische Sache empfindet. Die angespannte Lage im Land lässt keinen Raum für solche Zweideutigkeiten. Als Muḥammad bei einer aggressiven Rempelei auf offener Straße Partei für seinen Freund ergreift, ist das Maß voll. Am folgenden Tag findet man ihn erschlagen auf. Zwanzig Jahre später, im Rückblick auf jene Zeit, schreibt Christian:

> Angesichts des Blutes meines Freundes, der ermordet wurde, weil er sich nicht mit dem Hass verbünden wollte, wusste ich, dass mich der Ruf, Christus nachzufolgen, über kurz oder lang in jenes Land führen würde, in welchem mir ein Unterpfand jener größeren Liebe gegeben worden war, ‚qui pro vobis et pro multis effundetur'.[19]

---

[16] „Quand un A-DIEU s'envisage... Testament de Dom Christian de Chergé, ouvert le dimanche de Pentecôte *1996*", in: *La Croix* Nr. 134 (29. Mai 1996). Leichter zugänglich bei Christian de Chergé, *L'invincible espérance* (Textes recueillis et présentés par Bruno Chenu), Paris 1997, 221-224.

[17] Das Folgende in Anschluss an Marie-Christine Ray, *Christian de Chergé. Prieur de Tibhirine*, Paris 1998; Mireille Duteil, *Les martyrs de Tibhirine*, Paris: Brépols (1996). – Auf Deutsch liegen folgende Texte vor: Bernardo Olivera, „Mönch, Märtyrer und Mystiker: Christian de Chergé (1937-1996)", in: *Erbe und Auftrag* 76 (2000), 119-138; John W. Kiser, *Die Mönche von Tibhirine. Märtyrer der Versöhnung zwischen Christen und Moslems*, Interlaken 2002. Hingewiesen sei ferner auf den Film *Des hommes et des Dieux* von Xavier Beauvois, der das Drama der Mönche von Tibhirine auf eindrucksvolle Weise einfängt und bei den 63. Filmfestspielen in Cannes 2010 mit dem Großen Preis der Jury ausgezeichnet wurde.

[18] Vgl. Marie-Christine Ray, *Christian de Chergé*, 20f.; John W. Kiser, *Die Mönche von Tibhirine*, 43f.

[19] Marie-Christine Ray, *Christian de Chergé*, 59 (Dt. Übersetzung J.N.). Vgl. auch Bernardo Olivera, „Moine, martyre et mystique: Christian de Chergé *(1937-1996)*", in: Collectanea Cisterciensia 60 (1998) 279-294, hier 281. Anspielungen auf dieses Ereignis finden sich auch in Christian de Chergé, *L'invincible espérance*, 186 und 230.

Nach Paris zurückgekehrt, nimmt Christian seine theologischen Studien wieder auf. 1964 wird er zum Priester geweiht. Jedoch im Sommer 1969 ist der Entschluss, als Mönch in Algerien leben zu wollen, so unerschütterlich geworden, dass der Pariser Erzbischof seinen jungen Priester trotz der vielen Hoffnungen, die auf ihm ruhen, ziehen lassen muss: Ziel ist das Trappistenpriorat Notre Dame de l'Atlas in dem kleinen Dorf Tibhirine im Hohen Atlasgebirge.

Mit seiner am 14. September 1976, dem Fest „Kreuzerhöhung" abgelegten Profess ändert sich für das Priorat manches. Man überträgt Christian die Verantwortung für das Gästehaus. Schon bald bildet sich um den jungen Gastpater eine Gruppe von Christen und Muslimen, die sich in Fragen des alltäglichen Lebens austauschen, miteinander die Heiligen Schriften der Bibel und des Koran lesen, schließlich gemeinsam beten. Das Kloster trennt sich von seinem letzten Grundbesitz, um mit den Bewohnern des Dorfes in einer Kooperative Gartenbau zu betreiben. Den Muslimen wird ein leerstehendes Nebengebäude auf dem Klostergelände überlassen, um eine Moschee einzurichten, über die das Dorf bislang nicht verfügt. Seitdem rufen die Glocken und der Muezzin, je auf ihre Weise, gemeinsam zum Gebet. Zum Kloster gehört auch das Dispensarium, eine kleine Apotheke, die Frère Luc Dochier, der älteste der Mönche und von Beruf Arzt, betreibt. Hier findet jeder, der anklopft, Rat und Hilfe – unabhängig von Religion und Weltanschauung. Die Mönche sind nicht nur im Dorf, sondern weit darüber hinaus geachtet und respektiert.

Jedoch die Zeiten ändern sich. Der integralistische Islam, der seit dem Ende der siebziger Jahre in den Ländern der arabischen Welt spürbar an Boden gewinnt, lässt auch das säkulare Algerien nicht unberührt. Als im Frühjahr 1992 die Sammelbewegung „Front Islamique du Salut" (FIS) aus den Nationalratswahlen als stärkste politische Kraft hervorgeht, erkennt das algerische Militärregime das Wahlergebnis nicht an. Binnen weniger Wochen schlittert das Land in einen Bürgerkrieg. Die Mönche von Tibhirine verstehen sich als Gäste im Land und bemühen sich daher, den Vereinnahmungsversuchen beider Seiten zu widerstehen. Deshalb auch die auf den ersten Blick weltfremde, treuherzig anmutende Titulierung der miteinander verfeinden Gruppen: Die Mönche sprechen von den islamistischen Partisanengruppen als von den „Brüdern aus den Bergen"; und von den nicht minder brutalen Regierungstruppen als von den „Brüdern aus der Ebene".

Die Situation verschärft sich: Im November 1993 ergeht von Seiten der Partisanen die Aufforderung an alle nicht-muslimischen Ausländer, das Land binnen dreißig Tagen zu verlassen. Schon wenige Tage nach Ablauf des Ultimatums beweisen die Partisanen, wie ernst sie es mit ihrer Drohung meinen: Unweit von Tibhirine wird eine Gruppe von zwölf kroatischen Gastarbeitern, die den Mönchen freundschaftlich verbunden sind, auf entsetzliche Weise massakriert. Die Behörden fordern die Mönche auf, das Land wenigstens zeitweilig zu verlassen, da man nicht mehr für ihre Sicherheit garantieren könne. Nach eingehenden Beratungen beschließen die Brüder, zu bleiben. Ein Weichen vor der Gewalt empfänden sie als

Verrat gegenüber all jenen, die keine Möglichkeit zur Flucht haben. Die Dorfbewohner lohnen ihnen diese Solidarität mit lebhaftem Dank.

Dann zwei Wochen später, am Heiligen Abend 1993, eine erste lebensgefährliche Konfrontation. Die Mönche bereiten sich gerade darauf vor, die Vigil von Weihnachten zu singen, als eine Gruppe bewaffneter Partisanen in das Kloster eindringt. Christian de Chergé, zu diesem Zeitpunkt Prior des Klosters, stellt den Anführer der Gruppe zur Rede: „Wir bereiten uns darauf vor, die Geburt Christi zu feiern, des Friedensfürsten, und ihr dringt hier ein mit Waffen." Der Anführer der Gruppe, auf solche Vorhaltungen nicht gefasst, wird unsicher. Es gelingt Christian, ihn von seinem Vorhaben abzubringen, den ältesten der Brüder, den Arzt Luc Dochier, zu entführen. Der Anführer wendet sich nach einem längeren Wortwechsel zum Gehen, nicht ohne sich für die Störung des Gottesdienstes entschuldigt zu haben. Jedoch sein letztes Wort verfehlt seine Wirkung auf die Mönche nicht: „Wir kommen wieder!"

Die Mönche spüren instinktiv, dass sie nur knapp dem Tode entronnen sind. In den Tagen nach Weihnachten zieht sich Christian deshalb in die Einsamkeit zurück. Eine Reihe von Überlegungen, die er einige Wochen zuvor zu Papier gebracht hat, findet hier ihren Abschluss. Den Text sendet er seinem in Paris lebenden Bruder Gérard in einem versiegelten Briefumschlag zu mit der Anweisung, diesen zu öffnen, „quand un A-DIEU s'envisage...", wenn ein Lebewohl ansteht...

Knapp zweieinhalb Jahre später ist der Zeitpunkt für ein solches „A-DIEU" gekommen. In der Nacht vom 26. auf den 27. März 1996 dringt erneut eine Gruppe von Bewaffneten in das Kloster ein. Die Mönche werden im Schlaf überrascht, sieben von ihnen werden entführt. Vier Wochen später, am 26. April 1996, wird der Londoner Tageszeitung *Al Hayat* unter seltsamen Umständen ein Communiqué der „Groupes islamistes armés" (GIA) zugespielt, in welchem Algerien und Frankreich aufgefordert werden, im Gegenzug zur Freilassung der Mönche einige Hundert Islamisten aus den Gefängnissen zu entlassen. Die Verhandlungen ziehen sich hin. Weder die französische noch die algerische Regierung zeigen ein sonderliches Interesse am Leben der Mönche. Nach vier weiteren Wochen vermeldet ein zweites Communiqué der GIA, dass man die sieben Mönche am 21. Mai exekutiert habe. Drei Tage später, am Vorabend des Pfingstfestes, öffnet Gerard de Chergé den Brief seines Bruders. Er ruft die Familie zusammen, die, von Christians Testament tief berührt, zu dem Entschluss kommt, dass dieser Text nicht auf den privaten Kreis der Familie beschränkt bleiben dürfe. Am 29. Mai veröffentlicht die Tageszeitung *La Croix* „das Testament von Pater Christian de Chergé". Noch am selben Abend versammeln sich spontan einige Hundert Menschen zu einem Gedenkgottesdienst in der Pariser Kathedrale Notre Dame. Zwei Tage später, am 31. Mai 1996, werden unweit von Tibhirine die abgetrennten Köpfe der Ermordeten gefunden. Ihre Leichname sind bis heute verschollen.[20]

---

[20] Über das Drama der Entführung und Ermordung der Mönche von Tibhirine, das von offizieller algerischer Seite den GIA angelastet wird, die seinerzeit allerdings stark vom algeri-

Das Testament des Priors von Tibhirine besteht aus einem einzelnen Blatt Papier, beidseitig in gedrängter Handschrift beschrieben. Man hat in diesem Text nicht nur Christians Vermächtnis zu sehen, sondern das der Mönche von Tibhirine insgesamt. Der Text ist so eindrucksvoll, dass man ihn im Wortlaut wiedergeben muss:[21]

Wenn es mir eines Tages geschehen sollte – und das könnte schon heute sein –, ein Opfer des Terrorismus zu werden, der sich nun auch gegen alle Fremden in Algerien zu richten scheint, so möchte ich, dass meine Gemeinschaft, meine Kirche und meine Familie sich daran erinnern, dass mein Leben sowohl Gott als auch diesem Land GESCHENKT war.

Sie mögen anerkennen, dass der Meister allen Lebens diesem brutalen Hinscheiden nicht fremd gegenüberstehen kann.

Sie mögen für mich beten: Wie sollte ich würdig sein für ein solches Opfer?

Sie mögen diesen Tod im Zusammenhang mit so vielen Toden sehen, die ebenso gewalttätig waren, aber in der Gleichgültigkeit dieser Zeit namenlos geblieben sind.

Mein Leben hat keinen höheren Wert als ein anderes; es hat freilich auch keinen geringeren.

Auf keinen Fall aber hat es die Unschuld der Kindheit bewahrt. Ich habe genügend lange gelebt, um zu wissen, dass auch ich Komplize des Bösen geworden bin, das – leider Gottes – in der Welt die Oberhand zu behalten scheint, Komplize gar dessen, der mich dereinst in blinder Wut erschlagen wird.

Ich möchte, wenn dieser Augenblick kommt, so viel ruhige Klarheit haben, dass ich die Verzeihung Gottes und meiner Menschenbrüder anrufen kann, aber ebenso, dass ich dem aus ganzem Herzen vergeben kann, der mich umbringen wird.

Ich kann einen solchen Tod nicht wünschen. Es scheint mir wichtig, dies klarzustellen.

Ich sehe nicht, wie ich mich freuen könnte, dass dieses Volk, das ich liebe, ohne Unterschied wegen meiner Ermordung angeklagt wird.

Was man „die Gnade des Martyriums" nennen mag, ist zu teuer bezahlt, wenn man sie einem Algerier schuldet, wer immer dieser auch sei. Vor allem dann, wenn er sagt, er handle aus Treue zu dem, was er für den Islam hält.

Ich weiß wohl, wie sehr man die Algerier mit Verachtung belegt hat. Ich kenne auch die Karikaturen des Islam, die ein gewisser Fundamentalismus hervorgerufen hat. Es ist zu

schen Geheimdienst unterwandert waren, sowie über die politischen Hintergründe des algerischen Bürgerkrieges seit der Annullierung des Wahlsieges der FIS im Frühjahr 1992 durch das algerische Militärregime vgl. die Dokumentation von René Guitton, *Si nous nous taisons... Le martyre des moines de Tibhirine*, Paris 2001, sowie den Text des seitens der Angehörigen der ermordeten Mönche und der Ordensleitung der Trappisten vorgebrachten Antrags auf gerichtliche Untersuchung in Frankreich vom 9. Dezember 2003: *„L'enlèvement et l'assassinat de sept moines français à Tibhirine, en Algérie, en 1996"*, URL: http://algeria-watch. de/fr/article/just/moines/plainte (zuletzt aufgerufen am 28. Mai 2006). Vgl. dazu auch die einschlägigen Artikel in der französischen Tageszeitung „Libération" vom 10. Dezember 2003 sowie das Feature *Tod der sieben Mönche. Was wussten Algier und Paris?* von Marc Thörner, gesendet auf WDR 5 am 30. April 2006. Vgl. zum letzten Stand der Dinge Michaela Wiegel, *„Am Ende der falschen Fährte. Frankreichs Präsident [Nicolas Sarkozy] will, dass die Wahrheit über einen Mord an sieben Mönchen in Algerien von 1996 ans Licht kommt. Darüber zu schweigen war für lange Zeit Staatsraison"*, in: FAZ Nr. 156 (09.07.2009), 3.

21 Christian de Chergé, *„Quand un A-DIEU s'envisage"*. Deutsche Übersetzung von Martin Kopp (Concilium. Internationale Zeitschrift für Theologie 32 [1996] 379f.) im Abgleich mit dem französischen Original vom Vf. an einzelnen Stellen leicht korrigiert.

leicht, sich ein ruhiges Gewissen zu machen, indem man den religiösen Weg des Islam mit dem fundamentalistischen Integralismus und seinen Extremisten gleichsetzt. – Algerien und der Islam: für mich ist das wie Leib und Seele!

Ich habe es oft genug beteuert: Im Hinblick auf alles, was ich erhalten habe, glaube ich hier so oft den klaren Leitgedanken des Evangeliums wiederzufinden, welches ich damals auf den Knien meiner Mutter, meiner allerersten Kirche, gelernt habe, genau hier in Algerien, und damals schon im großen Respekt vor den muslimischen Gläubigen.

Mein Tod scheint denen recht zu geben, die mich immer schnell als naiv oder idealistisch abgeschrieben haben. „Er mag uns jetzt sagen, was er darüber denkt!" Aber jene, die so reden, müssen wissen, dass nun endlich meine brennendste Neugierde zufriedengestellt sein wird: Nun werde ich, wenn es Gott gefällt, meinen Blick mit dem Gottes, des Vaters, vereinen dürfen, um so mit Ihm seine Kinder aus dem Islam zu betrachten, und zwar so, wie Er sie sieht, ganz erleuchtet von der Herrlichkeit Christi, auch sie Früchte seines Leidens, angetan mit den Gaben des Geistes, dessen tiefverborgene Freude immer die sein wird, die Gemeinschaft zu begründen und die Ähnlichkeit wiederherzustellen, indem er mit den Unterschieden unter den Menschen spielt.

Dieses verlorene Leben, das so ganz meines ist, es wird ebenso ganz das ihre sein. Ich danke Gott, von dem mir scheint, er wollte dieses Leben ganz für diese Freude, gegen alles und trotz allem.

In diesen Dank, mit dem nun alles über mein Leben gesagt ist, schließe ich natürlich auch Euch ein, Freunde von gestern und heute, Ihr lieben Freunde von hier, zur Seite meiner Mutter und meines Vaters, meiner Schwestern und Brüder, hundertfach hinzugeschenkt, wie es versprochen war [vgl. Mk 10, 29f.; Mt 19, 29].

Und auch Du bist eingeschlossen, Freund meines letzten Augenblicks, der Du nicht weißt, was Du tust! Ja, auch für Dich will ich diesen Dank und dieses „A-Dieu", das Du mir [gegen Deinen erklärten Willen, denn in Gottes Antlitz sehe ich das Deine] bereitest.[22]. Dass es uns geschenkt sei, uns als glückliche Schächer im Paradiese wiederzusehen, wenn es Gott, dem Vater von uns beiden, gefällt. Amen. Insh'Allah.

Algier, 1. Dezember 1993
Tibhirine, 1. Januar 1994
Christian †

---

22 Dieser vorletzte Satz des „Testaments" ist kaum ins Deutsche übertragbar: „*Oui, pour toi aussi je le veux ce MERCI, et cet ‚A-DIEU' en-visagé de toi.*" Christian de Chergé will sagen, daß der Mord auf paradoxe Weise das Gegenteil dessen bewirkt, was der Mörder intendiert: Nicht Trennung von Gott, Verdammnis des Ermordeten bewirkt die Tat, sondern Heimkehr. Deshalb kann die Tat auf seiten des Täters die Qualität einer „felix culpa" annehmen: Der Abschiedsgruß „A-DIEU", den der Sterbende spricht, wird zum ehrlichen Segenswunsch, der dem Täter gilt: „Auch Du zu Gott!" Zugleich verbindet sich die Doppelsinnigkeit des „A-DIEU" mit der Doppelsinnigkeit des Wortes „en-visager" (einerseits „in Aussicht nehmen, beabsichtigen, planen; andererseits „ins Antlitz schauen, betrachten"). Der tödliche Hieb des Mörders wird überstrahlt vom Antlitz dessen, dem der Ermordete in seinem Sterben begegnet: Christus bzw. der göttliche Vater. Man beachte, dass die französischen Worte im Original mit Bindestrich geschrieben sind. Christian de Chergé wollte also wohl bewusst auf die Hintersinnigkeit beider Ausdrücke hinaus. (N.B.: Die vom Trappistenorden autorisierte englische Fassung übersetzt ähnlich wie wir: „And also you, my last-minute friend, who will not have known what you were doing: Yes, I want this THANK YOU and this ‚A-DIEU' to be for you, too, because in God's face I see yours." [In: Bernardo OLIVERA: *How far to Follow? The Martyrs of Atlas*, Kalamzoo/Mich.: Cistercian Publications 1997, 129].)

Der Text ist von solcher Wucht, dass es sich im Grunde verbietet, ihn auf die psychologischen Beweggründe seines Verfassers hin untersuchen zu wollen. Gleichwohl mag die Frage erlaubt sein, aus welcher Kraft ein Mensch in die Lage versetzt wird, sehenden Auges in den Tod zu gehen und dabei schon im Vorhinein demjenigen, der sein Mörder werden wird, nicht nur zu verzeihen, sondern ihm darüber hinaus liebevoll zugewandt bleiben zu wollen bis ins Äußerste, bis in die zum tödlichen Schlag erhobene Faust. Es scheint, dass eine Antwort auf diese Frage im intensiven Gebetsleben von Christian de Chergé gesucht werden muss. Obgleich selber von der Scheu beseelt, von den eigenen Gebetserfahrungen nur ja nicht zu viel preis zu geben, schildern ihn jene, die das Privileg hatten, ihn näher kennenzulernen, als einen außerordentlich anspruchsvollen geistlichen Menschen, der durchdrungen war von einer für den Außenstehenden geradezu unfassbaren Liebe zu Gott: „Man musste ihn nur einmal beten sehen: ausgestreckt auf dem Boden, demütig, arm. Eines Tages, als er mir über das Gebet sprach, brach es aus ihm heraus: ‚Nur ein paar Minuten, und ich bin ›weg‹.‘" [23]

In der täglichen Übung völliger Selbstüberlassung hat man denn wohl auch die Quelle jener inneren Freiheit, jener freundlichen Gelassenheit und klaren Entschiedenheit zu sehen, mit der Christian in das Antlitz eines jeden Menschen blicken wollte – selbst in jenes seines Mörders. In einem Exerzitienvortrag, den er im März 1996, wenige Wochen vor seinem Tod, in Algier hielt,[24] kommt Christian noch einmal auf jene unheilverheißende Begegnung am Vorabend des Weihnachtsfestes 1993 zu sprechen, als es ihm nur knapp gelungen war, seine Brüder und sich selbst vor einer Entführung durch die Maquisarden zu bewahren. In diesem Zusammenhang erwähnt er auch das Fünfte Gebot des Dekalogs „Du sollst nicht töten" und deutet es mit Hilfe eines Zentralgedankens von Emmanuel Lévinas, der ihm besonders wichtig war:

> Wenn gilt, dass alle Ethik überhaupt erst durch dieses Gebot [‚Du sollst nicht töten'] in die Welt gekommen ist, so ist zugleich deutlich, dass dieses Gebot sich mir im Antlitz des Anderen zuspricht, der mir durch seinen Blick auf stumme Weise zu verstehen gibt: ‚Achte mich!'[25]

Was aber, wenn ich im Antlitz des Anderen gerade nicht die stumme Bitte „Achte mich!" zu lesen bekomme, sondern das genaue Gegenteil: „Das war's, Freundchen! Sprich dein letztes Stoßgebet!"? – Diese Frage ist keineswegs ins Blaue hinein gestellt, denn es war sehr wohl denkbar, dass der „Freund meines letzten Augen-

---

[23] Zeugnis einer französischen Krankenschwester in Algier, übermittelt bei Marie-Christine Ray, *Christian de Chergé. Prieur de Tibhirine*, 124. (Dt. Übersetzung J.N.) Zumindest am Rande sei vermerkt, dass das anspruchsvolle geistliche Leben, dem Christian sich selber unterwarf, zuweilen für Spannungen innerhalb der Mönchsgemeinschaft sorgte, weil längst nicht jeder seiner Mitbrüder bereit war, dieses Programm mitzutragen.

[24] „L'Église c'est l'incarnation continuée", Christian de Chergé, *L'invincible espérance*, 289-318.

[25] Ebd. 305. (Dt. Übersetzung J.N.) – Vgl. Emmanuel Lévinas, *Totalität und Unendlichkeit. Versuch über die Exteriorität* [1961], Freiburg/ Br. et al. 1987, 285f.; ders. *Die Spur des Anderen. Untersuchungen zur Phänomenologie und Sozialphilosophie*, Freiburg/ Br. et al. 1998, 115-120, 198ff.

blicks", von welchem Christian in seinem Testament spricht, die Züge des Kommandanten jenes Überfallkommandos tragen würde, das die Mönche eine Woche zuvor heimgesucht hatte. Jener Kommandant, ʿAṭṭīya al-Sāyaḥ mit Namen, war als einer der Emire der GIA verantwortlich für die Überfälle auf die Dörfer um Tibhirine; seine Brutalität und sein kalter Fanatismus waren berüchtigt, und die Erfüllung der Drohung „Wir kommen wieder" somit keineswegs unwahrscheinlich. Angesichts dieser beängstigenden Perspektive um die Kraft zu bitten, in jenem Antlitz – durch die süffisanten oder hassverzerrten Züge des Mörders hindurch – immer noch den Blick dessen zu erkennen, der mein Bruder und insofern schutzbedürftig ist, läuft allen instinktiven Selbsterhaltungsmechanismen zuwider. Eine Selbstüberwindung der menschlichen Natur ist hier erfordert, die sich aus anderen als menschlichen Kräften speisen muss und die Anerkennung der letztlich metaphysischen Gründe jenes Appells voraussetzt:

> Der Grund, weshalb es [sc. in der Menschheitsgeschichte] überhaupt zu so etwas wie einem Tötungsverbot gekommen ist, liegt wohl darin, dass man das Bild Gottes tötet, wenn man tötet. In jedem Menschen lebt etwas Ewiges, das durch den Mord tangiert würde und von dem man im Falle einer Mordtat nicht mehr loskäme. Sich seinem Nächsten zu nähern, bedeutet, zum Hüter seines Bruders zu werden; Hüter seines Bruders zu sein, aber bedeutet, sich in eine Verantwortung hineingestellt zu finden, die sich nicht mehr abschütteln lässt, die mich nachgerade zur Geisel meines Bruders, meines Nächsten werden lässt.[26]

In dieser metaphysischen Überzeugung, die, wenn sie lebensgeschichtlich wirksam werden soll, nicht im Kognitiven verbleiben darf, sondern durch das beharrliche Gebet immer wieder neu verinnerlicht werden muss, liegt wohl auch der eigentliche und bestimmende Grund für jene ungeheure Versöhnungsgeste Christian de Chergés. Zugleich wusste er aber auch, wie sehr er selber der Zuwendung, ja der Vergebung bedürftig ist: *„Auch ich habe nicht die Unschuld der Kindheit bewahrt, sondern bin ein Komplize des Bösen geworden..."* Selbst durch den Mord kann die elementare Gemeinsamkeit von Opfer und Täter nicht ausgelöscht werden – jene Gemeinsamkeit, die (über alle eventuellen Komplizenschaften hinaus[27]) darin besteht, Kinder des einen Gottes zu sein. Als solche bleiben

---

[26] Christian de Chergé, *L'Église c'est l'Incarnation continuée*, 308. (Dt. Übersetzung J.N.) – Christian de Chergé zitiert hier, ohne näher darauf hinzuweisen, Emmanuel Lévinas. Vgl. *Jenseits des Seins oder anders als Sein geschieht* [1974], Freiburg/Br. et al. 1992, 260f.; *Die Spur des Anderen. Untersuchungen zur Phänomenologie und Sozialphilosophie*, Freiburg/Br. et al. 1998, 115-120, 198ff.; *Wenn Gott ins Denken einfällt. Diskurse über die Betroffenheit von Transzendenz*, Freiburg/Br. 1988, 208-215 und „Die Verantwortung für den Anderen", in: *Ethik und Unendliches. Gespräche mit Philippe Nemo*, Wien 1992, 72-79.

[27] Im Rahmen einer geistlichen Aufarbeitung des Überfalls am Vorabend des Weihnachtsfestes 1993 kreisen Christians Gedanken um das Geheimnis des christlichen Martyriums (vgl. *L'invincible espérance*, 225-251). Am Karsamstag 1994 kommt er auf „das Zeugnis der Unschuld" („le martyre de l'Innocence") zu sprechen, das einzig Jesus, dem Sündlosen, zukomme (vgl. ebd. 231-237). Daraus schlussfolgert er: „Angesichts dieses ‚Martyriums' sind der Heilige und der Mörder nur zwei Schächer, die auf die gleiche Vergebung angewiesen sind. Manchmal fehlt nur wenig, und man könnte sie verwechseln." („Obscurs témoins

beide, Opfer wie Täter, gleichermaßen auf die göttliche Vergebung angewiesen: *„Dass es uns geschenkt sei, uns als glückliche Schächer im Paradiese wiederzusehen, wenn es Gott, dem Vater von uns beiden, gefällt. Amen. Insh'Allah."*

IV. Zur Frage nach der Bedeutung existentieller Zeugenschaft in postsäkularer Zeit

Blicken wir zurück, so ist deutlich, dass die genannten vier Kriterien christlicher Zeugenschaft im Martyrium der Mönche von Tibhirine allesamt präsent sind: von außen kommende Nötigung zum Zeugnis, vergebungsbereite Gewaltlosigkeit, allein aus Gott sich schöpfende christusförmige Machtlosigkeit, öffentliches (und insofern auch politisch relevantes) Bekenntnis. Insbesondere aber sind die Fallibilitäten christlicher Zeugenschaft, wie wir sie anhand unserer Analyse der frühchristlichen Märtyrerakten vorfanden, im Lebenszeugnis der Mönche von Tibhirine weitestgehend vermieden: Weder wird der Gegner um der Herausstreichung der eigenen religiösen Wahrheit willen herabgesetzt (im Gegenteil!) noch ist hier ein fragwürdiger Heroismus, eine depressive Leidverliebtheit oder gar eine lebensuntüchtige Todessehnsucht am Werk. Nicht zuletzt deshalb gilt das Lebenszeugnis der Mönche von Tibhirine vielen als Beispiel christlicher Zeugenschaft par excellence.

Natürlich kann man auch dieses Zeugnis noch einer Hermeneutik des Verdachts unterziehen. Da uns der Anruf Gottes immer nur im Widerhall der Antwort des Menschen vernehmbar wird – da m.a.W. göttliches Wort uns immer nur in der Gestalt des Zeugnisses entgegenkommt, das Menschen, die sich von ihm ergreifen lassen, von ihm ablegen, ist Wahrheit niemals als sie selbst zu haben, sondern immer nur in der Gestalt, welche das menschliche Zeugnis ihr verleiht. Und so könnte man natürlich auch angesichts eines Zeugnisses wie jenem der Mönche von Tibhirine fragen, ob hier nicht der Zeuge seinen eigenen Projektionen aufgesessen ist. Ist sein Reden und Handeln nicht vor allem Echo seiner religiösen Vorurteile bzw. der kulturellen Klassenverhältnisse, denen er angehört? Schon die bloße Tatsache, dass die Mönche von Tibhirine als Angehörige der ehemaligen französischen Kolonialmacht im muslimischen Algerien das Evangelium bezeugen, provoziert ja eine gewisse Ambivalenz in dem ganzen Entführungsdrama. Und könnte es nicht sein, dass der Wunsch, als christlicher Mönch französischer Herkunft dem algerischen Islam möglichst respektvoll zu begegnen, von altruistischen Wiedergutmachungsphantasien begleitet, also gar nicht so uneigennützig ist, wie es auf den ersten Blick erscheint? Man könnte mit solchen Insinuierungen problemlos fortfahren.

---

d'une espérance" [17. Juli 1994], *Sept vies pour Dieu et l'Algérie. Recueil de lettres et bulletins des sept moines de Tibhirine*, hg. von Bruno Chenu, Paris 1996, 136. [Dt. Übersetzung J.N.])

Stattdessen sei hier folgender Frage nachgegangen: Wird durch die Einsicht in die kulturelle Relativität menschlicher Zeugenschaft deren argumentatives Potential notwendig hinfällig? Wohl kaum! Mir scheint vielmehr, dass hier eher eine Hermeneutik des Verdachts, die vor dem religiös imprägnierten Wahrheitsanspruch ethischer Überzeugungen ständig warnen zu müssen glaubt, unter Rechtfertigungsdruck gerät. Zwar will auch die durch Jan Assmann prominent gewordene Monotheismus-Kritik nicht einer Aufhebung der kritischen Unterscheidung von „wahr" und „falsch", „gut" und „böse" das Wort reden; sie meint aber, diese Unterscheidung diskursiv verflüssigen zu müssen:

> An der Unterscheidung zwischen Wahr und Falsch, an klaren Begriffen dessen, was wir mit unseren Überzeugungen als unvereinbar empfinden, werden wir unter allen Umständen festhalten müssen, wenn anders diese Überzeugungen irgendeine Kraft und Tiefe besitzen sollen. Nur werden wir diese Unterscheidung nicht mehr auf ein für allemal festgeschriebene Offenbarungen gründen dürfen, sondern immer wieder neu aushandeln müssen.[28]

Seltsam – wie kann man beides logisch zugleich behaupten: Man müsse „unter allen Umständen" (also unbedingt) an „klaren Begriffen" festhalten (nämlich in Hinsicht auf die Unterscheidung von „Wahr und Falsch", mit unseren politischen oder ethischen Überzeugungen „vereinbar" oder „unvereinbar"), und gleichzeitig auf ein Unbedingtes (nämlich „Offenbarung") verzichten und alles „immer wieder neu aushandeln"? Zwischen dem unbedingten Festhalten an etwas und dem „immer wieder neu Aushandeln" kann es kein „sowohl als auch" geben, sondern nur ein „entweder–oder".[29] Eine unbedingte Verpflichtung setzt nun aber die Annahme eines Unbedingten voraus, sei es (biblisch formuliert) einer Offenbarung der den Menschen in die von ihm zu verantwortende Freiheit setzenden göttlichen Gnade, sei es (in philosophischer Sprache) eines mir eingeschriebenen Sittengesetzes (vgl. Röm 2, 14ff.), das eben deshalb einer metaphysischen Fundierung bedarf.[30] Sowohl die Vorgabe gnadenhafter Berufung des Menschen zur Freiheit als auch die eines metaphysisch fundierten Sittengesetzes müssen zwar immer wieder neu plausibilisiert werden, können aber gerade wegen der ihnen innewohnenden Selbstperformanz nicht einfach „immer wieder neu ausgehandelt werden", will man sie nicht unter das ihnen eignende Verbindlichkeitsniveau fallen lassen.

---

28 Jan Assmann, *Die mosaische Unterscheidung*, 165.

29 So die berechtigte Kritik von Karl-Josef Kuschel, „Moses, Monotheismus und die Kultur der Moderne. Zum Gespräch über Jan Assmanns ‚Moses der Ägypter'", in: *Die Mosaische Unterscheidung*, hg. von Jan Assmann, 273-286, hier 274.

30 Kant wusste um diese Zusammenhänge sehr genau, weshalb die Erfahrung einer unbedingten Verpflichtung des „moralischen Gesetzes in mir" (*Kritik der praktischen Vernunft*, A 289, in: *Werke*, hg. von Wilhelm Weischedel, Bd. 6, 300), reformuliert im Kategorischen Imperativ, für ihn nicht anders denkbar war denn unter dem Postulat bzw. regulativen Prinzip der Vernunft, dass ein Gott sei, in welchem das Natur- und das Sittengesetz auf eine ihre Verbindung begründende höchste Einheit und auf einen Grund dieser Einheit übereinkommen.

Assmann schreckt vor beiden Konsequenzen (sowohl vor der explizit biblisch-mosaischen bzw. jesuanischen als auch vor der kantisch moderierten) zurück, weshalb die an und für sich erfreuliche Revision, der er seine Monotheismuskritik unterzogen hat,[31] für die uns hier beschäftigende Problematik nicht ausreichend ist. Könnten es nicht gerade geschichtliche Krisensituationen sein, wie sie das katastrophische 20. Jahrhundert zur Genüge geboten hat, um sich des Wertes jener Grenze, die die biblische Offenbarung aufgerichtet hat, zu vergewissern?[32] Womöglich lernt man nur hier, dass es Situationen gibt, da ein Zurückweichen hinter das einmal als gültig Erkannte alles verriete, was man als wertvoll erachtet. Wo hingegen in apodiktischer Sprache konstatiert wird, dass an Offenbarung zu glauben „uns" intellektuell nicht mehr möglich sei, dass „wir" dies nicht mehr „dürfen", sondern dass „wir" statt dessen immer wieder von neuem „auszuhandeln" hätten, was uns als „mit unseren Überzeugungen" noch vereinbar erscheint und was nicht, da rückt uns das Problem postmoderner Velleität auf den Leib: die Furcht vor der den Menschen womöglich das Äußerste abverlangenden Entscheidung, was ethisch richtig ist und was falsch. Dass solche Entscheidungen nicht willkürlich getroffen werden dürfen, dass man sie vielmehr argumentativ zu verantworten hat und dass gerade deswegen Offenbarung und Vernunft keineswegs einen Widerspruch darstellen müssen, wie Assmann insinuiert, sondern die Vernunft durch eine unwiderruflich ergangene und kritisch reflektierte Offenbarung womöglich über sich selbst aufgeklärt worden sein könnte: genau das scheinen er und seine Epigonen nicht wahrhaben zu wollen, weswegen sie in jenem äußersten Zeugnis, das die theologische Sprache „Martyrium" nennt, den Aufschein einer Intransigenz religiös formierter Vernunft erblicken, angesichts derer man nur warnend seine Stimme erheben könne.

Dagegen hat Paul Ricœur wenige Jahre nach dem Zweiten Weltkrieg die Zusammenhänge, vor welche uns das Zeugnis der Mönche von Tibhirine führt, auf folgende biblisch fundierte und philosophisch reflektierte Formel gebracht:

> Ich mache die Entdeckung, dass mein Lebenswille der Todesangst nur in dem Augenblick entgeht, in dem meine Gründe zum Leben über mein Leben selbst gesetzt werden, in dem die konkreten Werte, die den Sinn meines Glücks und meiner Ehre bilden, den Gegensatz von Leben und Tod selbst überwinden. Es versteht sich von selbst, dass dieser Akt der Transzendenz nur in der Haltung des Opfers vollendet wird; im Opfer ist mein Leben zugleich gefährdet und transzendiert, gefährdet durch den Tod in der Katastrophensituation, und transzendiert durch seine eigenen Gründe zum Leben, die zu Grün-

---

[31] Als eine solche will Assmann sein Buch *Die mosaische Unterscheidung oder Der Preis des Monotheismus* [2003] verstanden wissen, in welchem er die Thesen aus *Moses der Ägypter. Entzifferung einer Gedächtnisspur* [1997/98] einer vorsichtigen Retraktation unterzieht.

[32] Genau darauf macht ja ein *in theologicis* so unverdächtiger Romancier wie Thomas Mann aufmerksam: „Das Gesetz" [1942/44], in: *Die Erzählungen*, Frankfurt/M, 1986, 961-1037. – Vgl. dazu Karl-Josef Kuschel, *Moses, Monotheismus und die Kultur der Moderne*; sowie ders., „Weltethos und die Erfahrungen der Dichter. Thomas Manns Suche nach einem ‚Grundgesetz des Menschenanstandes'", in: *Wissenschaft und Weltethos*, hg. von Hans Küng et al., München et al. 1998, 455-492.

den zum Sterben geworden sind. Aber das ist leichter gesagt als gelebt, und die Reflexi-on braucht die Unterstützung leuchtender Beispiele, mit denen eine Gefahrenepoche wie die unsere vollgestopft ist.[33]

Was Ricœur hier tastend umschreibt, hat Abraham J. Heschel, dessen Familie in den nationalsozialistischen Konzentrationslagen fast vollständig ausgelöscht wur-de, auf folgende eindrückliche Formel gebracht: „Wir können die Wahrheit nur leben, wenn wir auch die Kraft besitzen, für sie zu sterben"[34] (das jüdische „Kid-dusch haSchem" klingt hier an[35]) – ein Satz, der nicht zuletzt an Kierkegaard ge-mahnt, der die Frage nach der Wahrheit bekanntlich unter das Kriterium gestellt hatte, ob man bereit sein könne, sich für sie gegebenenfalls auch totschlagen zu lassen,[36] und zwar nicht aus der verbohrten Intransigenz eines religiösen oder ideologischen Fanatismus heraus, sondern – um mit Albert Camus zu sprechen – aus der Erkenntnis, dass „einen Grund zum Leben" zu haben „ein ausgezeichne-ter Grund zum Sterben" ist, ist doch „die Frage nach dem Sinn des Lebens die dringlichste aller Fragen".[37] Den Sinn meines Lebens kann ich mir freilich nicht selber geben. Nicht um ein weltanschauliches Problem geht es hier, zu dessen Lö-sung ich mich aus eigener Kraft ermannen bzw. das man immer wieder einmal „neu aushandeln" könnte: Vielmehr „[d]er Begriff des Sinns involviert Objektivi-tät jenseits allen Machens; als gemachter ist er bereits Fiktion, verdoppelt das [...] Subjekt und betrügt es um das, was er zu gewähren scheint."[38] Insofern ist tatsäch-lich allein, was mir das Leben ermöglicht, jenes, wofür sich zu sterben verlohnt, aber nicht aus einer fragwürdigen Todesverliebtheit heraus, sondern aus dem un-bezwingbaren Wunsch, zu leben. Hans Urs von Balthasar hat diese Zusammen-hänge folgendermaßen auf den Punkt gebracht: „[...] Zeugenschaft, *martyrion*, [ist] weniger eine Sache des Sterbens als des Lebens in jedem Augenblick"[39] – hier leuchtet die den Tod transzendierende Macht existentieller Zeugenschaft auf, von welcher Ricœur sprach und wie sie im Lebenszeugnis der Mönche von Tibhirine an den Tag kommt: Selbst noch (oder gerade dann), wenn man an dem, was ei-nem das Leben ermöglicht, „bis hinein in den Tod" (Offb 12, 11) festhält, schöpft man sich aus ihm – und allein so lebt man. Lässt sich ein solcher „unter allen Umständen" festzuhaltender, lebensstiftender Sinn „immer wieder neu aushan-deln", wie Assmann meint?

---

[33] Paul Ricoeur, „Wahre Angst und falsche Angst" [1953], in: Ders.: *Geschichte und Wahrheit*, München 1974, 319.

[34] „We can only live the truth if we have the power to die for it." Abraham J. Heschel, *Who is Man?*, Stanford 1965, 92.

[35] Vgl. Verena Lenzen, *Jüdisches Leben und Sterben im Namen Gottes*, Zürich et al. 2002.

[36] Sören Kierkegaard, *Hat ein Mensch das Recht, sich für die Wahrheit totschlagen zu lassen?*, in: *Ge-sammelte Werke 21.-23. Abtlg., Kleine Schriften 1848/49*, Düsseldorf et al. 1960, 77-114.

[37] Albert Camus, *Der Mythos von Sisyphos. Ein Versuch über das Absurde*, Reinbek bei Hamburg 1982, 9.

[38] Theodor W. Adorno, *Negative Dialektik*, Frankfurt/M. 1988, 369.

[39] Hans Urs von Balthasar, „Martyrium und Mission", in: ders.: *Neue Klarstellungen*, Einsie-deln 1979, 172.

Aus der Perspektive christlicher Theologie liegt die Antwort auf der Hand: Blickt man auf das Leben und Sterben derer, die die abendländische Tradition als „Zeugen der Wahrheit" bezeichnet, so wird deutlich, dass sie die besseren Argumente liefern. Ohne des Sokrates Vernunftbesessenheit, die angesichts des drohenden Todes ihre ganze Stärke offenbart, wäre nicht das leibhaftige Beispiel dafür in der Welt, dass die Vernunft, jenes die Menschen von den Tieren unterscheidende Vermögen zur Abstraktion, auch eine die menschlichen Entscheidungen und Handlungen durchgängig bestimmende Kraft sein könnte. Und ohne den Gerechtigkeitssinn derer, die selbst angesichts von Verfolgung und Bedrohung an ihrer kritischen Einsicht in die Inhumanität von Faschismus oder Stalinismus festhielten, wüssten wir nicht, was Humanität, Solidarität oder Gerechtigkeit sein könnten. Und schließlich ohne das Glaubenszeugnis derer, die sich in ihrem Leben und Sterben auf jenen Gott verließen, „der die Toten lebendig macht und das, was nicht ist, ins Dasein ruft" (Röm 4, 17), wüssten wir nichts von Ihm. Insofern ist über Ricœur noch hinauszugehen: Nicht nur braucht „die Reflexion [...] die Unterstützung leuchtender Beispiele, mit denen eine Gefahrenepoche wie die unsere vollgestopft ist"; es scheint, dass nicht zuletzt an jenen Beispielen sich sowohl die ethische wie die religiöse Reflexion entzündet (hat), sind doch sie es, die ihr immer wieder aufs neue zu denken geben. Insbesondere hierin, so scheint mir, liegt die unaufgebbare, das menschliche Denken und Handeln humanisierende Bedeutung eines Lebenszeugnisses wie jenes der Mönche von Tibhirine.

Gandhi and the Sovereignty of Death

Faisal Devji (Oxford)

"We love death the way you love life."[1] These words were uttered by Shehzad Tanweer, one of the London suicide bombers, in a video released on the first anniversary of the attacks in July 2006. Other terrorists have gone further in claiming to love death more than their enemies do life, but whatever its form this striking statement appears calculated to challenge the primacy given to life in contemporary definitions of humanity. Although such a primacy has roots in the Christian sanctification of life, it is fundamentally modern in its overwhelming reference to the present, since the kind of humanity that is defined by humanism, humanitarianism and human rights tends to be strictly positive and contemporary in nature, eschewing any notion of an afterlife for instance. In other words: we are not dealing with a metaphysical conception of humanity that includes both the dead and the unborn, or a philosophical conception that would treat it as a regulative ideal, but rather with humanity as a global fact amenable to technical manipulation and administrative measures.

However, by erasing the past as much as the future from its definition and confining humanity, future generations included, to a purely empirical existence, we end up making it much more vulnerable to attack. Humanity thus becomes the eternal victim of history, always teetering on the brink of an apocalypse, whether of an atomic, environmental or even terrorist kind. It was the threat of nuclear war that first transformed humanity into a planetary fact, whose empirical existence alone made it capable of becoming an historical victim – and therefore potentially an historical actor as well. So the proliferation of fantasies about alien invasions and mutant infiltrations during this period only underlined humanity's vulnerability in the age of the atom bomb and the moon landing. Indeed these fantasies often rendered the earth into a kind of prison for the human race, a home under siege from hostile forces, or even a dead planet that a few lucky individuals bearing the future of their race might escape in a spaceship. Humanity thus assumes its mortal reality in popular imagination only within a war of the worlds.

The primacy given to life in the definition of a planetary humanity makes it prey to every kind of fear and anxiety. Moreover, the militant negation of life as humanity's defining feature provokes all these fears and anxieties by challenging it as a category familiar to us from the language of humanitarianism and human

---

 "American Al-Qaeda Operative Adam Gadahn, Al-Qaeda Deputy Al-Zawahiri, and London Bomber Shehzad Tanweer in New Al-Sahab/Al-Qaeda Film Marking the First Anniversary of the 7/7 London Bombings", *Middle East Media Research Institute*, Special Dispatch Series, no. 1201, 11.07.2006, 2, URL: http://www.memri.org/report/en/print1738.htm://memri.org/bin/opener.cgi?Page=archives&IDSP120106 (retrieved 21.07.2013)

rights. What the hysteria over militant Islam's "death cult" or "nihilism" entails then, is an attempt to re-draw humanity's borders around the love of life in such a way as to deprive those who would love death of their status as human beings. So the novelty of the legal measures put into place in America and Britain to imprison people accused of being potential terrorists, if only because of the things they say or read, lies in their assumption that such people are automatons who can be set off on a murderous rampage by the slightest provocation, and who are more dangerous than wild animals because they do not value their own lives.[2] These men indeed resemble Hollywood's robots in the imagination of their enemies – killing machines set off by some invisible switch like bit-part Terminators. Yet in placing so much emphasis on the love of life that they profess to find the love of death incomprehensible, the humanists of our time divorce their conception of humanity from Christianity more than they separate it from Islam, since the love of death is arguably more familiar in the former than the latter.[3]

In any case, life has not always provided the definition or even the ideal of humanity, so that in Roman Antiquity for example, there were many circumstances in which life was not considered worth living. And in these circumstances suicide was not only accepted but also seen as a noble act manifesting the quintessence of all that is human. I do not mean to equate Muslim terrorists with Roman suicides, only to claim that, when confined to life, humanity becomes a much narrower category than it ever was in the past. For even as a global fact, the human race can be and is indeed divided into a hierarchy of those more or less human than others, whether by moral, legal or medical criteria, since the inhuman always lurks behind any empirical definition of humanity as its shadow. It is even possible to claim that the more civilised a people is, the more stringent its criteria for humanity will be, and therefore the more likely it will be to condemn others to the status of the inhuman.[4] No better example can be given of this than the impassioned debates among modern humanists as to militant Islam's evil and inhuman nature. By contrast, the militants themselves entertain no ideas of the West's evil or inhuman character, no matter how much they may loathe and despise its representatives.

The Christian concept of evil is not one that exists in the rhetoric of militancy, and certainly not as a kind of external force, its place being taken by the Muslim's own sin in refusing to sacrifice himself for humanity. And since this humanity is not conceived of merely in terms of life as an empirical fact, being half in love with easeful death, it cannot become a category of exclusion but includes both friends and enemies within its embrace. Is this why Islam's terrorists always insist on referring to their enemies in the most familiar of ways, to the ex-

---

[2]   See for this Judith Butler, *Precarious Life: The Powers of Mourning and Violence*, London 2004.

[3]   For this see Talal Asad, *On Suicide Bombing*, New York 2007.

[4]   This is an argument made by Carl Schmitt in *The Concept of the Political*, trans. George Schwab Chicagon 1996, 54.

tent of joking about their hatred of each other? The paradox of loving death more than others love life is that in doing so the militant ends up rejecting humanity's status of victim together with the evil that produces it, since dying for him no longer figures as the negation of all that is human. Indeed, terrorist accounts of martyrdom invariably describe the militant's corpse as being far more beautiful than his living body ever was, becoming in this way more human than the human being it had once belonged to, and even exuding a perfume that made it seem more lifelike than its own life.

Rather than seeing in such statements a pre-modern religious inheritance, or examples of moral and psychological perversion, I want to link them to a tradition of anti-humanist political thought. The militant's contempt for life becomes meaningful as part of a general challenge to concepts like humanitarianism and human rights, which today dominate the rhetoric of global politics. To reject the priority given to life in such a politics is, of course, to move decisively beyond the accusations of "hypocrisy" that terrorists are not alone in levelling against the claims, made by Western powers in particular, to defend it. While an illustrious lineage of anti-humanist European thinkers exists, from Friedrich Nietzsche to Michel Foucault, very few if any of these men have challenged the politics of life by focussing on the love of death. And yet, simple though it may seem, such an inversion is surely an important part of any critique to which humanism might be subjected, especially given the value still placed on sacrifice in even the most humanitarian of societies.

I. Mahatma and Militant

In this essay I want to look at the way in which Gandhi, another militant who, as we shall see, advised people to love death more than life, might have been the most original critic of humanism in the history of modern politics. Although he was a critic of terrorism as well, I will explain how the Mahatma recognised that a complex relationship existed between its violence and his own advocacy of non-violence. Gandhi's language of sacrifice drew upon a number of traditions, including Hindu, Muslim and Christian, taking from the latter two roughly equivalent terms like the English martyrdom and the Arabic *shahāda*. Indeed, his ideas of self-sacrifice were largely indebted to this monotheistic terminology, since the Hindu tradition does not possess an independent conception of martyrdom. Instead, Sanskrit terms like *tyaga* or *tapasya* refer to renunciation and penance, while *yagnya* or *balidan* mean an offering that is distinct from the person making it. In modern times, *balidan* has come to include martyrdom among its implications, probably as a borrowing from Christian and Muslim notions, though the Arabic *shahāda* still remains the most common word for self-sacrifice in all north Indian languages. And like monotheistic conceptions of the term, the Mahatma's view of sacrifice placed witnessing at its centre. Not only did the nonviolent protestor bear witness to the cause he supported by his suffering, but more importantly this sacrifice had to be witnessed by others so as to be capable of convincing and converting even his enemies to the ways of righteousness. In this way Gandhi, himself an early star of the international press, turns out to have created an inadvertent precedent for the globally mediated witnessing and conversion of terrorist forms of sacrifice in our own times. And indeed Gandhi was not averse to comparing nonviolent suffering with revolutionary terrorism, not least because both courses of action resulted in the courting of arrest, punishment and even death. For as he put it to some companions in Bengal in 1946:

> Bengal had tried the method of violence for a long while. The bravery of the revolutionaries was beyond question, but it had failed to instil courage in the mind of the common man. But although the non-violence of the past twenty-five years had been of an indifferent quality, yet nobody could deny that it had succeeded in elevating the character of the whole nation to a certain extent.[5]

While Gandhi's is not a name to be uttered alongside that of a militant like Osama bin Laden, he, too, spoke of the necessity of bloody sacrifice in the cause of justice. In doing so the Mahatma was responding, in the early days of his career, to the Indian terrorists whose arguments, as he recounted them, bear a remarkable similarity to those that "experts" of all kinds attribute to the jihad movements of our own time:

> At first, we will assassinate a few Englishmen and strike terror; then, a few men who will have been armed will fight openly. We may have to lose a quarter of a million men, more or less, but we will regain our land. We will undertake guerrilla warfare, and defeat the English.[6]

To this political argument Gandhi offers the following religious response, which to my mind is far closer to the response that suicide bombing offers us today: "That is to say, you want to make the holy land of India unholy. Do you not tremble to think of freeing India by assassination? What we need to do is to kill ourselves."[7]

If the Mahatma so frequently advocated killing oneself for a just cause, this was not because he thought it an effective and ethical way of achieving some end, but rather because sacrificing one's life could not in fact be an instrumental act and was thus thrown back upon itself to become not a means so much as an end unto itself. Choosing death therefore transformed political acts into religious ones by demonstrating their unworldly and disinterested nature. Gandhi was quite clear that the terrorists of his day partook of sacrifice in its religious form, though they did so in a perverted way. Referring to one such suicidal assassin he wrote: "Dhingra was a patriot, but his love was blind. He gave his body in a wrong way; its ultimate result can only be mischievous."[8]

---

5   Nirmal Kumar Bose, *My Days With Gandhi*, New Delhi 1999, 106.
6   M.K. Gandhi, *Hind Swaraj and Other Writings*, Cambridge 2003, 77.
7   Ibid., 77.
8   Ibid., 78.

By the time Gandhi's movement of nonviolence had achieved maturity, the mutual violence between Indians had far outstripped their combined violence against the British. But this only made the Mahatma more determined on sacrifice. While not advocating the killing even of noisome insects, he was, in other words, willing to countenance the voluntary sacrifice of a million human lives for righteous ends. Indeed, towards the end of his own life, Gandhi longed for as many such Hindu and Muslim deaths as possible, so that these rival communities might cement their unity in blood. As it turns out, Gandhi, who was assassinated by a Hindu militant, ended up shedding his own blood to mix the cement of this unity. Gandhi's ideas of sacrifice were meant to retrieve another sense of the human from the idea of humanity that informed terrorist as much as humanitarian acts. After all, it was no accident that the Mahatma's assassin described his own act of violence as a "humanitarian" one, since he identified Hinduism with a statistical conception of humanity: "For, is it not true that to secure the freedom and to safeguard the just interests of some thirty crores of Hindus constituted the freedom and the well-being of one-fifth of [the] human race?"[9]

Faced with the increasingly murderous enmity between Hindus and Muslims in the India of the 1940s, the Mahatma was determined to transform this violence, not by futile pleas for harmony, but by turning it inwards in acts of sacrifice that would invite, if not compel, a different kind of response from those spoiling for a fight. The purpose of this sacrifice, which Gandhi had also mobilised against the British rulers of India, was to lay claim to the noblest human virtues such as courage and fearlessness, and so provoke the collapse or conversion of those who were bent on violence. All this was to be achieved not by prating about non-existent ideals, but instead by separating the already existing practice of sacrifice from that of murder, and this was to be done by emphasising it to such a degree that the courage and fearlessness of sacrifice were turned into gestures of hospitality.

In other words, for Gandhi, the display and witnessing of sacrifice was not important as a way of engineering sympathy and conversion among bystanders and opponents. Instead, the Mahatma could only tolerate violence and value suffering because he thought the nonviolent resistance they displayed constituted moral as well as political sovereignty in its own right. Indeed, he frequently described such resistance as the "sovereign method" or the "sovereign remedy" for every kind of political ill. And if we define as sovereign any authority that can ask people to kill and die in its name, then we must recognise that what Gandhi did was to split the concept of sovereignty down the middle. By separating dying from killing and prizing the former as a nobler deed, the Mahatma was doing nothing more than retrieving sovereignty from the state and generalising it as a quality vested in individuals. For while such individuals might be unequal in their ability to kill, they were all equally capable of dying and, therefore, able to demonstrate the universal-

---

[9]   Nathuram Godse, *Why I Assassinated Mahatma Gandhi*, Delhi 1998, 26 (parenthesis mine).

ity of suffering and sacrifice over violence of all kinds. And because he had fragmented sovereignty in this way, Gandhi held that the nonviolent hero's most intimate rival could only be the revolutionary terrorist willing to kill and die for India's freedom. What was sovereign about the terrorist's act, after all, was the fact that it already represented freedom and did not serve merely as an instrument for its realisation in some undefined future. Indeed, the Mahatma believed that the sovereignty of terrorism resided in its sacrificial immediacy, which was what gave it nobility in the eyes of other Indians, and not in the murderous element that merely obscured it with the rhetoric of instrumentality. Hence, in a speech delivered in 1916, Gandhi blamed the militants of his time for degrading the truly sovereign act of dying, achieving it by killing:

> I honour the anarchist for his love of the country. I honour him for his bravery in being willing to die for his country; but I ask him: Is killing honourable? Is the dagger of an assassin a fit precursor of an honourable death?[10]

The Mahatma can therefore be described as a philosophical anarchist, since he not only disconnected sovereignty from the state, but also believed that, as a willingness to suffer and die, it lay in the grasp of anyone who wanted it. As early as *Hind Swaraj* or "Indian Self Rule", his manifesto of 1909 which by no coincidence is structured as a dialogue with a violent revolutionary, Gandhi had made it clear that freedom and thus sovereignty was immediately available to anyone fearless enough to accept suffering and death by withdrawing cooperation from an unjust order. Indeed, only that freedom was real which possessed this existential and therefore individual character, even if the rest of India remained in chains.[11] Departing in this way from the long-awaited collective utopias of revolutionary politics elsewhere, Gandhi linked his movement to the kind of immediate gratification that arguably inspires all mass action at some level.

II. Throwing Life Away

Early in July of 1937, a well-known Nazi journalist, SS officer and advisor to Hitler named Roland von Strunk visited Gandhi at his ashram in Segaon. As befitted a National Socialist concerned with the cultivation of a nation's health and power, Captain Strunk was interested in the Mahatma's criticism of machinery and modern medicine. In the course of their conversation, Gandhi pointed out what he thought was the fundamental contradiction in the attention that Europeans paid to the preservation of life:

---

[10] M. K. Gandhi, "Hindu University Speech", in: *Speeches and Writings of Mahatma Gandhi*, Madras 1922, 256.

[11] See M. K. Gandhi, *Hind Swaraj and Other Writings*, ed. by Anthony J. Parel, Cambridge 1997, 73.

> But the West attaches an exaggerated importance to prolonging man's earthly existence. Until the man's last moment on earth you go on drugging him even by injecting. That, I think, is inconsistent with the recklessness with which they will shed their lives in war. Though I am opposed to war, there is no doubt that war induces reckless courage. Well, without ever having to engage in a war I want to learn from you the art of throwing away my life for a noble cause. But I do not want that excessive desire of living that Western medicine seems to encourage in man even at the cost of tenderness for subhuman life.[12]

Having expressed his horror of the hatreds sweeping Europe, the violence of Spain's Civil War, in which he had accompanied Franco's Army on its march to Madrid, and even what he said was the "overdone" targeting of Jews in Germany, Strunk must have been surprised to hear that Gandhi was in some ways even more contemptuous of life than Hitler. For the Mahatma's desire to learn from the "reckless courage" of European warfare was not in the least premised upon the need to protect one's own life, nor indeed the lives of one's countrymen, racial brothers or partners in civilisation, as was true both of the Nazis and their enemies. In fact, Gandhi was clear that justifying war by means of the conventional link between taking life in order to save it could in no sense be considered rational. What the Mahatma found disturbing, in other words, was not that an inordinate concern with preserving life stood opposed to its casual disposal in battle, but rather that one led to the other in such a way as to make the love of life itself guilty of the desire for death. Only by giving up the thirst for life that was represented in modern warfare and medicine alike, he suggested, could the urge to kill be tamed.

From the kind of "subhuman life" that modern medicine sacrificed in its vivisections, to men and women rendered "subhuman" and thus available for fascism's killing machines, Gandhi blamed humanity, or at least its definition in terms of life as an absolute value, for the massive scale of modern violence. And this not only allowed him to put the Nazis in the same category as their enemies as far as the espousal of such a value was concerned, but also to hold humanitarians and pacifists equally responsible for its violence. Indeed, in some ways those dedicated to the cause of peace and humanity were even more culpable than the rest, if only because they might value life in far greater measure than others who were at least willing to sacrifice it in war. For in the very recklessness of this sacrifice the Mahatma saw the possibility of going beyond and even destroying life as an absolute value. The kind of violence that entailed risking one's life, in other words, was capable of providing an opening for nonviolence, something that preventing war in the name of life's sanctity never could. And this was why Gandhi wanted to learn the art of throwing one's life away from those parts of European warfare that still involved such risk. As if convinced by the Mahatma's words, Ro-

---

[12] M. K. Gandhi, "Interview to Capt. Strunk", in: *Harijan*, 03.07.1937, in: *The Collected Works of Mahatma Gandhi* (hereafter *CWMG*), New Delhi 1976, vol. LXV, 361.

land von Strunk died in Germany a few months later, the casualty of an old-fashioned duel fought with pistols, which resulted in Hitler banning the custom altogether.

It was only by refusing to treat life as an absolute value that Gandhi was able to accomplish his aim and spiritualise politics, for he thought that as long as life remained its basis, political action could never answer to moral principles.[13] After all, the preservation of life was an aim that all political actors shared, and therefore no moral principles could be drawn from it, these having been reduced merely to second-order justifications for valuing some lives over others. The courage of a Nazi, for instance, would be deemed in this way to possess less value than that displayed by an American or Russian soldier fighting him, but only because it was dedicated to taking life for an immoral cause. The paradoxical thing about the Mahatma's glorification of sacrifice in the name of an ideal rather than a gross reality such as life, however, is that its rejection of this reality as an absolute value also entailed protecting it. Only by disdaining life could it be saved, while even politics in its most sacrificial forms, including the Cold War doctrine of "mutually assured destruction," continued being devoted to life's preservation. By disregarding the saving or protection of life as a justification for sacrifice, Gandhi of course managed to exit the monotheistic narratives of martyrdom that otherwise provided him with so much of his conceptual vocabulary. For in line with the Hindu teaching of "desireless action" as expounded in an ancient text like the *Bhagavad-Gita*, which was one of the Mahatma's chief sources of inspiration, sacrifice could only be dedicated to the cause of truth in its own right and not defined by the sordid calculation of means and ends that would make something merely instrumental of it. Martyrdom, then, even when undertaken in somebody's defence, had to be informed by duty alone, this being the only way in which it could set limits to the instrumentality of everyday action that yet remained unpredictable and prone to failure.

The Mahatma was not being idealistic, I think, in calling for sacrifice in the name of duty, since such an invocation is familiar enough in the figure of the soldier who is also asked to die out of duty, such a task taking strict legal priority over his propagandistic role in saving or protecting the lives of his countrymen. But this form of sacrifice is perhaps more visible in the suicidal acts of contemporary terrorists, who in places like Iraq, Afghanistan or Pakistan can rarely be said to behave in the way that counter-terrorism analysts say they should: by disposing of their lives in an asymmetric way, with one suicide bomber bringing about as much death and destruction as possible. The fact that this happens so infre-

---

[13] In a brilliantly provocative essay, Shruti Kapila has argued that truth rather than nonviolence was the key to Gandhi's politics. And this meant that not only life but morality itself had to be subordinated to the imperative of truth as the only absolute value. See Shruti Kapila, "Gandhi before Mahatma: The foundations of political truth," in: *Public Culture*, vol. 23, no. 2, Spring 2011, 431-448.

quently should be attributed not to any misjudgement on the militant's part, but instead on his or her deployment of martyrdom in a non-instrumental way. Indeed, this is borne out in al-Qaida documents, which often speak of potential martyrs having to be restrained in the offering of their lives on any occasion. And rather than seeing these frustrated martyrs simply as the deluded instruments of others, we might do better to reflect upon the non-instrumental form their sacrifice takes, something that gradually deprives the militant's cause itself of any conventionally political character.

Gandhi went further than asking people not to love life, if only because he wanted them to love death more. Thus in his response to a letter from Bengal describing the exodus of Hindus from what had in 1947 become East Pakistan, he claimed that by loving death those in peril could avoid the cowardice that might save their lives but leave them consumed by shame and the consequent hatred of Muslims that was meant to atone for it:

> Man does not live but to escape death. If he does so, he is advised not to do so. He is advised to learn to love death as well as life, if not more so. A hard saying, harder to act up to, one may say. Every worthy act is difficult. Ascent is always difficult. Descent is easy and often slippery. Life becomes liveable only to the extent that death is treated as a friend, never as an enemy. To conquer life's temptations, summon death to your aid. In order to postpone death a coward surrenders honour, wife, daughter and all. A courageous man prefers death to the surrender of self-respect.[14]

A life devoted solely to self-preservation, in other words, would not be one worth living. Though he was willing to tolerate spectacles of sacrificial destruction, Gandhi did not pay as much attention to such events in places like Stalingrad, Dresden or Hiroshima as did the politicians who waged war in the name of life. Instead, his disregard for life in the name of principles took far more quotidian forms. Thus, during the time he spent in Noakhali just prior to India's partition trying to make possible the return of Hindu refugees there, the Mahatma repeatedly forbade private persons and charitable organisations to provide them with help. This was in order to compel the Muslim League government of Bengal to fulfil its responsibilities in caring for this displaced and terrorised population, while at the same time teaching the latter to behave as the citizens of a democracy. Nirmal Kumar Bose, in his luminous account of Gandhi's days in Calcutta and Noakhali during this period, makes it abundantly clear that the Mahatma's concerns were not in fact humanitarian at all but political, since it was in politics that the root of violence as well as its potential for conversion was lodged:

> But, in spite of the magnitude of material damage, Gandhiji was more concerned about the political implications of the riots. Later on, he told me one day that he knew, in any war brutalities were bound to take place: war was a brutal thing. He was therefore not so

---

[14] M. K. Gandhi, "Death–courageous or cowardly", in: *Harijan*, 30.11.947, in *CWMG* (1984), vol. XC, pp. 87-8.

much concerned about the actual casualties or the extent of material damage, but in discovering the political intentions working behind the move and the way of combating them successfully.[15]

The conversation with some friends who had come on behalf of the Gita Press of Gorakhpur had more than a usual interest. They came with an offer of blankets worth a lac of rupees for distribution among the evacuees. But Gandhiji wished them to hold back the gift for the present. He said, it was the duty of the Government to provide warm covering, and it was within the rights of the evacuees to press their demand. If the Government failed, and confessed that it had not resources enough, then only could private organizations step in to help the evacuees. Unless the people were conscious of their political rights and knew how to act in a crisis, democracy can never be built up.[16] Gandhiji dealt with the problem as a whole and explained that we should proceed in such a manner that the Government might be put in the wrong and the struggle lifted to the necessary political plane. Whatever steps had to be taken, whether it was relief or migration, should be taken only after the Government had been made to confess that they were unable to do anything more for the sufferers, or had failed to restrain the rowdy Muslim elements. If, in the meantime, which he hoped would not be more than a week or so, a few of the sufferers died of exposure, he was hard-hearted enough (main nirday hun) not to be deflected from his course by such events. The whole struggle had to be lifted to the political plane; mere humanitarian relief was not enough, for it would fail to touch the root of the problem.[17]

My purpose in quoting Bose's text so extensively is not only to show that Gandhi's politics of nonviolence was as far removed from humanitarianism and its cult of victims as it could possibly be, but also to demonstrate how it was that his idealism was the least "idealistic" of things. His response to suffering was thus not in the first instance to ameliorate it, but instead to make sure that those who had been wronged behaved like moral agents and not victims, thus allowing them to enter into a political relationship with their persecutors. These men, after all, were themselves in need of a moral transformation, for which their victims were to be made responsible, preferably without the humanitarian intervention of any third party. If the spiritualisation of politics meant anything, it was this eminently realistic dedication to an ideal that took precedence over life's own reality. And in fact the nihilistic or even apocalyptic elements in modern politics all seem to derive from the fears of those who value life either in its weightiest forms, as represented by the survival of nations, races and even species, or in its lightest and most impoverished ones, such as the desire to safeguard one's profit, lifestyle or wellbeing, both forms being part of the same continuum. For it is the fear of this value being threatened that makes possible a defensive politics with no limits as far as its violence is concerned.

---

[15] Nirmal Kumar Bose, *My Days with Gandhi*, New Delhi 1999, 43.
[16] Bose, *My Days with Gandhi*, 43.
[17] Ibid., 87f.

III. The End of Human Rights

When in 1947 he was asked to express his opinion on what might go into a report for the United Nations Human Rights Commission in Geneva, which was
to draft the Universal Declaration of Human Rights, Gandhi rejected the whole
idea of inalienable rights. Chief among these, of course, was the right to life,
which like all other rights the Mahatma would instead make dependent on duties, since these had nothing passive about them and involved dealing with violence in an effort to convert it.[18] Indeed it was precisely in violence that Gandhi
claimed to discover the possibility of its overcoming, something that the great
revolutionary figures of the past two centuries had always maintained, though
none in his intensely moral if idiosyncratic way. It was the moral relationship between enemies rather than friends that created rights, which meant that such relationships had to be prised despite the violence they entailed, and not what the
Mahatma considered the deeply suspect ideal of life as an absolute value. It
might be appropriate, then, to end this essay with a passage from Gandhi's letter
to Julian Huxley, the first Director of UNESCO, condemning the rights of man:

> I learnt from my illiterate but wise mother that all rights to be deserved and preserved
> came from duty well done. Thus the very right to live accrues to us only when we do
> the duty of citizenship of the world. From this one fundamental statement, perhaps it is
> easy enough to define the duties of man and woman and correlate every right to some
> corresponding duty to be first performed. Every other right can be shown to be usurpa-
> tion hardly worth fighting for. I wonder if it is too late to revise the idea of defining the
> rights of man apart from his duty.[19]

If Gandhi's vision of nonviolence is to be taken at all seriously today, we ought
to acknowledge that one of the great challenges facing its proponents is to think
about what a "citizenship of the world" might look like that does not invoke the
rights of man as its justification. For unlike rights, which can only be guaranteed
by states and are thus never truly in the possession of those who bear them, duties belong to individuals and cannot be stripped from them.[20] They represent in
this sense the inalienable sovereignty of men and women, and therefore stand
alone in their ability to create rights. Yet first among all duties, of course, is the
disposal rather than preservation of life, something that is familiar enough from
our own notions of morality and politics, or at least such of them as stand outside the demesne of rights. Indeed, it is even possible to say that duty is dominated by death and the individual as right is by life and the collective. And in
this sense the Mahatma's nonviolent idea of individual duty bears comparison to
al-Qaida's violent conception of militant activity as a *fard al-ʿayn* or individual

---

18 For Gandhi's conception of duty and criticism of rights, see Richard Sorabji, *The Stoics and
Gandhi: Modern Experiments with Ancient Values*, Oxford 2011, chapter 5.

19 Gandhi, "Letter to Julian Huxley, May 25, 1947", in *CWMG* (1994), vol. XCV (supple-
mentary vol. 5), p. 142.

20 I am grateful to Ramin Jahanbegloo for this insight into Gandhi's idea of duty.

moral duty like praying and fasting. For unlike the *farḍ al-kifāya* or collective obligation, within which category jihad has generally been placed and which has a political and therefore instrumental purpose, the individual duty glorified by militants today is clearly denuded of such a function. Like the militants of our own day then, by thinking of duties before rights Gandhi was able to think of sovereignty beyond the state and its violent politics of life.

III.
Visual Representations:
Ritual, the Arts and New Media

Performing a Massacre

Murder and Martyrdom in *taʿziyih*

Maryam Palizban (Berlin)

Fig. 1: *Ḥurr*[1] *Taʿziyih*, Ḥurr's army entering *takyih* (the *taʿziyih* space), Gaz, 2010.

Taʿziyih has been performed in Iran for nearly 400 years as a ritualistic theatre form, rooted in the Islamic Shiite religion; however, it has developed to a level where it needs to be considered as more than a mere religious ritual. At first it was performed only in Iran, followed later in almost all Shiite countries such as Iraq, Lebanon and Bahrain; nonetheless, the most developed theatrical form is still performed in central Iran. It is a performance involving dozens of actors and children as well as featuring both manmade and real animals.

With the Shiite Ṣafawīd dynasty (1501-1722), the historical story of Ḥusayn's oppositional movement and the tragic outcome of his rebellion against the ruling caliph of the time, *Yazīd*, developed into a self-reflecting, powerful source

---

[1] Al-Ḥurr was a high-ranking general in the army of Yazīd (Ḥusayn's enemy) who switched sides in favour of Ḥusayn and became a martyr on his side.

that connected all oppositional movements in the Shiite community against all kinds of tyranny.[2]

The conflict that ends with the massacre of Ḥusayn, his family and his companions had a tremendous impact. The mourning over their catastrophic demise was readily adopted into older forms of mourning rituals already existent in every region. During the 18th century these gently gave birth to a form of theatre structured around the polarisations of Ḥusayn's story and the definitions of *mukhālif khawānī* (antagonist) and *muwāfiq khawānī* (protagonist).

It is necessary to differentiate between the *taʿziyih* or other mourning-sacrificial rituals and the processions during the mourning months of *Muḥarram* and *Ṣafar*. This necessity rises from the vague discussion of different phenomena in studies neglecting the characteristics defining each medium. This essay will focus particularly on the ritualised theatrical performance – the *taʿziyih* – which takes place at particular places at particular times as a happening, in short as an "event that takes place".[3]

Mourning, as it happens in *taʿziyih*, is the code turning the spectators into interactive players, resulting in a "bodily co-presence of actors and spectators".[4] The grief over the *murder* is not in response to the murder of a single individual; rather, the life line of an entire community is interrupted. It is about a *mass murder.*

But performing a historical massacre is a challenge when considering everyday life. It is not only a historical narration but a fictive happening lasting hours on end. Free from the unity of place and time, it welcomes the use of modern technology. Microphones have been integrated into the *taʿziyih* as a means to solve practical problems without any fear of compromising authenticity.[5] "Man and woman alive" and their "ongoing developing and declining processes of interpersonal and intergroup behaviour in communities and network",[6] turn the sacred figures and their death on the stage of the *taʿziyih* into a theatrical system that adapts itself to fit into the present.

What a *taʿziyih* narrates is the murder of Ḥusayn – the grandson of Muḥammad, the Islamic Prophet – with his family and followers at Karbalāʾ at the hands of the army of the Sunnite caliph, a battle lasting just one day that ended up in a massacre of all men, including Ḥusayn and even children. A *taʿziyih* concentrates on this paramount moment in Shiite history. It is performed over several days with different storylines, all of which revolve around the Karbalāʾ massacre. Every theatre performance ends with the martyrdom of one of the famous characters

---

[2]   For more detail, see Hamid Dabashi, "Taʿziyeh as Theatre of Protest", in *The Drama Review*, 49 (2005), 91-99.

[3]   Max Hermann, "Das theatralische Raumerlebnis", in: *Raumtheorie - Grundlagentexte aus Philosophie und Kulturwissenschaften*, ed. by J. Dünne et al., Frankfurt 2006, 153.

[4]   Erika Fischer-Lichte, *Ästhetik des Performativen*, Frankfurt 2004, 45.

[5]   It is customary nowadays for every *taʿziyih* participant to use a microphone, held in one hand as a fixed accessory.

[6]   Victor Turner, *The Anthropology of Performance*, New York 1987, 21.

connected to Ḥusayn; it is therefore named after the main protagonist to be killed last on stage.

Similar to the Greek tragedies, the *taʿziyih* audience is familiar with the stories. The spectators can distinguish the *antagonists* from the *protagonists* by the colours of their costumes and the music. The protagonists sing their texts from a small notebook, which they carry in their hand, while the antagonists declaim. The colours of the male protagonists are green, white and orange, while the females wear black and the antagonists are dressed in red, gold, etc.

I. Ḥusayn and Siyāwush

Taʿziyih as a theatrical form has its roots in ritual.[7] Later it was established as a theatre form, similar to its present-day manifestation.[8] Linked to the mourning rituals of a God sacrificed in winter and reborn in spring, *taʿziyih* protagonists are deeply connected to Siyāwush, the Persian prince of the mythical Kiyāniyān dynasty and the mourning rituals associated with his sacrificial death.[9]

The figure of Siyāwush, in a textual and performative context, has been transformed in many basic elements of a *taʿziyih*: black functions as the colour of mourning;[10] horses, as totemic symbols, are always present beside the protagonists and the antagonists in the vengeful actions consequent to the murders of

---

[7] For further studies about the origin of theatre: Jane Ellen Harrison, *A Study of the Social Origin of Greek Religion*, Cambridge 1912.

[8] Cf. ʿAli Ḥusūrī, *Siyāwushān*, Tehran 2000, and Ehsan Yarshater, "Development of Persian Drama in the Context of Cultural Confrontation in Iran", in: *Iran: Continuity and Variety*, ed. by Peter Chelkowski, New York 1971.

[9] Siyāwush's story in Firdawsī, Shāhnāmih, Tehran 2005. Rustam, the mythical Persian hero, raises him and brings him – a young noble man eligible to become king – to the royal court of his father, Kāwūs. Sūdābih, the queen and wife of Kāwūs, ignites a passion for Siyāwushand repeatedly approaches him, to no avail. Having been rejected and now vengeful, Sūdābih goes to Kāwūs and falsely accuses Siyāwush of rape and assault. To prove Siyāwush innocence he is tested with fire (a ritual indicating sacredness of fire in ancient Iran; the accused had to walk cross the fire and the innocent would not burn), and he has to cross through the fire on his black horse. Once proven innocent, Siyāwush asks his father to forgive Sūdābih and goes into self-imposed exile to fight the Tūrāniyāns and eventually retreats to Tūrān. Siyāwush is popular even in the land of his enemies. He marries Farangīs, daughter of Afrāsiyāb, and establishes a pristine and heavenly town in Tūrān. But the popularity of this stranger is costly. Provoked by his men, especially his brother, Afrāsiyāb orders Siyāwush to be beheaded. The period of peace ends and, as Siyāwush had predicted, an age of revenge begins. Siyāwush is one of the most important sacrificed figures in Central Asia where a disposition to demigods is evident.

[10] The colour black is originally more an Iranian symbol for mourning and not so prevalent in the Arab world and the Islamic tradition. ʿAlī Ḥusūrī, *Siyāwushān*, 89. Both figures, Ḥusayn and Siyāwush have mythical horses. *Dhu'l-Janāḥ*, which means Pegasus, is Ḥusayn's horse and *Shabrang*, which means black horse as symbol for a male horse (totem), belongs to Siyāwush.

both Ḥusayn and Siyāwush;[11] and most importantly, the mourning rituals performed for the sacrifice of the holy demigod/God.[12] Narshākhī in *History of Bukhārā* states: "There are special songs of the people about the killing of *Siyāwush*.
The musicians called these *Kīn-i Siyāwush*... from now (332/943) it was three
thousand years ago."[13]

This is one of the oldest pieces of evidence of *Siyāwush-Khawānī*, the annual
mourning tradition played out to mark Siyāwush's death, as a ritual. *The History of
Bukhārā*, a reliable source on the subject of mourning and elegy recitation rituals,
describes in detail all significant issues with regards to the history of this ritual.

But what is the sense of performativity that these protagonists share in ritual
to theatre?[14] What is the process through which historic-mythic-cultural figures
transform into performative characters of a collective memory?

1. Ḥusayn

In a *taʿziyih* interpretation Ḥusayn is mostly a father figure, a man with his children or simply a man with his brother and sisters. Even as a husband, his role is
reduced to that of a family head, a shepherd defending his flock. Ḥusayn is accompanied by a large number of people on the stage. He bears responsibility for
all. He is always present, even if he is not the main protagonist or even if his
story is absent, as is in fact the case in some important *taʿziyihs*. He remains the
fundamental element of cultural memory in the *taʿziyih*.[15]

Like Ḥusayn, *taʿziyih* protagonists exist on two different levels: that of the
taʿziyih text and the actual performance. The so-called protagonists – the *taʿziyih*
martyrs – are presented in both *textual* und *performative* discourses. Here I will focus here on *taʿziyih* protagonists, specifically Ḥusayn – also famous as the *Lord of
Martyrs* –, in terms of how they portray the character in their performance, leaving aside the literary representation. In other words here we will discuss the *martyrdom in its performative context*.[16] The mourning rituals revolving around both
figures are connected. Siyāwush, as an earlier martyr figure, is still strongly con-

---

[11] Post-Karbalāʾ movements like the rebellions of Mukhtār and Tawwābūn. The whole Shāhnāmih (977) after the death of Siyāwush is more or less about the revenge and the following war.

[12] According to Ḥuṣūrī in *Siyāwushān*, 25-53, Siyāwushān turns to be a totem in Central
Asia, but also the narration of his story in later versions all point out his demigod existence and his holiness.

[13] Abū Bakr Muḥammad b. Jaʿfar Narshākhī, *Tārīkh-i Bukhārā* [332/943], trans. by Abū Naṣr
Qubādī (Persian), Tehran 2009, 59. Translation by the author.

[14] As far as the protagonists concerned, in a *taʿziyih* Ḥusayn is only one of thousands. Scores
of historical und fictive figures are involved in a *taʿziyih*.

[15] There are many *taʿziyih* stories with no direct connection to Karbalāʾ however; in these
taʿziyihs Ḥusayn and his fate are also mentioned implicitly or explicitly.

[16] See Erika Fischer Lichte, *Theater als Modell für eine performative Kultur*, Universitätsreden,
Saarbrücken 2000, 46.

nected with nature: it is from his blood, which drops to the earth while he is murdered, that plants grow.[17] The mourning ritual devoted to him thus replaces the spring festivities.

This refers in turn to another mythical figure: Tammūz, the Sumerian God of Vegetation. These two early figures – Siyāwush and Tammūz – come from different traditions: the Siyāwush myth is originally from Transoxiana while Tammūz, who also seems to be an older counterpart, is based in Mesopotamian culture. With their central theme of the sacrificed god, the mourning rituals connected to them and last but not least, their strong performative and literary backgrounds, they furnish sufficient evidence that a cultural transmission took place which brings Mesopotamian and Transoxianan traditions together in the *ta'ziyih*.

All three characters are based on the principle of *duality*.[18] As far as the myth of Tammūz is concerned, these two poles are represented in Tammūz and his spouse Inanna. While Inanna kills Tammūz so as to survive, soon after she starts to mourn the loss of Tammūz and this continues until he returns to earth.[19]

If we follow the thesis of William Robertson Smith, who argued that "the myth was derived from the ritual and not the ritual from the myth",[20] then the basic action can be traced back to the act of sacrifice in all these myths. The main difference between the newer (Husayn and Siyāwush) and the older version (Tammūz) is how the mourners and murderers are separated into two groups. In the oldest version these two characteristic features belong to the same figure: in the Tammūz-Inanna myth, Inanna is the one who kills Tammūz and is, at the same time, the one who mourns him; in the later versions however, the murders and the mourners are separated from each other. It is out of this very separation into antagonists (as murderers) and spectators (as mourners), witnessing the emergence of a theatre-ritual out of a mourning ritual, that the *ta'ziyih* originates.

The main question that arises here is the identification between the antagonists and the spectators, between the *mourners* and the *murderers*. Robertson Smith's thesis shows that the oldest counterpart of our myth, rooted in a ritual, had given its antagonist both *mourner* and *murderer* roles. Although in a *ta'ziyih*

---

[17] The plant is called *Par-i Siyāwushān*.

[18] Duality here may be defined as *moral duality*.

[19] The other important aspect is rebirth. Mehrdād Bahār has written on this: "The presence of *Kay-Khusraw* as the son of Siyāwush in fact represents the resurrection and rebirth of the martyred god. If we accept that Siyāwush is the Iranian example of *Dumūzī* (Tammūz) of Mesopotamia, in that case the death of Siyāwush equals the descendent of Dumūzī or Tammūz to the netherworld. But Dumūzī/Tammūz returns to life whereas this part is missing in the story of Siyāwush. The escape of *Kay-Khusraw* from *Tūrān* to Iran in fact is the return of Dumūzī to the world and his kingdom represents the renewed godliness of this vegetation deity and fertilization." *Sukhanī čand dar bārih-yi shāhnāmih*, ed. by Katāyūn Mazdāpūr, Tehran 1979, 226.

[20] William Robertson Smith, *Lectures on the Religion of the Semites*, ed. by Adam and Charles Black, London Elibron [1894] 2005, 18.

both roles are specifically separated and clearly contoured, the older counterpart seems to have no problem with an undefined state as to the *mourners*.

At the same time, the spectators see themselves reflected in the protagonists who, having gone through the transformation the holy family into an elementary *social icon* – the family –, in turn moves the mourners to identify with the protagonists. The whole aforementioned complex creates an enormous sense of ambivalence in the theatre space. We need to explore this issue in more detail.

II. *Antagonists in the* taʿziyih: *Evil on the Stage*

In the *taʿziyih* we are dealing with evilness on two levels: firstly, there is evil as an act of malice, or in the words of Paul Ricoeur: "when one experiences himself as a victim of the evilness of others";[21] secondly, we are faced with discovering evil in one's own self (as a spectator). These two aspects of experiencing the phenomenon of the *evil* are circularly connected with each other in the *taʿziyih*. Hence, the first interaction is not the empathic dialogue with the *good* – the protagonists – but with the *evil*, the antagonists.

It is the discovery of passiveness in the spectator as an experience of one's own fate when facing injustice: the experience of watching on – and only being able to watch – while others are murdering someone fully incapable of defending themselves and engaging in a fair fight (much like a child), of being condemned to the position of a mere spectator when the situation actually demands intervention. This is the result of the limits imposed by the stage, what we may term 'the theatrical dictatorship'. Moreover, witnessing murder more or less implicates the viewer in the deed committed, turning them into an accomplice, if not indeed making them (partly) guilty. The situation causes a perception of suffering when *the others* are suffering,[22] und the most extreme examples of this experience are scenes of child murder in some of the important *taʿziyihs*.

The key to discovering this evil dimension are the antagonists. They are alone, unaccompanied by women, children and families. The antagonists are also unmusical, i.e. they are not given a musical theme. While the protagonists sing and proudly show off their highly-qualified voices, the antagonists shout and unleash their voices as loud as they can, for antagonists are rulers and represent authority. They are the manifestation of sovereignty on the *takyih*, the *taʿziyih* space. Here, under this aspect, *mourners* and *murderers* become *masses* and *sovereigns*, respectively.

Takyih as the *taʿziyih* space consists of three concentric circles (see the figure below). The central circular space belongs to the protagonists. Most of the action takes place in this space, the space afforded Ḥusayn and his family. All this centres around a family (*masses*), the holy family of Ḥusayn, which represents the

---

[21] Paul Ricoeur, *Das Böse*, Zürich 1986, 19.
[22] Ibid., 18.

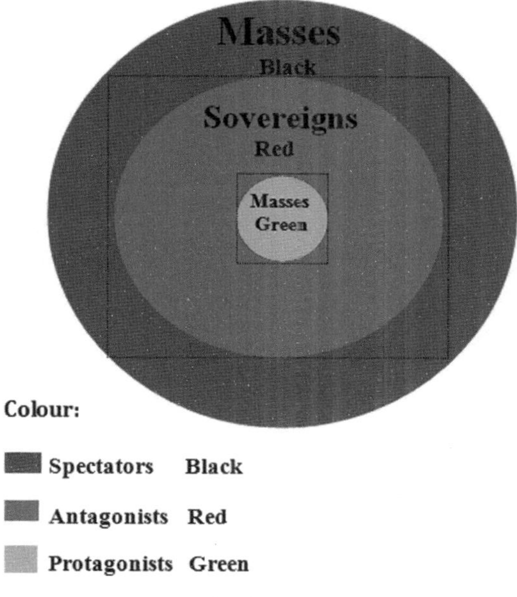

Colour:

Spectators   Black

Antagonists   Red

Protagonists   Green

Fig. 2: The territories of the *takyih* stage

society. The masses in the outer space are thus watching a mirroring of their own fate in the inner space of the stage (protagonists' space).

The second or middle circle belongs to the antagonists. The antagonists never leave this space, except for the murder scenes. Finally, the largest space is afforded to the spectators. This system enables the masses to observe their *sovereigns,* a situation impossible outside this theatrical space. If we leave the *takyih* we are entering the territorial domain of the sovereign or the authorities.

III. A Collective and Its Shadows

These circles are the key to understanding this unique system. How every internal circle reflects on the outer circle, the relationship between the different circles and, more importantly, the dominant circle, which belongs to the spectators and holds both circles within itself – these elements together construct what we may call a performative system. We are dealing with a society that is facing its protagonists on stage. The most significant protagonists are undergoing the process of becoming a martyr. The antagonists are those who enable this process of metamorphoses from mere protagonist to martyr.

Majlis is a title indicating a specific performance of the *taʿziyih*: *majlis-i shahādat-i imām ḥusayn* is one of the thousands of performances and it can be translated as *The Performance of the Martyrdom of Imam Ḥusayn.* While literature is confined to seeing martyrdom as a predefined phenomenon, the figuration of martyrdom in a *taʿziyih* creates a completely different case. In literature the process of becoming a martyr is already completed when it reaches and is received by the reader, whereas in a *taʿziyih* performance, presenting the process of becoming a martyr, it is the spectators who define and declare the moment and the figure of martyrdom.[23] Spectators are the rulers over the rhythm of the whole *taʿziyih*. Their interest and attention decides, indirectly, the best time for arranging the climaxes and how much effort needs to be put into it.

Martyr figures, as a part of cultural memory, transcend all expected norms in the act of becoming a martyr. In the *taʿziyih* we cannot ignore the dominant interactive presence of the spectators. They are free to stay or leave anytime they want, the auditorium is never darkened but always remains light, and they are allowed to drink and eat as they wish. The spectators' reactions are essential to first establishing and then changing the rhythm of the *taʿziyih*. Almost every scene – expositions, rising actions, climax, falling actions and dénouements – depend on the spectators' reactions, for instance their crying or expression of appreciation. Here the spectators rule and by exercising this rule they reclaim the cultural memory in the name of an *interactive cultural memory*.

On the performative level the martyr is tied up in "the materiality of theatre, that is, from the semiotics of movement, tones, silences, costumes, and spatial arrangements onstage, as well as from the reactions of spectators in the auditorium."[24] In this case, the martyr and his sovereign act, facing the limitations and dictatorship of the theatrical space, turns into the sacrificial death of the innocent, becoming the victim of a collective murder which in the case of a *taʿziyih* renders them as the victim of both spectators and antagonists.

Ḥusayn and the other protagonists straddle two different layers; naturally enough they are manifestly present as protagonists in a *taʿziyih*; but they are also represent, on the other side as it were, the collective memory of the spectators.

1. The taʿziyih*'s manifestation of the protagonists*

In a *taʿziyih* the manifestation of the protagonists is based on a paradox: the character structure of each figure is established independently of the historical holy figures. The figuration of the protagonists, especially Ḥusayn, takes place without any specification of age and bodily appearance; while it is a norm to cover the faces of holy figures in all other art mediums, here no veils are employed to cover faces.

Furthermore, everything on the stage defines itself autonomously in the process of the unfolding events. Faces and voices are what glimpsed first and these fascinate the spectators. A protagonist with a perfect singing voice and a young,

---

[23] Max Hermann, "Das theatralische Raumerlebnis", 502.

[24] Sandra L. Richards, "Writing the Absent Potential: Drama, Performance, and the Canon of African-American Literature", in: *Performativity and Performance*, ed. by Andres Parker et al., New York et al. 1995, 72.

charming face is the key to success of the whole *ta'ziyih* troop. The ambivalence of performing a holy figure with a face which could belong to anyone is an important characteristic of the *ta'ziyih*, and it has always raised a number of challenges. The paradox comes into existence the very moment when the holiness vanishes behind the ordinary face of an actor, who shifts between being and not being the protagonist, a feature that also applies to the antagonists.

2. The cultural memory of the spectator

To understand the cultural memory affiliated to the *ta'ziyih* protagonists, we need to keep in mind that the *ta'ziyih* originated in a culture where the performative and textual maintained a close and strong connection with each other. In this cultural background the most intricate subjects of the humanities und philosophy were (and still are) part of the everyday lives of ordinary people.[25] Among these are the mystic interpretations of the religious concept of *shahīd* (martyr) and the mystic concept of *'ishq* (love), which taken together create the concept of the *martyr of love, shahīd-i 'ishq*, a key concept among the mystics.

The two following poems by two famous mystic poets encapsulate the problem of war, love and martyrdom:

> The warrior strives in the way of becoming a martyr,
> Ignorant that the martyr of love stands higher than him
> On judgment day, how can one compare the two
> One is killed by the enemy and the other by his (her) lover. [26]

> The butterfly said to the candle: Your festivity is joyful.
> Sacrifice me, while dissolving in you is my pleasure
> All your promises and rewards are dear to me
> You are my witness and I am your martyr. [27]

Shahīd-i 'ishq is a model for a clear and deliberate decision for death; however, it is not to be compared with a decision for suicide. On the eve of the murder of his family and friends Ḥusayn says that everybody should leave him, for it is not a battle that awaits them but a brutal and cruel death.

On the performative level however, the question arises whether somebody would come to help him. At the same time though, in the *Performance of Ḥusayn's Martyrdom (majlis)* he refuses – so as to avoid any interference – to accept the help of the armies of ghosts, angels, animals, prophets and demons. He refuses any help for he fears being charged with creating an unjust war. He thus saves innocence, but this innocence itself will be destroyed along with him.

---

[25] For example the books of Ḥāfiẓ and Firdawsī, two very important cultural figures, are firmly embedded in the normal life of Iranians.

[26] Abū Saʿ id Abū al-Khayr, *Rubāʿiyāt*, [C4/5th - C9/10th], Hamadān 1998, 19. Translation by the author.

[27] Farīd al-Dīn ʿAṭṭār, *Mukhtārnāmih*, [C6/7th - C12/13th], Tehran 2007, 232. Translation by the author.

Fig. 3: Ḥusayn *Taʿziyih*, The dead and the ghosts rise up to help Ḥusayn, Khulanjān, 2010.

Ḥusayn redefines himself as being a winner and not a loser of war when, after hours of the supernatural army's march, he then refuses their help. Through this position ("He could win if he wanted but he doesn't") his character gravitates even closer to the definition of a martyr of love. He has not been killed by his enemy but he has decided to die. As a result, Ḥusayn's actions and his death in a *taʿziyih* challenge the spectator even more.

The spectator looks at the evilness in two main ways. Every event on the stage is already known to him. In other words, there is no surprise on the levels of text and cultural memory, but the excess of the performative act is for him – the spectator – an immensely shocking fright, a vital shudder.

The performative murder, the massacre, draws the border between spectators and actors (antagonists and protagonists). Up to this time they play together the role of the spectator. Up to the point of the murder, the *taʿziyih* actors (antagonists and protagonists) dissociate themselves from their roles in different ways: openly holding the text, they act freely and impromptu, suddenly engaging in private conversations with spectators and other actors, drinking tea or delivering direct comments such as: "I am myself one of you! Only a humble follower of Ḥusayn!"

And then the constructive act of violence by the evil person in a *taʿziyih*: the act of murder which leads to martyrdom on the performative level. *The act of murdering* separates the actors (antagonists and protagonists) from the spectators.

Murder and martyrdom – the order seems to set up quite literally the construction. Is in a *taʿziyih murder* the *ritual* and, at the same time, *martyrdom* the *theatre*? Is in a *ta'ziyih* the act of murder definable as the ritualistic part, and at the same time its result, the declaration of martyrdom on stage, the theatrical dimension? Does it make sense at all to try to analyse rituality and theatricality as two distinct spheres in the *ta'ziyih*? Erika Fischer-Lichte has discussed the same question regarding spiritual plays of the Middle Ages:

"A systematic distinction between theatre and ritual, which can be applied to ritual and theatre of all cultures and times, seems [...] to be neither possible nor meaningful. If a distinction is to be made, then it should be drawn on the basis of the historical background, whereby the question is: what specific functions has a particular culture assigned to theatre and ritual at a particular time, and what differences has it identified between them."[28]

In the *ta'ziyih* the shift from the sacrifice-ritual to a *theatre of martyrdom* should be considered an essential function. It is not the difference between theatre and ritual that is important, but how they co-exist and how they restructure and intervene in each other. The martyrdom, as it is identified in the Shiite context, supports the separation of theatre from ritual as a theatrical necessity.

Furthermore, the double role of the spectators as participants in a sacrificial ritual and as passive killers supports the same detachment. The spectators, confirming the role of the antagonists – as figures of the tyrant on the stage, maintain their function when their role as a ritual participant is transferred into a co-existing presence with the actors in a theatrical space.

If the discussion is limited to sacrificial ritual, the roles would be reduced to victims and murderers. But here we are also concerned with a *mourning-sacrificial ritual*. The grief, the act of weeping, is stressed by the religious participants as *thawāb*: who cries for the martyrs is recompensed by his God. This statement however is a dissimulation of what the origin of the grief was.

How can it come about that we have *mourning* as an *act*, integrated in a theatrical space and not just as a *sympathetic reaction*, or a sort of reaction which would stay only in the individual spaces? If there were no guilt feelings, why is there such a strong collective process of regret and remorse? Our key to understanding the concepts of innocence, evil, martyrdom and murdering has always revolved around the constant presence of a feeling of guilt, or the constant absence of a concept (guilt) which has been present already while we have argued its counterpart (innocence).

The murder/sacrifice scene still remains, as a part of the ritual, forceful and shuddering. The participants experience an extreme case of cruelty, a fundamental crime, in the infanticide scenes that a child, almost like a sacrificial animal, is to be decapitated with a knife by an antagonist.

---

[28] Erika Fischer-Lichte, "Theater und Fest, Anmerkungen zum Verhältnis von Theatralität und Ritualität in den geistlichen Spielen des Mittelalters", in: *Transformationen des Religiösen*, ed. by Ingrid Kasten et al., Berlin 2007, 8.

Fig. 4: *Ḥusayn taʿziyih*, Shimr killing ʿAbdullāh, Khulanjān, 2010.

Apart from any connection to Ḥusayn's history or religious references, child murder fundamentally shakes society. Interestingly, in *the performance of the martyrdom of Imam Ḥusayn* the murder of his nephew ʿAbdullāh – the climax which induces the participants to cry – is shown earlier than the murder of Ḥusayn. Therefore, the martyrdom of Ḥusayn loses its performative significance and necessity, and his martyrdom is disguised and symbolised by releasing pigeons.

The innocence of Ḥusayn and his family, as well as of all the other martyr figures in a *taʿziyih*, lies at the heart of the feelings of guilt, the feelings of *mass guilt* in the participants of this sacrificial ritual. Theatricality generates a martyr from the body of the ritualised victim. The result of this consideration of the *taʿziyih* as a theatrical ritual is a recognition that the *taʿziyih* is a projection screen for the *collective guilt* associated with the martyr.

The Mystical Notion of the Perfect Man

Discourses of Iranian Revolutionary Painters and the Portrayal of Martyrs

Alice Bombardier (Paris)

As a result of contemporary conflicts, the 1980s onwards sees the emergence of numerous "neo-martyrs" in Middle Eastern countries. In sacrificing their lives, these neo-martyrs demonstrate the merits of their cause and, through their act, sanctify it. The Koran, the Hadiths of the Prophet, and the Imams delineate the martyr canonical privileges,[1] which include the intrinsic purity of the body and dispensing of all funeral ablution, direct access to upper levels of Heaven without the torments of Purgatory, and the ability to intercede for other men.[2] As such, neo-martyrs are imbued with paradigmatic force, which is particularly acute in Iran, as martyrdom elevates them to an upper rank of humanity. Falling squarely within this trend, a cult of martyrs was established in Iran in 1979 by the Islamic Republic to extend after death their spiritual and moral influence. Murals or canvas paintings reflecting Islamic-revolutionary norms are key conveyors of this cult. They participate in the commemoration of this privileged category, called by Eric Butel a pantheon of "quasi-saints" given that the Iranian martyr's saintliness is mutilated by its political exploitation.[3]

In 2009 in Tehran, I conducted interviews with several Iranian painters, participants in the Revolution from the outset, as part of a sociological survey on their artistic practices and their representations of art, society, and State.[4] During these semi-structured interviews, which were conducted in Farsi in the privacy of their workshops, three of these revolutionary artists revealed that they were inspired by the same heroic and mystical imaginative figure. "The Perfect Man" (*insān-i kāmil*), and to a lesser extent "the Ideal Man" (*insān-i īdih-āl*), were two denominations emphatically carried by these three painters to designate the artist

---

[1] Denis Gril, "Les fondements scriptuaires du miracle en islam", in: *Miracle et Karama*, ed. by Denise Aigle, Louvain 2000, 237-50.

[2] Eric Butel, "Martyre et sainteté dans la littérature de guerre Irak-Iran", in: *Saints et héros du Moyen-Orient contemporain*, ed. by Catherine Mayeur-Jaouen, Paris 2002, 307.

[3] Ibid, 312.

[4] The interviews with Iranian painters to whom I refer here were conducted by me in 2008 and 2009 as part of a PhD research entitled *La peinture iranienne au XXème siècle (1911-2009). Historique, courants esthétiques et voix d'artistes. Contribution à l'étude des enjeux de l'art en Iran à l'époque contemporaine*, PhD: Paris/Genève: EHESS/Université de Genève, 2012. The corpus of 19 interviews is available in its entirety in the appendix to the thesis (vol. 2). See "Madame O", 158-61; "Monsieur P", 162-67; "Monsieur R", 168-74. The anonymity of the artists was preserved.

in his creative process, as well as the new *homo islamicus* shaped by Islamic-revolutionary values and the notion of the ideal citizen in the Islamic regime.

These three painters clearly shared the same cognitive universe and values. In 1979, they were among the founding members of the Centre of Thought and Islamic Art (*ḥawzih-yi andīshih wa hunar-i islāmī*), the artistic and political matrix of the Islamic regime. As part of this work, I will highlight the specificity of the rhetoric that was particular to the Centre of Thought and Islamic Art (CTIA) in the 1980s. This rhetoric, heavily influenced by revolutionary Shiite ideology, was directly inspired by the teachings of Ali Shariati (1933–1977) – an Iranian sociologist whose thought spread primarily through numerous lectures held in Iran from 1965 to 1973. Shariati had a strong effect on the members of the Centre as well as on an important part of the Iranian population. The discourse of the painters is deeply rooted in this rhetoric, which also served to inspire their paintings devoted to the praise of martyrdom. The power of persuasion that this rhetoric demonstrated in the early 1980s in Iran, prompting many Iranians to march to their death, leads to the study of some of its primary characteristics. One of the most important is the recurrent notion of the Perfect Man that stems from Islamic esoteric mysticism.

This study will commence with a presentation of the careers of the three painters in question. From here, I will show how the mystical notion of the Perfect Man was revived by revolutionary Shiite ideology.[5] In this vein, I will parse out the recurring usages or reformulations of the notion of the Perfect Man present in this ideology. First, in focusing on the painters themselves, an original reformulation of the concept of the Perfect Man linked to the status of artist emerges in their discourse. Moving on to analysis of paintings of martyrs, I will emphasise the parallel drawn in the early 1980s between the process of martyrdom and the spiritual ascent to the Perfect Man. This parallel marks another reformulation of the Perfect Man, here understood as a model for the martyr in which mortality is manifest. Through these plural explorations – semantic, discursive, and iconographic – I will highlight the complex "apparatus"[6] connecting mystical concepts, revolutionary Shiite ideology, and representation, which was established in Iran in the 1980s and which supported these reformulations of the mystical notion of the Perfect Man.

---

[5] By "ideology", I mean a coherent, organised, and epoch-dated system of ideas that explains the existing social order with reasoning based on nature or religion and which serves as a guide to action.

[6] By "apparatus", I mean an arrangement of wordings and images required to operate strategically in a given field of forces: "the idea of apparatus (*"dispositif"* in French) suggests the connection between formal and semantic choices and the set of constraints, conditions, and practices that characterise a given historical situation". Bernard Vouilloux, "Du dispositive", in: *Discours, image, dispositif,* ed. by Philippe Ortel, Paris 2008, 31.

I. From Artisan to Artist, from the Centre of Thought and Islamic Art to Sūrih University: An Initiation Journey

The three artists highlighted here, Mrs. O, Mr. P, and Mr. R, all present the particularity of hailing from families of craftsmen. All three were able to break with their background as a result of university studies: the success each achieved in the late 1970s in the national competitive exam to enter the Faculty of Fine Arts at the University of Tehran signalled their transition from artisan to artist. This biographical and social data – their modest and traditional backgrounds nonetheless linked to artistic creation – was proclaimed by each as absolutely decisive in their chosen vocation of artist. Indeed, this was mentioned in the first minutes of every interview and explicitly connected to their inclination for painting and art in general. Mrs. O and Mr. P were both born in rural towns from families of weavers and carpet designers who were able to convey to them what Mrs. O called "the taste for the arts" and Mr. P "the power, the capacity to create".

> What may have led me to art came from my father and my mother. I grew up in a family where we practiced artistic activities: drawings on carpets. My father drew and my mother wove. My siblings and I, we all developed a taste for the arts. [...] I got a degree of accountancy but I had no desire for it. I wanted to do art. This is why I started university in that field. (Mrs. O, 2009)

The early experience of home life described as particularly warm, dignified, and talented was complimented, according to Mr. P, by the contribution of a pedagogically effective institution ("the library"). A few years after having entered the Faculty of Fine Arts at the University of Tehran, Mr. P participated in the Revolution and, subsequently, became involved in the Iran-Iraq War. Stationed at the front, he contributed to the war effort in his capacity as an artist by portraying the soldiers.

> My father was a driving monitor, then he sold tyres. But he loved literature and poetry. He went to the coffee houses, listened to the storytellers and, in the evenings, told us the stories or poems he had heard. He loved poetry, but as he had to bring us up he worked at the bazaar. [...] I often wonder: why did I make these works? [...] I was lucky. What I loved and what delighted me was art. Up to eighteen years old, I wrote plays and played them, especially in the children's library [of my town]. Then I made films. Throughout my childhood, I was making artistic things. I loved tinkering. This is thanks to the atmosphere that prevailed in the library [of the city] where I was born. If this library had not existed, maybe I would never have gone in for a career in art. In this library, I met people who taught me things and told me there was a Faculty of Fine Arts in Tehran. [...]
> When I tried the competitive exam of the University, I received first. The best! [in English]. They were surprised because the others had grown up in Tehran while I came from the provinces. It was surprising that a student from the provinces received first at the competitive exam of the University of Tehran. This is due to the fact that for six years I had worked there every day, every day. I was also admitted at the Faculty of Psychology but I did not go. I chose. The inclination for art has perhaps its roots within the human being, then the family comes into the picture, and then the genes.

> I think that in my family there were artistic genes from both sides, from my father and from my mother. My grandmother was an expert in carpet weaving [...]. She had many students. She had the title of "master" in the workshop where she worked. Her husband died very early. She had to bring up her children alone with carpet weaving, all her life. My mother was also a weaver. As a child, I sat next to my grandmother when she was weaving. She sang at the same time very sad songs. Because she had to work hard to bring up her children alone, you know? The voice of my grandmother has always stayed with me. When she would sign and weave. During weaving, the colour yarns would get mixed up. I was asked to separate them. Green on one side, red on the other. And I gave them to the weavers. Maybe by doing this I increased very early my awareness of colours. [...] This was my first experience of creation, that the human being can create things with his hands. The power, the capacity to create from human beings was the lesson my family gave to me, my grandmother in particular.
> Then [...] I was accepted at the Faculty of Fine Arts of Tehran. Almost simultaneously, the Revolution occurred. [...] The Revolution [...] ushered me into a professional atmosphere, and finally the war, where I went to the front, all that influenced me. (Mr. P, 2009)

Mr. R, for his part, comes from a family of what can be termed folk painters. He converted the workshop of his father, who practiced Coffee house painting (*naqqāshī-i qahwih-khānih*), into a museum, in full awareness that he himself was part of an artistic process that started before him and that he had inherited. Mr. R specified that he received training from the miniaturist Mahmoud Farshchian before entering university. He committed himself wholly to the Revolution, the fervour and the ideals of which he tried to convey during the interview.

> My father was a painter. He painted in the coffee house style. He painted religious subjects, the Shāhnāmih, Firdawsī's stories. With the Revolution, the ideals I mentioned appeared. We worked in the Centre of Thought and Islamic Art (ḥawzih). [...] I was for two years a pupil of Farshchian. Before the university, I was in a secondary school specialised in art (hunaristān). [...] I have studied here for three years. Then I was accepted at the university. After two years, the Revolution occurred. At the time when I was at secondary school, I also worked with my father. (Mr. R, 2009)

In addition to entering the university, the Islamic Revolution of 1979 represented a significant breaking point in the life of these three artists. During the revolutionary period, their activities converged. All three contributed to the founding and functioning of the CTIA. Mr. R described the atmosphere of effervescence that prevailed during the Revolution and the promising sociopolitical context that led to the creation of the Centre.

> At the beginning of the Revolution, I was twenty-seven, no twenty-five. We were students at the University of Tehran. At night, we worked in our bedrooms. The Revolution was not victorious yet. Around the university sat the army. They did not know that at night, we lit candles and painted for the Revolution. We were creating posters, paintings. When the Revolution was victorious, we carried all that to Ḥusayniyyih Irshād. [...] We sat in the basement of the mosque (shabistūn), where they settle in winter. There were miles of queues. We called our group "Salmān", from the name of one of the companions of the Prophet. We had borrowed two jeeps from a TV channel with a large truck. We carried our works to other cities. First Qum: it was the first time an exhibition of paintings was held in Qum. People had never seen any artistic exhibition before. And

Iṣfahān, Shīrāz, Ahwāz, Ābādān, Kirmānshāh, Sanandaj, Urūmiyyih, Tabrīz, Gīlān, Māzandarān, Mashhad, Tehran. And the children (bačih-hā, [affectionate term]) got together to found the Centre of Thought and Islamic Art (ḥawzih). [...] We painted on what I said, on the past, the struggles of the Iranian people, the Shah's regime and on Islam, the ideal society, and the ideal man. I, Hossein Khosrojerdi, Ḥabīb Ṣādiqī, Nasser Palangi... They were numerous. Mr. Ḥalīmī also, but later. Mr. Rajabī. And some women. Students. In the cinema, there was Mohsen Makhmalbaf, you know him in the West. (Mr. R, 2009)

The Centre of Thought and Islamic Art was created as a result of this foundational exhibition of paintings, inaugurated February 11, 1979 in Tehran's Ḥusayniyyih Irshād. In this religious space dedicated to Imam Ḥusayn, Ali Shariati and Mihdī Bāzargān had initiated a series of lectures in 1969, one year after the publication of Ali Shariati's first volume of his major work entitled *Islamology (islāmshināsī)*.[7] This first exhibition of Islamic-revolutionary painting, featuring the social and political struggles of the Iranian people, the struggle against the Shah, the rejection of Western imperialism, and especially the religious and political commitment that culminates in martyrdom, attracted many enthusiastic artists, poets, writers, and filmmakers who rallied to the group, which led to the creation of the multidisciplinary Centre.[8] Initially non-governmental, the CTIA was attached in 1982 – after the outbreak of Iran–Iraq War – to the Organisation of Islamic Propaganda (*sāzmān-i tablīghāt-i islāmī*), opening an era of exploitation by the Islamic Republic of the martyr's figure for the benefit of political and communications strategies.[9] Also consisting of workshops and exhibition spaces, the Centre left its mark on contemporary Iranian art production by its edicts on the definition and the value of Islamic-revolutionary art and by the exclusive subsidising of artists who subscribed to this creed. It remains above all at the origin of the fundamental pattern of official propaganda, based on the figure of the martyr.

Within the CTIA, the three painters participated in the theorisation of the pictorial Islamic-revolutionary norm, characterised by the overexposure of the martyr's body or its attributes (such as dove and wings), or symbols such as the tulip (*lālih*). The martyr is the key element of Islamic-revolutionary thought. It is the rallying sign, an identity marker. The quasi-exclusive representation of revolutionary values, the martyr's body in official paintings is a call for political, military, and patriotic commitment. It symbolises the qualities of self-abnegation and self-sacrifice that belong to the ideal citizen as advocated by Islamic authorities.[10]

Almost simultaneously with the establishment of the CTIA, Sūrih University, whose artistic orientation exclusively responded to the new Islamic-revolutionary

---

7   Ali Rahnema, *An Islamic Utopian. A Political Biography of Ali Shariati*, London 2000, 226-42.
8   Hossein Khosrojerdi, "The Islamic Revolution in Contemporary Iranian Art", in: *Ṭāwūs*, 1 (1999), 91-99.
9   Ziba Jalali-Naini, "L'art islamique révolutionnaire. Naissance et agonie", in: *Les cahiers de l'Orient. Revue d'Etude et de Reflexion sur le Monde arabe et musulman*, 49 (1998), 125-128.
10   Alice Bombardier, "Iranian Revolutionary Painting on Canvas: Iconographic Study on the Martyred Body", in: *Iranian Studies*, 4 (2013), 583-600.

standards, was created within it. This university was among the few that remained open during the political, social, and cultural upheavals in Iran in 1980-1983. During this period, the academic system was completely paralysed in order to reform programs and teaching;[11] however, the new institutions created during the Revolution represented an exception and thus remained operational. Sūrih University in the CTIA and the new Museum of Martyrs (*mūzih-yi shuhadā'*), which included a teaching section led by Dr. Zarīnqalam, former director of the Faculty of Decorative Arts, were particularly active.[12] During these three years of transition, Mrs. O, Mr. P, and Mr. R followed the instruction of Sūrih University. After 1983, they went back to the Faculty of Fine Arts at the University of Tehran, but continued to study in parallel at Sūrih University. The link woven with this new university remained particularly important as some later chose to teach within its walls.

Between 1980-1983, Sūrih University played the role of pilot university in the artistic field. In this capacity, and in keeping with Islamic-revolutionary ideals, new programs, including the painting of martyrs, were developed. These programs spread with the particular intensity of post-revolutionary effervescence, but also within the troubled context of the beginning of the Iran–Iraq War. The dominance gained over the academic system by Sūrih University, along with the rhetorical eloquence mixed with ideology of its programs, contributed symptomatically to the emergence of a paroxysmal form of martyr painting. The modality of speaking and painting in a specific language, which was particular to these revolutionary circles and was to be shared first by the group and then by the masses, produced several considerable effects. In a "performative" and persuasive manner, it lent to the act of creation an elevated dimension, close to the divine, and drove into the heart of the Iran–Iraq War through repeated invocations of martyrdom, urging deadly or even suicidal behaviours. This rhetoric, mixed with bloody paintings advocating sacrifice, influenced many Iranians at a loss for points of reference; as shown by the sociologist Farhad Khosrokhavar, this almost forced them down a "martyropathic" process to self-sacrificial violence.[13]

As of 1981, among the circle of committed artists who attended this new university, many were promoters of this Islamic-revolutionary form of painting with its deadly overtones. At that time, some of these works were even published as postcards by the Organisation of Islamic Propaganda. Reproduced and distributed in number, these paintings were representative of a "dead-conveying Shiism"[14] developed in the second year after the Revolution, with Sūrih Univer-

---

[11]   See Bombardier, *La peinture iranienne au XXème siècle.*

[12]   Alice Bombardier, "La peinture murale iranienne: genèse et evolution. Enjeux de la spatialisation artistique dans le processus d'affirmation et de pacification des pays du Moyen-Orient", in: *Standing on the Beach with a Gun in my Hand. Eternal Tour 2010 Jérusalem*, eds. Noémie Etienne and Donatella Bernardi, Genève-Paris 2011, 119-20.

[13]   Farhad Khosrokhavar, *L'islamisme et la mort*, Paris 1995, 26-30.

[14]   *Ibid*, 37.

sity steering the theorisation and spread of their rhetorical and pictorial form. I will refer further to some of these pictorial reproductions in order to better understand the impact of the idea of the Perfect Man on painting of martyrs in Iran.

II. The Mystical Notion of the Perfect Man and Revolutionary Shiite Ideology

The notion of the Perfect Man has long been a reference for Persian miniaturists, which perhaps partially explains its success among revolutionary painters. According to Mehdi Mohammad-Zadeh, faces of Shiite saints in Persian miniatures are unique in their portrayal of similar or even identical features corresponding to the face of the Perfect Man.[15] "The Imam", stated the Prophet, "is the person who physically and morally most resembles me" and "his portrait is mine".[16] Mohammad Ali Amir-Moezzi confirms that the notion of the Perfect Man is rooted in the figure of the Imam as conveyed by the oldest Shiite sources.[17] A tacit agreement was thus adopted among the miniaturists to represent the saints with a featureless face, as was commonly accepted in religious literature.

The idea of the Perfect Man was especially developed in the theosophical writings of Andalusian Sufi thinker Ibn al-ʿArabī (1165–1240).[18] Henry Corbin, in *Cyclical Time and Ismaili Gnosis,* writes about the following development of the concept in earlier stages of Ismāʿīlī Shiism, wherein the Gnostic idea of the Imam as "Perfect Anthropos" prevailed.[19] In Shiism, where the esoteric dimension of Islam is highly developed through Imamology and the theology of *wilāyat* (divine friendship, later rendered "power" in the doctrine of Ayatollah Khomeini), a spirituality close to Sufism occupies a substantial place and is bolstered directly with great Sufi works including those of Ibn al-ʿArabī.[20] It must be noted, however, that Sufi doctrine as such is criticised in Iran by the Shiite clergy, who perceive it as illegitimate in the context of doctrinal competition. Many Shiite ʿulamāʾ denounce the non-compliance of Sufis with the doctrinal and social rules of Islam. Indeed although the obligations of Islamic worship (prayer, fasting, pilgrimage, ritual almsgiving) are not abolished, they are none-

---

[15] Mehdi Mohammad-Zadeh, *L'iconographie shiite dans l'Iran des Qadjars. Emergence, source et développement,* PhD: Geneva–Paris: University of Geneva–EPHE, 2008, 35.

[16] Shaykh Ṣaddūq, *Ikmāl al-dīn wa itmām al-niʿma,* vol. 1, 286. Quoted in Mohammad-Zadeh, *L'iconographie shiite dans l'Iran des Qadjars,* 35.

[17] Mohammad-Ali Amir-Moezzi, *Guide divin dans le shiisme originel,* Paris 2007.

[18] Prior to Islam, the origin of the notion of the Perfect Man can be compared to Gnostic conceptions, which took many forms before converging in the Manichaeism with the doctrine of the First Man. According to the disciples of Zoroaster and Mani, this prototypical man has to fight evil and darkness. Roger Arnaldez, "Al-Insān al-Kāmil", in: *Encyclopédie de l'Islam,* Leiden et al. 1971, 1271.

[19] Henry Corbin, *Temps cyclique et gnose ismaélienne,* Paris 1982, 57-8.

[20] Yann Richard, *Le Shiʿisme en Iran: Imān et révolution,* Paris 1980, 93.

theless secondary in this cult reserved for initiates.[21] This is why Shiite theologians in Qum prefer the term "gnosis" (*ʿirfān*) rather than "Sufism" (*taṣawwuf*) to denote the commonalities existing between Shiism and Sufism.[22] Yet, according to Henry Corbin, various Shiite thinkers, mostly Siyyid Ḥaydar Āmulī (born c.1320), Ibn Abī Jumhūr (born c.1401) and Ṣāʾin al-Dīn ʿAlī Turkih Iṣfāhānī (died c. 1426-1433), who wrote a comment on Ibn al-ʿArabī's *Fuṣūṣ al-Ḥikam* (*Gems of Wisdom*), were interested in the concepts developed by Ibn al-ʿArabī and integrated some aspects into Shiite dogma.[23]

Philosophical, religious, and moral, the notion of the Perfect Man was notably reinvigorated in the twentieth century by Muḥammad Ḥusayn Ṭabāṭabāʾī (1903–1981). In his widely circulated book, *The Principles of Philosophy and the Realistic Method*, Ṭabāṭabāʾī advocates a spiritual philosophy.[24] Ayatollah Khomeini (1902–1989) himself, who taught mysticism and philosophy at Qum until the early 1950s, referred to the doctrine of the Andalusian Sufi.[25] However, Ali Shariati differed from his predecessors by giving to the notion of the Perfect Man a social, political, and ideological dimension. A sociologist committed to the religious opposition of Mohammad Reza Shah Pahlavi's regime, and considered one of the major ideologues of the Islamic Revolution, Ali Shariati was influenced both by nationalist and religious circles. He studied in Mashhad, then in Paris between 1959 and 1964; on his return from France, he attempted to reconcile his Western education with the religious beliefs of his country. Shariati conceived a new Islamic idiom, putting emphasis on the social and political dimension of Islam, which he expounded upon in 1968 in the first volume of his major book, *Islamology (islāmshināsī)*, then again in 1973 in a second volume.[26] Between 1969 and 1973, Ali Shariati also conducted lectures that benefited from a wide audience in the conference centre he founded with Mihdī Bāzargān in Ḥusayniyyih Irshād. These lectures prompted his arrest by the political police of the Shah, as well as that of many of his students; Shariati spent eighteen months in prison. After being released in March 1975, he was allowed to go into exile in England, where he died shortly after his arrival and a few months before the outbreak of the Revolution. His ideas largely influenced the revolutionary fighters and the new regime that was established during the Revolution.

According to Ibn al-ʿArabī, the idea of the Perfect Man – whose primary meaning is "prophet" or "vicar of God on earth" in the Koranic verses of Light (IX, 32

---

[21] Yann Richard, *L'Islam chi'ite: croyances et idéologies*, Paris 1991, 76.

[22] Henry Corbin, *En Islam iranien*, I, 11; III, 153. Quoted in Richard, *L'Islam chi'ite*, 81.

[23] Henry Corbin, *Histoire de la philosophie islamique*, Paris 1986, 455-59.

[24] Muḥammad Ḥusayn Ṭabāṭabāʾī, *Uṣūl-i falsafih wa rawish-i riālīsm* [The principles of philosophy and the realistic method], ed. by M. Muṭahharī, 5 vol., Tehran, 1953-54; *Shiʿite Islam*, trans. S. H. Nasr, Albany 1975.

[25] Richard, *L'Islam chi'ite*, 81.

[26] Ali Shariati, *Islamshināsī*, vol.1, Tehran 1968; vol. 2, Tehran 1973.

and LXI, 8)[27] – was above all understood as a symbol of the human being, the ontological meaning of human existence that the thinker chose to illustrate with the figure of the first man, Adam.[28] In the opinion of Masataka Takeshita, the Perfect Man in Ibn al-ʿArabī's philosophical treaty *Fuṣūṣ al-Ḥikam* could also refer to the figure of the Gnostic Sufi who had reached the upper threshold of his mystical journey, the possessor of divine knowledge (*maʿrifa*) who sees the appearance of the Divine Names in all forms of earthly existence.[29] By this ability, the Gnostic Sufi is the only one in Ibn al-ʿArabī's treaty, according to Takeshita, who can be called "human being" in the true sense of the term.

After 1969, one of Ali Shariati's lectures delivered in Ḥusayniyyih Irshād was *ʿAlī, the Perfect Man*.[30] The idea of the Perfect Man, as elaborated upon by him in the contemporary era, was henceforth inseparable from the Shiite spiritual tradition. By reinterpreting in a decidedly militant fashion the founding principles of Shiism, Ali Shariati wanted to transform Islam into a progressive, liberating, and revolutionary religion. In the first volume of *Islamology (islāmshināsī)*, several pages are also devoted to the Ideal Man, the "theomorphic man in whom the spirit of God has overcome the half of his being".[31] The reference here is thus not to the Imam ʿAlī but rather is understood in a broader sense as every man encompassing the qualities of "truth, goodness and beauty – in other words, knowledge, ethics and art".[32] These writings had particular influence on the revolutionary youth[33], who could easily identify with this Ideal Man and adapt the mystical idea of the Perfect Man to the socio-political realities of contemporary Iran. The description of the human qualities of the Ideal Man – "pure" and "pious", whose heart is dedicated to the inner life and the mysteries of the spirit but whose body participates in the struggle for freedom – is followed by an illustration of his lifestyle based on stories recounting the lives of the prophets.

Following these parables, Ali Shariati's reflections on art, which he argued must be used as a creative tool in the hands of the Ideal Man and not as a "toy",[34] deserves to be highlighted. The attention he turned to the virtues of art in the context of Islam and mystical philosophy was new:

---

[27] Arnaldez, "Al-Insān al-Kāmil", 1271.

[28] Masataka Takeshita, "The Theory of the Perfect Man in Ibn ʿArabī's Fuṣūṣ al-Ḥikam", in: *Orient* 19 (1983), 91.

[29] Ibid, 95-97.

[30] Ali Shariati, *On the sociology of Islam. Lectures by Ali Shariati,* trans. Hamid Algar, Berkeley 1979, 35.

[31] Ibid, 121.

[32] Ibid, 124.

[33] A slogan that could often be read on banners in protest marches during the Iranian Revolution also came from Ali Shariati's work *Shahādat*: "Karbalāʾ is everywhere; every month is *Muḥarram*; every day is *ʿĀshūrāʾ*", Ali Shariati, *Shahādat*, Tehran 1972, 104. See Heinz Halm, *Shīʿa Islam*, Princeton 1997, 136.

[34] Shariati, *On the sociology of Islam*, 123.

> Art is not a plaything in [the] hands of [the Ideal Man]; it is not a means for gaining pleasure, for diversion, for stupefaction, for the expenditure of accumulated energy. It is not a servant to sexuality, politics, or capital. Art is the special trust given to man by God. It is the creative pen of the Maker, given by Him to his vice-regent so that he might make a second Earth and a second paradise, new forms of life, beauty, thought, spirit, message, a new heaven, a new time.[35]

The artists who converged on the CTIA clearly founded the renewal of their status along these lines. It allowed them to present themselves as life guides and justified the new educative, religious, and political mission they sought. For this group of artists, such philosophical underpinnings translated into the assertion of their importance in the transmission of the new Islamic-revolutionary values and legitimised their profession.

In support of the same mystical tradition as his predecessors, Ali Shariati popularised in Iran the use of the word "ideology", understood as a body of doctrines inspired by religious beliefs but guiding social and political action. Shariati clearly distinguished Islam as an ideology, in the sense of active enforcement of beliefs, from Islam as a religious culture preserving tradition. He claimed that it was in the principles of Islam to link religion and politics. This use of the term "ideology" was reconfirmed by the authorities of the Islamic Republic, who adapted the notion to establish what became Shiite revolutionary ideology. If Shariati praised the human, moral, and religious merit of the Ideal Man in an ideal society (the *umma* according to him),[36] the Islamic regime went one step further by exploiting the principle of the Perfect Man – and through him the martyr – to achieve its aims of internal consolidation. The various usages of the mystical notion of the Perfect Man, which heavily influenced the discourse of the CTIA painters, are an exemplary illustration of the Islamic regime's ideological reformulation of a spiritual legacy in the service of its own interests. Indeed, the Islamic regime diverted from their original context the fundamental principles on which the authority of the Imami religion is based. The revolutionary Shiite ideology, derived from these reformulations, led the Islamic regime to significantly increase its political, social, and economic influence, which reached its peak in the 1980s. The painting of martyrs, which expanded throughout this period, is among the most effective expressions of this ideology. This ideological influence was still perceptible in 2009 in the discourse of the revolutionary painters interviewed here.

III. The Resurgence of the Notion of the Perfect Man in the Discourse of Revolutionary Painters

In 2009, thirty years after the Revolution, the discourse of these three painters maintained a strong ideological tone that reflected the teaching of the CTIA and

---

[35] Ibid, 123f.
[36] Ibid, 119-20.

its satellite, Sūrih University, as evidenced by their somewhat scripted shared formulations. The Persian term *"Ḥawzih"*, which designates the CTIA, literally means "Islamic school". Within this religious school dedicated to art, Ali Shariati's writings and teachings occupied a central position and were implemented through the principle of "revolutionary self-training" as defined in the early pages of *Islamology*.[37] Revolutionary self-training consists of developing a person's potentialities in close relation to his social and political context. As stated by Nouchine Yavari-d'Hellencourt, "Revolutionary self-training according to Ali Shariati, it is to rise up in a revolutionary manner, it is to accept a fundamental principle, to adhere to a noble goal which is none other than the determination to move towards man's existential perfection. Revolutionary self-training is for Shariati what allows to rise up just like Ali."[38] It is thus not surprising that the notion of the Perfect Man is so deeply engrained in the minds of these three painters, who referred repeatedly to it during the interviews. This notion is used not only in the sense of Shariati in *Islamology* (i.e. the ideal of the pious man seeking godly perfection in intellectual and political struggle) but also in the more specific context of the artist group as a form of self-justification or sanctification of their mission. Indeed, celebrated by Ayatollah Khomeini,[39] the ideologically committed artists were key players of the Revolution.[40] In this vein, Mr. R uses of the term "Ideal Man", as directly inspired by Shariati, to describe the content of the works presented at the founding exhibit of Ḥusayniyyih Irshād.

> Yes, the first event of the Revolution was pictorial. We painted on what I said, the past, the struggles of the Iranian people, the Shah's regime and Islam, the Ideal society and the Ideal man. (Mr. R, 2009)

In line with Shariati's teachings, the Perfect Man is mobilised by Mr. R to establish a new scale of values within Iranian society. During the interview, Mr. R conveyed the force that drove the actors of the revolutionary utopia in its original purity. Mr. R explicitly associated the notion of the Perfect Man with the Iranian Revolution, thus conferring a sacred dimension on the political event. According to him, the notion of the Perfect Man is the future promise of a reconstruction of post-revolutionary society via mysticism. The Perfect Man is equivalent in his discourse to the ideal citizen of the Islamic Republic, "where everything is centred around God". In other words, the *homo islamicus* that Mr. R – along with many Iranians involved in the Revolution – hoped would finally be embodied.

> The ideals of the Revolution... Well, I... I was... a painter of the Revolution. I believe in these issues. Everyone believes in something. Men pursue ideals. Worldwide. Our Revo-

---

[37] Ali Shariati, *Histoire et destinée*, trans. F. Hamed and N. Yavari d'Hellencourt, Paris 1982, 38.

[38] Ibid, 38.

[39] Agnès Devictor quotes a declaration of Ayatollah Khomeini defending cinema and filmmakers, who "bring up the people". Agnès Devictor, *Politique du cinema iranien*, Paris 2004, 24.

[40] The story of the Revolutionary events made by Mr. R and also quoted above, gives a concrete image of what these artists undertook, especially in Qum where no art exhibition had never reached such a scope.

lution had two ideals, which were derived from Islamic past culture, actually the Iranian culture: to achieve the Perfect Man, and that the society becomes perfect too. A perfect society is a society that has pure human and divine ethics. That is the time of justice, spiritual love, and kindness and where everything revolves around God. For example, in the centre of a circle, there is a point. We say that this central point is God. So all behaviours that exist in a society must be linked to God. In the Shiite belief, when the Imam of the Time returns and calls the end of the world with his horn, this event occurs. Its base becomes God. The foundation becomes the contentment of God. The morality of men becomes respect for God, piety. Do you know what that means? Respect for God, it means a behaviour without sin. Morality becomes divine.

With these words, Mr. R gives access to the inner mystical dimension of human experience that he lived during the Revolution: through the experience he *was*; it transported him and caught him in a collective movement of total commitment. In this lived experience, he and the "children of *Ḥawzih*" (hinting at the members of the CTIA), as well as the Iranian people as whole, seemed to be within reach of the Perfect Man. For him, the Revolution was an event that ushered in a new era. He legitimised his "ideals" by referring to the "Islamic past culture" and "Shiite belief".

More unexpectedly, and perhaps more specifically to the circle of committed artists who attended the CTIA in the early 1980s, two of the painters also referred repeatedly to the notion of the Perfect Man when they evoked their own artistic careers. In their eyes, the Revolutionary artist does not content himself with simply conveying the ideal of the Perfect Man in pictorial representations; rather, it is embodying the Perfect Man in his own life as an artist that is also essential. In line with what Ali Shariati wrote on art as an instrument in the hands of the Ideal Man, the painters asserted that the revolutionary artist devotes himself to the creation of an artwork – which places him equal to God through his creative act – while at the same time rendering his own life an artwork.

Similarly, Mr. P drew his inspiration directly from the doctrine of Ibn al-ʿArabī to define the artist worthy of the name. The human faculties that Mr. P mentioned at the beginning of the interview (extract below) refer to the twenty-six perfect behaviours defined by Ibn al-ʿArabī in *Fuṣūṣ al-Ḥikam*. These perfect behaviours, according to Ibn al-ʿArabī, must be developed by man over the various paths that lead to perfection. Ibn al-ʿArabī described in detail these paths and faculties, embodied by legendary prophets. Along with these faculties, Mr. P emphasised the need for mystical elevation. This kind of knowledge can be linked to *maʿrifa*, the upper branch of knowledge in the doctrine of Ibn al-ʿArabī. Moreover Mr. P used the terms of the latter to describe how one should proceed to move closer to perfection: the artist must open the eyes of the heart (*qalb*), which are reason (*ʿaql*) and imagination (*khayāl*).[41]

---

[41]　William C. Chittick, "Ibn al-ʿArabī", in: *Encyclopedia of Islam and the Muslim World*, ed. by Richard C. Martin, New York 2004, 333.

> It is complicated and long to define what is a true artist but in a few sentences, I would say it is someone who is himself. Who sees what he likes. We are wearing masks. The artist knows himself. He transforms his individuality in creation. Strength, which becomes creation, is in man himself. Man must develop these faculties: imagination (khayāl), reflection (tafakkur), sensitivity (iḥsās), intelligence (taʿaqqul), thinking (wahm), inspiration (ilhām)... The man who develops these faculties becomes a Perfect Man. Otherwise he sleeps and eats, that is all. The artist is a man who knows his inner energy and uses it so that it becomes art: music, painting...
>
> I accept also the mystical vision. I think many works that are shown are only technical works. But I think that spirituality and art are one. Someone who has a mystical vision of things is also an artist. Without that, he is only a technician. Only skilful. The ordinary person sees with the eyes of the head, he has only a vision of physical things. A vision somewhat higher comes from the beholder of the mind's eye. The third eye is the eye of the heart. Mystics have this third eye. [...]
>
> I think an artist is someone who sees from three eyes: head, mind, and heart. He is awake, open, he sees. In the mystical culture, we say baṣīrat (voyance, insight, intelligence). Ḥāfiẓ and Mawlānā say: ṣāḥibnaẓar (perceptive, lucid). [...] One of the conditions to be an artist is to have the third eye. [...] (Mr. P, 2009)

In these words, the contradiction between the Ideal Man, an artist who has faculties moving him closer to divine wisdom and towards the Perfect Man, and the man who, according to the painter, "eat and drink, that is all", is radical. This allusion to a man concerned only with basic needs, placed at the bottom of hierarchy by Mr. P, can be compared to the idea of Animal Man developed by Ibn al-ʿArabī as a counter-model of the Perfect Man.

The same inspiration is visible in the discourse of Mrs. O. Her comments can also be compared to the writings of ʿAbd al-Karīm al-Jīlī (1366–1424). Upholder of Ibn al-ʿArabī's thought in the fourteenth century and author of *The Universal Man*, ʿAbd al-Karīm al-Jīlī presumed that the Perfect Man is the pole around who turn all spheres of existence, from the first to the last.[42] According to Mrs. O, an artist must "improve all the dimensions of his life".

> A true artist is a Perfect Man. A human being who manages to make perfect the four dimensions of life: his soul, his body, his mind, his heart. An artist is not just someone who paints well, writes well... This is someone who has an elevated soul, a soul full of kindness. Who knows public relations. Who has good friends. Kindness is part of his art and his language. This is a man who improved all the dimensions of his life. He can talk, make friends, laugh, cry. The dimensions of his existence becoming perfect are reflected in his art. If he is an accomplished man, all he does is artistic. If he paints, he paints artistically. Artists are Perfect Men who have a perfect existence. (Mrs. O, 2009)

Beyond this, Mr. P also specified that the link existing between the artist and the Perfect man is etymologically inscribed in the Persian language itself: "*Hunar* (art) comes from Sanskrit: *hu* = *kāmil* (perfect) and *nar* = *insān* (man). At first, they said *sunar* in old Persian language. Then, it became *hunar*." (Mr. P, 2009)

---

42   Arnaldez, "Al-Insān al-Kāmil", 1272.

According to Mr. P and Mrs. O, art constitutes in itself a way to perfection. Stemming from these ideological and doctrinal positions, art is from then on presented by them as a means to access truth and transcendence. For these painters, the relationship with God comes no longer directly under spiritual guides (Imams) or human guides (mystical poles, or *quṭb* in the Sufi congregations), but through the individual's search for the "Imam of his being", the Perfect Man potentially existing in each person that art has the power to help uncover. This viewpoint gives a new stature, both missionary and paradigmatic, to the revolutionary artist: the mission of the artist is sanctified and his status is significantly increased. This reference to mystical tradition inserted artistic practice into the new Islamic regime by rendering it praiseworthy and attractive, but also by submitting it to the ideology of the latter, and if necessary, by using it as a political instrument.

The comments of these painters regarding the deeply rooted notion of the Perfect Man hint at the reformulations at play in the early 1980s in revolutionary Shiite ideology, as well as their implications. The reading of Ali Shariati constituted a significant theoretical foundation that allowed these newly formed artists exposed to modernity to fully come to terms with their vocation without losing their traditional identity of persons of faith.

IV. The Influence of the Notion of the Perfect Man
on the Painting of Martyrs

At the beginning of the Iran–Iraq War, between 1980 and 1983, when most of the revolutionary painters practiced their art at the CTIA and followed classes at Sūrih University, the figure of the martyr became omnipresent in their works. Perhaps as a result of the people's growing distress in witnessing the misconduct of the Revolution and its sacred utopia,[43] much of the murals and canvas paintings attested to increasingly doleful representations of martyrs reaching a point of martyropathic escalation.

Analysis of paintings produced at this time by the CTIA revolutionary painters demonstrates how each proceeded to represent the martyr.[44] Through descriptions of the works, I will highlight what is conveyed in these paintings and how the concept of the Perfect Man spread within the CTIA, and in turn how this is connected to the representation of martyrdom. Printed by the Organisation of the Islamic Propaganda in the early 1980s, four paintings are analysed.[45]

In the first painting, martyrdom is in progress. In *Submission to God (qunūt)* (c.1981, see fig. 1), Hossein Khosrojerdi portrays an ethereal and evanescent

---

[43] Khosrokhavar, *L'islamisme et la mort*, 26-30.

[44] See also Bombardier, "Iranian Revolutionary Painting on Canvas", 583-600.

[45] See Khosrokhavar, *L'islamisme et la mort*, 288-303. Khosrokhavar carried out a socio-anthropological analysis of some of these postcards.

Fig. 1: Hossein Khosrojerdi, *Submission to God (qunūt)*, c.1981 (170 × 120 cm)

man, a mirage on the edge of the living world, standing in a pose of prayer (open hands covering the face). He is wearing green trousers, the colour of Islam, rolled up mid-calf and revealing a red lining. The top of the trousers, whose sides seem to be going up in smoke, his hands and wrists, as well as a nest in place of the head where two doves are nestled, are all glowing as if ready to burn out. This man is standing with his bare feet joined, floating in a pure white haze. His shirt is also white, fraying on both sides. His face is absent, as his entire head is overshadowed by the pair of nestling doves standing in place of his spirit. The posi-

Fig. 2: Hossein Khosrojerdi, Light of History, c.1981 (160 × 130 cm)

tioning of the two birds is well balanced and harmonious, with their eyes oriented in the same direction.

The yearning for martyrdom has eclipsed all other thoughts. The painter insists here on the call of Heaven, the need for this man on the path of transmutation to free himself from the chains of existence, which now lie on the ground but remain enclosed before his ankles. Martyrdom and prayer are juxtaposed. The yearning for martyrdom seems to consume the man from inside. The two peaceful doves cover (or mask?) his feelings and symbolically represent that for which he yearns.

In *Light of History* (c.1981, see fig. 2), another painting by Hossein Khosrojerdi, the martyr is represented at the moment of his killing.

Two men in uniform – or rather, two postures of a single man, their legs intertwined – occupy the foreground. The persuasive power of the work is enhanced by the use of a figurative and scaled narrative, featuring a body in motion. The body is split in two to represent two key steps it goes through. First kneeling, the soldier is shown like someone in prayer ready to bow down, in an pose that seems to represent the step of the "liberating explosion"[46] of martyrdom, symbolised by the flash of light flowing from the gun. Death is considered equivalent to

---

[46] Terms used in the wills of Iranian martyrs of Iran-Iraq War. See Eric Butel, *Le martyr dans les mémoires de guerre iraniens. Guerre Iran-Irak (1980-1988)*, PhD: Paris, 2000, 521.

mystical ecstasy. The second moment of death is depicted by the soldier who has fallen forward. This is the time of the settling, experienced as the liberation from the body, rendered an empty shell. Face against the ground, the soldier remains braced with both hands on his rifle, which he keeps on holding at arm's length. When moving towards death, the kneeling soldier is serene, disconnected from his suffering. Yet, he is wounded: under the rifle he hugs, blood is flowing. This fighter is already removed from the world. He faces Earth, which is humanised, transformed into a head with a green band tied around the forehead, which Iranian soldiers wore before attacks and which the fighter also sports. Paralleling the fighter, Earth is also injured and bleeds from under the headband. This earth, which symbolises the desire for unity and totality of the soldier society, is not represented as a dead or inert substance but rather as a source of vital strength. This is a sphere impregnated with supernatural power. Changing the scale of the earthly creatures and of the space that encompasses them allows for the representation of a new world, to be shaped by metaphysics. The work is entirely painted through a filter of blood, whose red colour covers even the green of Islam in the uniforms and headbands.

Death is directly conjured up by the injured body, lying lifeless. In this way, violence is fully sublimated and thus converted into a mystical ecstasy. The soldier's weapon constitutes his injury, killing, martyrdom, and ecstasy (as depicted by the light emanating from the gun). Although death is present, it is reinterpreted as the mystical experience of martyrdom, which is announced by the posture of prayer. As such, martyrdom and prayer are once again superimposed. The enemy is not designated nor are the circumstances that justify the battle; nonetheless, another actor is visible: the Earth, which also fights and bleeds. The painting's title, for its part, evokes a guide leading the path.

The two remaining paintings invoke the aftermath of martyrdom.

Nasser Palangi's *Shroud of Blood* (c.1981, see fig. 3) portrays a minimalist representation of martyrdom. Interdependent bloody shrouds placed side by side in several rows – expressing some type of collective – symbolise the transcendence of an ideal society based on self-denial. Their vertical position seems to indicate that the martyr is not passive in death but rather the active witness of a higher cause. The bloodied shrouds form the background while an immaculate white shroud bearing a sword with a bloodstained tip is positioned in the foreground. The shrouds cover headless bodies. This incomplete presence of the body, breaking with the normal human form, refers to a traditional representation of the martyr's body in Iranian revolutionary iconography: the headless martyr recalls Imam Ḥusayn, who was beheaded in Karbalā' in 680 (hence the tears at the neckline of the shroud) and whose severed appendage was sent to the Umayyad caliph in Damascus. The flight of the soul is symbolised by the upward movement of a dove taking flight at the bottom of the painting. Although the bird is white, its right wing is also bloodstained.

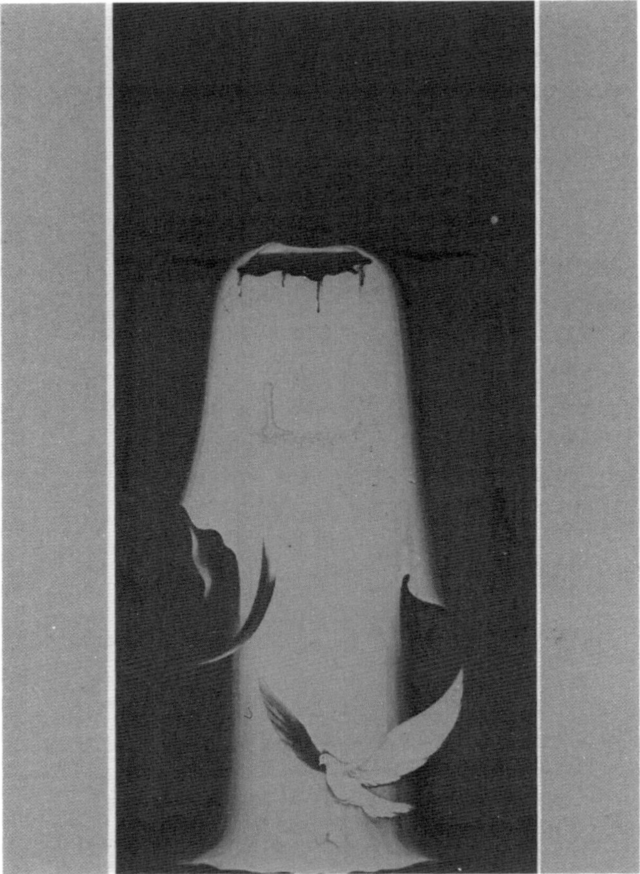

Fig. 3: Nasser Palangi, Shroud of Blood, c.1981 (300 × 140 cm)

In this painting, the abstract and symbolic dimension of martyrdom predominates. This "community in death"[47] expresses a striving for the ideal society, where martyrs would serve as mediators between the ordinary human reality and the Perfect Man. The predominance of the theme of bloodshed, the depiction of a community of martyrs, as well as the title itself all indicate the gap where ideology emerges. This is a hijacking of religion and an exploiting of art for the purpose of political strategies that promote the repetition of deadly behaviors.

Finally, in his mural painting entitled *Self Sacrifice* (c. 1981, see fig. 4), full of symbols and structured as a choreography, Kazem Chalipa illustrates the same dimension of martyrdom as shown in Nasser Palangi's work. Martyrdom corresponds here again to the expression of a collective united in common values and faith. A woman dressed in black, her stony face frozen with pain – likely a mother figure – holds a lifeless body covered in a white shroud. She is located in

---

[47] Khosrokhavar, *L'islamisme et la mort*, 292.

Fig. 4: Kazem Chalipa, Self Sacrifice, c. 1981 (300 × 200 cm)

the centre of the painting and serves to separate two distinct areas, one above her where the colour white prevails and the other below her, bathed in a glowing red atmosphere. To her right, a long line of the dead man's comrades-in arms and co-religionists moves forward with rifles in hand. To her left, a perfectly symmetrical row of red tulips, symbols of martyrs, moves toward the viewer. In the first flower, the semi-transparent petals reveal at their heart a golden light, and a kind of embryo of a future martyr. At the bottom of the painting, we perceive the outline of a grave where another red tulip seems rooted. Its vast corolla forms an altar supporting the arms of the woman who is carrying the body of the martyr as an offering. Above the two symmetrical processions, twisted figures of tortured or shot men attached to posts bring forth the image of an excruciating conflict. In the upper portion of the painting where the colour white prevails, we can identify behind the woman the figure of Imam Ḥusayn riding a white horse. Paragon of the martyr in Shiism, Imam Ḥusayn wears a dark grey coat over his shroud. Instead of a head, however, a circle of light emanates from his neck. He holds a book, the Koran most likely, in his left hand and a sword in the right. Beyond him, occupying the upper third of the work, two distinct rows of beheaded martyrs face the viewer. These spectra, representing perhaps his seventy-two companions, wait with serenity for Judgment Day. At this level of reading, the figure of the Imam of Time, who it is thought will appear at the end of time on a white horse, seems to be superimposed on the figure of Imam Ḥusayn.[48] In the middle of the upper portion of the painting, a light seems contained in white petals, which conjures up once again the form of a tulip outlining the sky. At the heart of this light, a closed hand appears with its forefinger pointing upward in the direction of Heaven. Finally, the painting (mural) is framed by religious calligraphic writing in the shape of a doorway or threshold.

In this fourth and last painting, martyrdom is already accomplished, the "door" crossed. The martyr is encircled in a multitude of symbolic, religious, and collective references. He is part of a larger configuration to which he contributes and brings his blood, but which revolves around him. The divine hand pointing in the direction of Heaven seems to pull the world upwards; at the same time, however, the reality of suffering and war is not obscured but rather is reflected on the stony face of the woman. The assassination of Karbalāʾ which is a foundation of Shiism, is mentioned here not merely as an example to follow, that of "self-sacrifice", but as a struggle for faith to be practiced alongside the Imam, the incarnation of the Perfect Man in the first Shiite sources.[49]

These paintings of the early 1980s featured the repeated representation, or indeed the overexposure, of the martyr's body, which became a new symbol of martyrdom.[50] To this point, the personal fate of the martyr within the context of the battle is ignored. Instead, emphasis is placed on the dying or dead body that reflects the accomplished sacrifice and becomes the subject of celebration. Martyrdom as staged in these paintings makes reference to the founding elements of the Shiite religion and its theological particularities: the revolt of Imam Ḥusayn, the eschatological expectation of the Savior Imam, the Last Judgment as justification for rebellion against an unjust authority, the wait for the great revolution of the end of time, and the triumphant return of the Twelfth Imam and advent of his kingdom of justice and truth. It is also staged through the mediation of an

---

[48]   Ibid, 289.
[49]   Mohammad Ali Amir-Moezzi, "Réflexions sur une évolution du shi'isme duodécimain: tradition et idéologisation", in: *Les retours aux écritures: fondamentalismes présents et passés*, ed. by Evelyne Patlagean et al., Louvain et al.1993, 68.
[50]   See Bombardier, "Iranian Revolutionary Painting on Canvas", 583-600.

edifice of signs and symbols. What appears emphatically as a leitmotiv is related to bereavement and mourning. The grief that follows the martyr's death is ritualised and established as a cult. Death as martyr, central in these four paintings, appears in glorious veneer as an ideal to achieve, as a means to transcendence and divine perfection.

In these paintings, the notion of the Perfect Man is associated with what is identified as a deadly vision of religion: the pursuit of perfection in death is achieved when the individual is driven by a yearning for martyrdom. The martyr in his journey towards death, a hallmark of revolutionary thought, is rightly described by Farhad Khosrokhavar as the "Pilgrim of the Absolute".[51] The notion of the Perfect Man is superimposed on the figure of the martyr, in the sense that the martyr accepts to the point of death the role of protector of faith, as well as the role of Revelation destined to the Perfect Man.

The reformulation of the mystical notion of the Perfect Man highlighted here gives a privileged status to the martyr, who becomes a kind of prototype of the Perfect Man. The frequent declarations by Ayatollah Khomeini on the subject are particularly instructive. In 1982, in a message to families of martyrs, he declared: "Martyrdom in the way of God is not something that can be evaluated with human criteria and tangible objectives [...] because the great value and higher status of martyrdom need divine criteria. We, earthly creatures, are quite incapable and the heavenly creatures are also unable to grasp the essence of martyrdom, because it is part of the attributes of the Perfect Man [...]. Martyrs are beyond our understanding".[52] Earlier, in 1981, inside the walls of the Foundation of Martyrs, his declaration was even more acute: "In the tradition reported in the *Kāfī*,[53] the same rank is given to the prophets and to the martyrs, so that the glory expressed for the prophets is the same that is shown to the martyrs. The martyr also contemplates the face of God; he tears the veil in the same way that prophets have torn theirs, and this is the last stage permitted for a man to achieve. We were promised that, for the martyrs, it would be the same stage as for the prophets".[54]

Ayatollah Khomeini explicitly uses here the notion of the Perfect Man to root the rhetoric of martyrdom in revolutionary Shiite ideology. By comparing the martyr to the Perfect Man and the prophets, he fills the desire for recognition and promotion of the young soldiers that the Islamic regime encouraged, both on the domestic scene and on the front of the Iran–Iraq War, and continues to encourage them to sacrifice themselves on behalf of the ideals of the Revolution.

---

[51] Khosrokhavar, *L'Islamisme et la mort*, 294.

[52] Ruhollah Khomeini, "Message aux familles de martyrs, prisonniers, disparus, invalides et blessés, 31 Shahrīwar 1362-22 Septembre 1983", in: *Ṣaḥīfih-yi Nūr* 18, 119.

[53] The book *Al-Kāfī fī ʿilm al-dīn (What is Sufficient in the Knowledge of the Faith)* is a Twelver Shiite Hadith collection compiled by Muḥammad Yaʿqūb Kulaynī.

[54] Ruhollah Khomeini, "Message à un groupe de responsables de la Fondation des Martyrs, 20 dey 1359–10 Janvier 1981", in: *Ṣaḥīfih-yi Nūr* 13, 272-274.

Ibn al-ʿArabī described the paths that lead to the Perfect Man; among them, martyrdom is not mentioned.[55] Similarly, Ali Shariati did not cite the model of the martyr as a possible incarnation of the Ideal Man. In his *Islamology*, he developed an ideal of life and not of death: "[The Ideal Man] seeks out mankind and thus attains God. He does not bypass nature and turn his back on mankind".[56] Under the auspices of revolutionary Shiite ideology, a semantic mutation of the notion was carried out. The idea of the Perfect Man was turned into a model of perfection via martyrdom. This mutation is closely related to Islamic mysticism, according to which the Perfect Man has attained the state of *fanāʾ*, the state of "mystical death". Yet, in revolutionary Shiite ideology, this mystical concept is redefined and reassessed. The mystical state of death is explicitly transformed into a state of physical death. In other words, real death is permitted and sanctified by the notion of martyrdom, and self-sacrifice is de-ritualised.[57]

Examining Indo-Muslim literature dating from the late 13th century, Annemarie Schimmel has commented on the connection made between the formula *insān-i kāmil = shahīd* and *fanāʾ = shahādat*, as in for example the poetry of Shāh ʿAbd al-Laṭīf of Bhit (1689–1752).[58] As she notes, Shāh ʿAbd al-Laṭīf explicitly specified that the heroes of his work, "who ha[d] never thought themselves, but only of love of God which makes them face all difficulties, ha[d] finally reached the goal: the *fanāʾ fiʾllāh*, annihilation in God and remaining in Him".[59] According to her, the poet had transformed the life of the Imams, and the death of the Imam Ḥusayn in particular, into "a model for all those Sufis who strive [...] to reach the final annihilation in God, the union which the Sufis so often express in the imagery of love and loving union".[60] If a link between Imam Husayn's martyrdom (*shahādat*) and the mystical death (*fanāʾ*) was metaphorically (yet explicitly) extended in the poetic work of this author, in the Shiite revolutionary apparatus sacrificial death is henceforth concretely demanded in service of the regime's interests.

V. Conclusion

In an article about the historical evolution of Shiism, Mohammad Ali Amir-Moezzi shows how Twelver Shiism after the Islamic Revolution in Iran became "one of the most politicised variants of Islam, a doctrine seeking to build an ideology of salvation, ideology taken in a political sense".[61] He explores how this trans-

---

55 Takeshita, "The Theory of the Perfect Man in Ibn ʿArabī's Fuṣūṣ al-Ḥikam", 87-102.
56 Shariati, *On the sociology of Islam*, 122.
57 Halm, *Shiʿa Islam*, 136.
58 Annemarie Schimmel, "Karbalāʾ and the Imam Ḥusayn in Persian and Indo-Muslim Literature", in: *Al-Ṣirāṭ*, 12 (1984), 29-42.
59 Ibid, 29-42.
60 Ibid, 29-42.
61 Amir-Moezzi, "Réflexions sur une évolution du shiʾisme duodécimain", 63.

formation of the traditional Shiite religion can be related to the historical evolution of its dogma. While in the original context of Shiism the term *ʿālim* (singular of *ʿulamāʾ*), translated as "wise initiate", was exclusively reserved for the Imam, this term from the late ninth century was synonymous with jurist-theologian.[62] At the same time, esoteric traditions with a metaphysical and mystical dimension were progressively rejected. From the Būyid dynasty, the "theological-legal rational tradition" emerged gradually as the mainstream of Twelver Shiism, relegating the "esoteric non-rational tradition" to an increasingly marginalised position.[63] Khomeini's doctrine and its central theory of the "power of the jurist-theologian" (*wilāyat-i faqīh*) should be contextualised in this historical and doctrinal evolution of Shiism. According to M. A. Amir-Moezzi, it can be regarded as the logical result of a process which ran during almost a millennium, from the divine wisdom of the Imam to rationalisation and finally to "ideologisation".[64] Even if regarded as a potential historical phenomenon, he nonetheless assesses this final stage ("ideologisation") as a revolution in traditional Shiism.[65] Said Amir Arjomand also conceives the *faqīh*-system as a deviation from classical Shiism,[66] in the same way that the political revolutionary interpretation of the tragedy of Karbalāʾ is considered by Heinz Halm as a new step in twentieth century Shiism.[67]

From his book published in 1944, *The Discovery of Secrets*, Ayatollah Khomeini's doctrine became increasingly important.[68] Ali Shariati participated in its strengthening by focusing his own thinking, from the late 1960s, on the political and ideological dimension of Islam. The revolutionary Shiite ideology of the 1980s, however, came to differ from the classic casuistry by inserting extremely simplified mystical concepts such as the Perfect Man. As explained by Amir-Moezzi, the rational theological tradition as opposed to the mystical tradition historically gained ground and culminated with the coming to power of Ayatollah Khomeini.[69] However, as shown in this work, revolutionary Shiite ideology as driven by the search for charisma presents the particularity of re-use and reformulation of certain mystical aspects of Shiite belief in order to accentuate influence and consolidate its power.

Aware of the impact of these reformulations, Ayatollah Khomeini encouraged many actors within the political scene, not just the *ʿulamāʾ*, to spread the revolutionary ideology. Both through their discourse and their works, the committed painters formed part of the eulogists of revolutionary Shiism. Through a comprehensive approach, I have correlated the discourse of three of these revolu-

---

[62] Ibid, 68-73.
[63] Ibid, 71.
[64] Ibid, 79.
[65] Ibid, 63.
[66] Said Amir Arjomand, *The Turban for the Crown*, Oxford 1988, 177-88.
[67] Halm, *Shiʿa Islam*, 137.
[68] Ruhollah Khomeini, *Kashf al-Asrār*, Tehran 1944.
[69] Amir-Moezzi, "Réflexions sur une évolution du shiʾisme duodécimain", 78-81.

tionary artists interviewed in 2009 with the analysis of paintings created in the early 1980s by the same narrow circle of committed artists.

For each of the three artists, it was paramount that the interview conveys their commitment to the ideals of the Islamic regime and to God. Their discourse reveals how the painting of martyrs was rooted in the revolutionary event, which is considered sacred by having potentially initiated the advent of a new world ruled by the mystical criterion of the Perfect Man. However, the revolutionary Shiite rhetoric – despite having constructed inter-human links and a closer relation to God – became blunt in its confrontation with the harsh reality and as a result of disillusionment.

> The Perfect Man makes what God appreciates. How can we achieve him? I thought that in a short period the world could change. But I got the idea that it does not happen like that. It was necessary to apply these principles in our own society. And it is already difficult. (Mr. R, 2009)

In 2009, the three painters finally confided that they had distanced themselves from their first matrix.

Through the discourse of these painters, it appears that the mystical notion of the Perfect Man, whose use was recurrent during the interviews, constitutes a key concept of revolutionary Shiite ideology. They frequently used the notion and applied it in their own field to describe the artist worthy of the name. Painting was first understood by these three artists as a privileged vector to complete political commitment and to a pure faith, which thus placed them on a path to a higher level of humanity as embodied by the Perfect Man. Within the CTIA, the committed artists sought confirmation of their legitimacy through Ali Shariati's ideology. The reformulation of the notion of the Perfect Man as applied to their own group allowed these artists to rise socially, as well as to insert and legitimise – for their benefit but also at their expense – art and artistic practice in the Islamic regime.

Finally, through the four paintings of martyrs analysed here, another ideological reformulation of the Perfect Man emerges in a vision of perfection culminating in death. Between 1980 and 1983, in the CTIA and Sūrih University, revolutionary painting was devoted, tirelessly, to the glorification of martyrdom. The force of persuasion that these paintings conveyed in the 1980s resulted partly from the mystical ideal of the Perfect Man in which they were rooted. The revolutionary painters translated through their art a political and religious utopia. The martyr, one of the main symbols of this utopia, conveyed hidden and esoteric truth that could only be achieved through death and that could, in turn, transform society.

Through these discourses and artistic works, the mystical notion of the Perfect Man, reformulated at several levels, can be considered an essential part of a broader ideological framework. This complex ideological apparatus succeeded in linking traditional mystical concepts, revolutionary Shiite ideology, and figurative representation, all in support of Ayatollah Khomeini's doctrine and the larger project of the Islamic Revolution.

Making Salvation Visible

Rhetorical and Visual Representations
of Martyrs in Salafi Jihadist Media

Silvia Horsch (Osnabrück)

In April 2003 the so-called media wing of al-Qaida, *al-Sahab*[1] (literally "the cloud"), published the first video in a series presenting the recorded testaments of some of the 19 men held responsible for the September 11 attacks of 2001. Its opening sequence shows a globe, with photos of the 19 men appearing in the outer space around the globe, one of which – that of Aḥmad al-Ḥaznāwī, whose testament is presented later in the video – approaches the viewer while a striking voice declaims in Arabic:

> Our words remain dead, waxen dolls of life, frozen, until when we die for what we believe, our words come to life and dwell among the living. Every word had been nourished on the heart of a human being, so it dwells among the living. For the living do not adopt the dead.[2]

There is no indication who is speaking; however, anyone somewhat familiar with Jihadist media will immediately recognise the voice of ʿAbdullāh ʿAzzām, the "Imam of Jihad". That only death will bring convictions and principles into existence is one of the central ideas in his concept of martyrdom, the basis for the martyr cult of contemporary Jihadist groups[3] – including those deploying suicide bombings and attacks even though ʿAzzām never supported their use. In this article I would like to examine how this concept has been represented in selected audios, images and videos in Jihadist media from recent decades.

---

[1] For *al-Sahab* see Jarret Brachman, *Global Jihadism. Theory and Practice*, New York 2009, 131-133.

[2] Translation according to the English subtitles given in the video with exception of the last sentence, which was not translated. Al-Sahab, *Waṣiyyat al-shahīd Aḥmad al-Ḥaznāwī* [The martyr Aḥmad al-Ḥaznāwī's last will], 2003, the video can be found at archive.org, URL: http://archive.org/details/Haznawi?start=2459.5 (retrieved 24.10.2012).

[3]. The terms Jihadists and Jihadism are controversial since they include the term "jihad" which is an important concept in Islam and has a broader meaning then military fighting. According to Jarret Brachman, it refers "to the peripheral current of extremist Islamic thought whose adherents demand the use of violence in order to oust non-Islamic influence from traditionally Muslims lands en route to establishing true Islamic governance in accordance with Sharia, or God's law." Jarret Brachman, *Global Jihadism*, 4. This definition still covers a very heterogeneous group of movements. It is important to bear in mind that this term does not designate a coherent set of convictions and strategies but a spectrum. It is evident for example that local groups like Hamas, Hizbullah and others who resort to violence in their struggle of liberation have to be distinguished from groups like al-Qaida. In this article mainly the transnational Jihadist movement is considered, with a focus on al-Qaida-related media.

I shall argue that in ʿAzzām's concept of martyrdom the personal salvation of the martyr and the collective salvation of the *umma* (the worldwide community of Muslims) are inextricably linked. Both dimensions, the personal located in the Hereafter and the collective in the here and now, are addressed in the Jihadist martyr cult not only verbally but also visually. Both the content of the Jihadist martyr myth and its visual representation prove to be an amalgamation of classical Islamic traditions and modern discourses. The use of modern technologies and media – from photographs and videos to digital image processing – not only makes it possible for a Jihadist martyr cult to exist at all, but moreover shapes it.

I. ʿAbdullāh ʿAzzām and Jihadist Media

ʿAbdullāh ʿAzzām (1941-1989), a Palestinian religious scholar, is held to be the leading ideological figure of what is today described as global Jihadism.[4] As Brachman sees it, "he provided the first modern hybridization of deep Jihadist ideological thinking with unswerving commitment to fighting and spreading the call of Jihad around the world."[5] He was the main organiser of the so-called Arab Afghans, Arab volunteers who joined the Afghan mujahidin in the war against the Soviets in Afghanistan (1979-1989). Together with Usama bin Laden, he led the "Service Bureau" (*Maktab al-Khidmāt*) in Peshawar, a drop-in-centre for the volunteers. Besides these activities he wrote, lectured and travelled widely on behalf of the Afghan mujahidin. His reputation rests on his training as a classical religious scholar at the Al-Azhar, his engagement as an activist in jihad, as well as to his own martyrdom (he was killed in a car bomb blast in Peshawar). Although he is still seen as one of the major inspirational figures for al-Qaida, his views differed in a number of points from the strategies and concepts of its leading figures.

The figure of the martyr occupies a central place in ʿAzzām's writings and lectures. This is not as self-evident as it may seem. While the martyr played a role in the writings of earlier Islamists, it was not accorded outstanding significance. It is with ʿAzzām's work that an Islamist martyr cult started to develop which eventually resulted in suicide bombings as its logical consequence.[6]

---

[4]   For an important criticism of the term, which tends to overlook the regional root causes of militant Islamism or terrorism, see Guido Steinberg, *Der Nahe und der Ferne Feind. Die Netzwerke des islamistischen Terrorismus*, Munich 2005, 9f. For a useful biography of ʿAzzām, see Thomas Hegghammer, "Abdullah Azzam, the Imam of Jihad," in: *Al-Qaeda in its own words*, ed. by Gilles Kepel et al., Harvard 2008, 81-101.

[5]   Jarret Brachman, *Global Jihadism*, 112.

[6]   See Hegghammer, "Abdullah Azzam", 101. This is not to say that this martyr cult is the only reason for deploying suicide bombings, to which militant groups resorted for military and strategic reasons. But the cult helps to gain acceptance (and recruits) for this practice, which amongst other things blatantly contradicts the norms of sharia as to the prohibition of killing of non-combatants and suicide.

ʿAzzām was not only influential in laying down the ideological basis of modern Jihadism; he was also a pioneer of Jihadist media. He and his followers made extensive use of modern media and technology at an early stage in their efforts to disseminate his message. Besides his journals *Al-Jihad* and *Lahīb al-Maʿraka* (Blaze of the Battlefield), which spread news of the Afghan War in Islamist circles around the globe,[7] he had his lectures and sermons recorded on audiotapes (a procedure he deployed or endorsed already in his time as a lecturer on sharia at the University of Jordan in the 1970s) and videotapes for distribution. According to Asiem El Defraoui, the media efforts undertaken during the time of the Afghan War constituted the first stage (1979-1989) in the development of Jihadist propaganda and were the preliminary for the later online Jihad.[8] As early as the Afghan War pictures of martyrs played an important role in the propaganda for the mujahidin. They were accompanied by cameramen who captured the clashes, taking photographs and videos of fallen fighters.[9] At that time relatively few videos were produced in the VHS format, but with the advent of digital technology both the numbers and the quality of videos increased remarkably.

The second stage, spanning 1990 to 2001, had its centre in London ("Londonistan") and was again closely associated with ʿAzzām's name: in 1996 the website azzam.com, promoting mujahidin in Bosnia, Chechnya and Afghanistan (Taliban), was established. Digitalised lectures by ʿAzzām could be accessed over the site and the first professional martyrdom videos were produced and distributed. The site followed the same aims ʿAzzām had pursued with his propaganda work for Afghanistan: recruiting fighters and raising funds.[10]

The third stage, the "globalisation of Cyberjihad" (2001-2006), started with the U.S.-led intervention in Afghanistan and later in Iraq.[11] It is characterised by the development of Jihadist media companies, which act more or less independently from Jihadist organisations, and an increase in video production made possible by the availability of low-cost digital cameras and video-editing programs.[12]

---

[7] *Al-Jihad* is considered the "most famous Jihadist periodical of the twentieth century [and] was produced almost single-handedly at first by ʿAzzām". Jarret Brachman, *Global Jihadism*, 112.

[8] Asiem El-Defraoui, *jihad.de. Jihadistische Online-Propaganda: Empfehlungen für Gegenmaßnahmen in Deutschland*. SWP-Studie, Berlin 2012, URL: http://www.swp-berlin.org/fileadmin/contents/products/studien/2012_S05_dfr.pdf (retrieved 24.09.2012). The description of the different stages follows El Defraoui.

[9] ʿAzzām describes in his martyrology how a camera operator, Yāsin al-Jazāʾirī, became a martyr himself in 1989, ʿAbdullah ʿAzzām, *Ushāq al-Ḥūr* [Lovers of the Paradise Maidens] (n.p., n.d.).

[10] The site was closed down in 2001 after the attacks of September 11. For more on the website, see Jarret Brachman, *Global Jihadism*, 122-125.

[11] Asiem El-Defraoui, *jihad.de*, 11.

[12] For an overview on the content and producers of videos, see Cecilie Finsnes, *What is audio-visual jihadi propaganda? An overview of the content of FFI's jihadi video database*, Norwegian Defense Research establishment (FFI), March 2012, URL: http://rapporter.ffi.no/rapporter/2010/00960.pdf (retrieved 20.10.2012).

Internet forums appeared facilitating the easy exchange of Jihadist material, while the use of languages diversified. Texts, audios and videos by ʿAzzām were (and still are) available on nearly every Jihadist website and excerpts from his lectures are included in numerous videos from this period.

The fourth and ongoing stage of Jihadist online propaganda was initiated with the development of Web 2.0. It is characterised by the use of social media and even smart phones. Older material is still reprocessed and often presented in a piecemeal way: short excerpts from longer video productions can be seen on *Facebook*, *YouTube* and elsewhere. ʿAzzām is still prominent on the contemporary stage of Jihadist media: a search for ʿAbdullāh ʿAzzām on *YouTube* generates more than 13 000 video clips, and these are only those in which ʿAzzām appears in the title.[13]

The extensive deployment of media and especially of images is by no means self-evident given the religious strand from which the Jihadists emerged. They have their roots in two reform movements of the 19th century, Salafiyya and Wahhābiyya.[14] Both movements are characterised by objections against the traditional *ʿulamāʾ* (scholars) and aim to reform Islam by turning to the pious forefathers (*al-salaf*). The Salafiyya movement, however, sought to catch up to Western achievements in civilisation and technology, while the Wahhābiyya viewed these achievements with suspicion, including photography. The Grand Mufti of Saudi Arabia, ʿAbd al-ʿAzīz Bin Bāz (1912-1999), declared in a fatwa based on a very narrow interpretation of prophetical Hadiths concerning images and statues that it is unlawful to take photographs and, indeed, to appear on a photograph. Television was introduced in the 1960s in Saudi Arabia against the fierce opposition of Wahhābī scholars, even resulting in violent demonstrations. The ban on public photography was first lifted in Saudi Arabia in 2006.[15] Accordingly, mujahidin also objected to pictures: ʿAbdullāh Anas, an Algerian who was one the founders of the Services Bureau in Peshawar and a son-in-law of ʿAzzām, has reported that a number of mujahidin were unwilling to appear on videos and photographs for religious reasons.[16] Such objections were obviously not valid in the mind of ʿAzzām and a lot of his followers, and this was even more so the case amongst leading figures of al-Qaida, like the late Usama Bin Laden and Ayman al-Ẓawāhirī, who used, and still use, video as a medium of cyber war on a regular basis. The propaganda value of images obviously outstrips any religious concerns, and the position towards images is determined rather by their usefulness.

---

[13] Search on 24.09.2012.

[14] Historically these are two distinct movements; today *Salafī* and *Wahhābī* are used interchangeably.

[15] Cf. Silvia Naef, *Bilder und Bilderverbot im Islam*, Munich 2007, 120-122.

[16] Interview with ʿAbdullāh Anas in the film *The Al Qaeda Code* by Abdelasiem El Difraoui, Germany/Canada 2008.

The usefulness or the necessity of pictures can be traced back to the argument articulated by Muḥammad ʿAbduh and Rashīd Riḍā, two of the most prominent proponents of the Reformist Salafi movement. Whereas ʿAbduh even allowed images for aesthetic reasons, his stricter pupil Riḍā confined their deployment to their usefulness. Prior to the advent of visual mass media, he gave no consideration to the propaganda value (which also always has an aesthetic aspect), condoning photographs in fields like natural sciences and medicine as well as espionage and weaponry.[17] One of the reasons to permit photographs is that they are considered to be a mechanical representation of the world and are therefore no rival to the power of creation, which belongs solely to God. The fallacy that mechanically produced images do not possess the character of an artwork but rather present nothing more than a pure depiction of nature – a fallacy which, as Mitchell has pointed out,[18] also prevails in Western thought – enables religious misgivings towards photography to be overcome. Images proved to be indispensable for the Jihadists for recruiting fighters and raising funds, and as the technical equipment and media production methods became more and more sophisticated the value of images even increased. Accordingly, a Jihadist Internet activist asks rhetorically: "What if the Mujaahideen had never carried a camera with them to the battlefield? [...] What if the Mujaahideen never had the appropriate program to make their videos look nice?"[19]

Martyrdom is one of the central topics in Jihadist propaganda[20] and with the technical developments in audio-visual media pictures of martyrs come to the fore. In the following I shall analyse representations of martyrs from these different stages and in different media with regard to ʿAzzām's idea of martyrdom.

II. Multimedia Martyr Biographies: Text, Sound and (Moving) Image

With his seminal martyrology *Lovers of the Paradise Maidens* (*ʿUshshāq al-Ḥūr*) ʿAzzām initiated a modern Sunni literary tradition that was later taken up in contexts as varied as the Second Palestinian Intifada, the cyber jihad of al-Qaida and the Arab uprisings which broke out in 2010. *Lovers of the Paradise Maidens* is a collection of martyr biographies, including their letters and testaments as well as letters by ʿAzzām to the families of the martyrs. The book contains stories of fallen mujahidin from different countries, mostly Arabic, and the aim is to present the martyrs as role models. A number of elements recur: arrival in Afghanistan, which is presented as a departure from the mundane world (sometimes de-

---

[17] See Silvia Naef, *Bilder und Bilderverbot im Islam*, 113-115.

[18] "What is natural is, evidently, what we can build a machine to do for us," W.J.T. Mitchell, "What is an image?" in: *New Literary History* 15, 1984, 524.

[19] Unknown Jihadist Internet propagandist, quoted from Jarret Brachman, *Global Jihadism*, 107.

[20] See Asiem Defraoui, *jihad.de*, 47f.

scribed in terms of a "divorce") and as a Hijra (emigration, an allusion to the emigration of the prophet from Mecca to Medina); the obstacles the mujahidin had to overcome in order to take part in the jihad (like the opposition of their parents or difficult journeys), anecdotes highlighting their devoutness, sincerity, humility, generosity and courageousness, as well as their love for their brothers in arms. The circumstances of their death are described, as are the details surrounding their funerals. Both the death and the funeral are frequently accompanied by miraculous events; recurrent motifs are a fighter (or that of another mujahidin) dreaming of coming death, the martyr's blood smelling like musk and his corpse not decaying.

A number of motifs link the deeds of the mujahidin to the generation of the first Muslims. The biographies are studded with Koranic verses (most prominently: "Think not of those who are killed in the way of Allah as dead. Nay, they are alive, with their Lord, and they have provision", 3:169) and Hadiths dealing with jihad and martyrdom. The biographies also include numerous poems praising the martyrs, and at the same time express sorrow and grief over the loss of comrades. Such poems follow the genre of *marthiya* (elegy), known from pre-Islamic times, which laments the death of a person, mostly a fighter, and praises his merits. Such allusions to the Prophet's time and connections to well-established genres of Islamic literature, together with the numerous citations of foundational Islamic texts and statements from scholars of earlier times, accumulate symbolic capital, crucial in winning support amongst fellow Muslims.[21]

ʿAzzām's *Lovers of the Paradise Maidens* is an extensive collection of several hundred pages and it cannot be read in a short time. Numerous excerpts and partial translations can be found in the Internet, presenting the most prominent martyrs or the most interesting stories. Another way to make the martyr stories more 'consumer friendly' are audios and videos, and these present only selected martyrs.

In the Hearts of Green Birds (1996)

One of the first and very influential examples is an audio cassette entitled *In the Hearts of Green Birds* released by Azzam Publications in 1996.[22] Just like *Lovers of the Paradise Maidens*, this title takes up a prominent motif from the martyr tradition: according to well-known Hadiths, the souls of the martyrs (or the martyrs themselves) reside in Paradise in the craw (or in the inside) of green birds.[23] On

---

[21] For the significance of symbolic capital acquired through references to the Islamic tradition, see Lohlker, *Dschihadismus. Materialien*, Vienna, 2009, 56-76, especially 60.

[22] A second part was released in November 1997 *Under the Shade of Swords*. Both tapes are available as audio files at archive.org and elsewhere in the Internet.

[23] This Hadith appears in several versions in different collections. An example is the following: [...] "We asked ʿAbdullāh about the Koranic verse: 'Think not of those who are slain

the tape – which starts with radio communication and gunfire from a real-life battlefield recording –[24] an English-speaking narrator presents the story of several martyrs from amongst the foreign fighters in Bosnia. The *nashīd* (chants, a form of vocal music considered lawful) on jihad and martyrdom makes up much of the run-time and it assumes the function of poetry in the textual martyrology, indeed becoming even more important due to the capacity of music (if only vocal) to transport and arouse emotions.[25] Most of the songs stem from an Afghan veteran who was killed in Bosnia in 1992 and whose story is the first one presented on the tape.[26] With the sounds of the war and the voices of the martyrs and fighters (albeit often in poor quality) the listener is virtually immersed into events. The voice of the speaker is accompanied by artificial reverberations designed to create an awesome atmosphere. The cassette did not fail to have an effect on listeners. An anonymous jihadist is reported as saying, "when I heard this cassette, I cried and cried."[27] A transcript of the tape was also printed in book form and this is available on the Internet.[28] *In the Hearts of the Green Birds* is considered a classic of Jihadist media and is still used as a source material in the production of new videos.

Two quotes taken from *In the Hearts of the Green Birds* show the two central themes of the Jihadist martyr cult. The first is a Hadith stressing the personal rewards awaiting martyrs in the afterlife:

> The Messenger of Allah (sallallaahu 'alayhi wa sallam) [peace and blessings be upon him] said: the Shaheed [martyr] is given seven special favors from Allah:
> 1- All his sins are forgiven at the first drop of his blood.
> 2- He sees his place in Paradise as soon as he is killed.
> 3- He is saved from the punishment of the Grave.

---

in Allah's way as dead. Nay, they are alive, finding their sustenance in the presence of their Lord.' (3:169). He said: 'We asked the meaning of the verse (from the Prophet) who said: 'The souls of the martyrs live in the bodies of green birds who have their nests in chandeliers hung from the throne of the Almighty. They eat the fruits of Paradise from wherever they like and then nestle in these chandeliers [...].'" Muslim b. al-Hajjāj al-Qushayrī al-Nīsābūrī, Abū l-Husayn/ al-Nawawī, Yahyā b. Sharaf: *Sahīh Muslim bi-sharh an-Nawawī*, Beirut ca. 1983, Vol. 13, 30-32; translation by Abdul Hamid Siddiqui, *Sahih Muslim*, New Delhi 2000, Book 20, Number 4651, with minor changes.

24 Recording of Operation "Miracle" in Zavidovic, North Bosnia, 21 July 1995 according to a transcript of the tape released by Azzam Publications, see http://www.sunniforum.com/forum/archive/index.php/t-8676.html (retrieved 26.09.2012).

25 For *anashīd* (sing. *nashīd*) and poetry see Rüdiger Lohlker, *Dschihadismus*, 130-141. For the motivational factor of *anashīd*, see Tilmann Seidensticker, "Jihad Hymns (Nashīds) as a means of self-motivation in the Hamburg group", in: *The 9/11 Handbook*, ed. by Hans G. Kippenberg et al., London 2006, 71-78.

26 Abū Zubayr Al-Madanī released a cassette with *anashīd* under the title *Qawāfil al-shuhadā'* (Caravans of Martyrs), considered a classic in Jihadist circles.

27 In the Jihadist forum Islamic Awakening, URL: http://forums.islamicawakening.com/f41/~*-smile-of-the-shuhada-*~-14820/index9 html#post145675 (retrieved 26.09.2012).

28 The transcript was also released by Azzam Publications, URL: http://www.militantislam monitor.org/article/id/258 (retrieved 02.11.2012).

148 SILVIA HORSCH

4- He is saved from the great Terror on the Day of Judgement.

5- There is placed on his head a crown of honor, a jewel of which is better than this whole world and all that it contains.

6- He is given intercession for 70 members of his household.

7- He is married to 72 women of the most beautiful women of Paradise.[29]

The second quote is a reference to ʿAbdullāh ʿAzzām:

> Sheikh Abdullah Azzam rehmatullah'alaih [God have mercy on him] said that Islamic history is not written, except with the blood of the Shuhadaʾ [martyrs] and except with the stories of the Shuhadaʾ.[30]

These two quotes, one of a foundational Islamic text, the other of a 20th-century religious scholar and militant activist, highlight two central aspects in the Jihadist concept of martyrdom which were combined most effectively by ʿAbdullāh ʿAzzām.[31] Whereas the idea of personal expiation through martyrdom is old, as the Hadith indicates,[32] the idea that martyrs build the foundations of history, nation or civilisation is a very recent one. Two other statements by ʿAzzām in this regard are inserted in the following stories of the martyrs, this time taken directly from his recorded lectures: "And with the likes of all these (the martyrs), nations are established, convictions are brought to life, and ideologies are made victorious." And: "Indeed, history is not recorded except with the blood of all these (the Shuhadaa'), except with the stories of all these, except with the likes of all these."[33] The twofold salvation – personal in the life to come, collective in the here and now – is what is expected from martyrdom and part of what makes it such a powerful idea in Jihadist discourse.

---

[29] Azzam Publications, *In the Hearts of Green Birds*, 1996. Translation and spelling here and in the following according to the transcript released by Azzam Publications. Additions are added in square brackets. The Hadith is also important in ʿAzzām's writings: it is included in his fatwa *Join the Caravan* as well in the renowned lecture "Martyrs. The Building Blocks of Nations", from which the following quote of ʿAzzām stems. Versions of the hadith can be found in Muḥammad b. ʿĪsā al-Tirmidhī, *Sunan al-Tirmidhī. Al-Jāmiʿ al-ṣaḥīḥ*, ed. Khalīl Maʾmūn Shīha, Beirut 2002, No. 1663; Muḥammad b. Yazīd b. Māja, *Sunan*, ed. Muḥammad Fuʾād ʿAbd al-Bāqī, Kairo 1975, Vol. 2, No. 2799. Aḥmad b. Muḥammad b. Ḥanbal, *Musnad*, ed. Ṣidqī Jamīl al-ʿAṭṭār (Beirut 1994, Vol. 6, No. 17182, see for another version without the possibility of intercession, No. 17798.

[30] Azzam Publications, *In the Hearts of Green Birds*, 1996.

[31] Ḥasan al-Bannā, the founder of the Muslim Brotherhood killed in 1949, allegedly by the Egypt secret service, had already described martyrs' blood as a sign of victory in this world ("Their pure blood is a symbol of victory in this world and the mark of success and felicity in the world to come", *Jihād fī l-Islām*; for the English translation see *Jihad in Islam*, URL: http://www.2muslims.com/directory/Detailed/227153.shtml, retrieved 19.10. 2012). However, in contrast to ʿAzzām, martyrdom is by no means as prominent in al-Bannā's writings.

[32] Although this idea is not without theological difficulties regarding the linking of bloodshed and expiation, see Silvia Horsch, *Tod im Kampf. Figurationen des Märtyrers in frühen sunnitischen Schriften*, Würzburg 2011, 186ff.

[33] *In the Hearts of Green Birds*, transcript released by Azzam Publications.

In *The Hearts of Green Birds* the personal dimension of salvation is more important, since the tape is nearly devoid of more comprehensive information about the war in Bosnia (only a few operations are described). The wish for martyrdom is presented to have been very strong: "He [the singer Abū Zubayr al-Madanī] did not used to think about anything except one thing, and he did not speak about anything except one thing, that is Jihad and martyrdom".[34] Again miracles and amazing stories play an important role and numerous dreams are narrated. One of the martyrs is reported to have seen Paradise before his death: "He was shot in the heart; and he continued to walk for a distance of 20 meters still holding his machine gun. And then he said to the brothers that were around him: 'Look in the sky! Look what I can see...!'"[35]

As in *Lovers of the Paradise Maidens*, it is often reported that the smell of musk emanated from the blood of the martyrs, that their bodies did not decay (in contrast to the bodies of the Serbs which decayed very fast) and that the martyrs smiled after dying. All these things serve as signs that the fallen had indeed reached the position of a martyr and bliss in the afterlife. As the narrator puts it: "This is a sure sign of his Shahada [martyrdom] and this is a sign for the other brothers as well, that this is the right path that they are on."[36]

The Martyrs of Bosnia (1997)

Shortly after the sequel audiotape (*Under the Shades of Swords*), the first professional martyr video was released by Azzam Publications, *The Martyrs of Bosnia* (1997). In contrast to *In the Hearts of Green Birds*, it is a history of the Bosnian War from the perspective of the mujahidin and places the conflict in the broader framework of 'Western wars against Muslims'. It is for this reason that the collective dimension of salvation becomes more important.

The narrative structure of the video is of outstanding importance for its effect on the audience and the significance ascribed to the martyrs. Consisting of two parts, both about 70 minutes long, the video begins with a sequence of some 20 minutes showing the brutality of the wars waged against Muslims all over the world – as of course the narrative sees it. Six places are at the forefront: Afghanistan, Tajikistan, Chechnya, Kashmir, Palestine and Bosnia. The suffering of the Muslim civilian population is shown in extremely graphic images: disoriented and scared little children and elderly people in hospitals with severe injuries, babies with amputated limbs, rows of bodies of children wrapped in white shrouds awaiting their funeral. In short: helplessness and despair in every respect. All these pictures are accompanied by *anashīd*. Several sequences are particularly

---

[34] *In the Hearts of Green Birds*, transcript released by Azzam Publications.
[35] Ibid.
[36] Ibid.

hard to endure, like recordings of abuses inflicted on the Palestinian civilian population, probably during the First Intifada, and a sequence of three whole minutes showing injured and dead Bosnian civilians, probably in Sarajevo after one of the bombings of the Markale market.[37] Long sequences showing the dead and wounded, several of them in mortal agony, in haunting close-ups create a feeling of utter helplessness. One can imagine that this helplessness is easily turned into rage demanding action. The pictures of the Markale massacres are accompanied by a *nashīd* with the recurrent line "Where is the army of the Muslims?" (*Ayna jund al-muslimīn?*) The underlying message is clear – it is only by the way of action that the sense of powerlessness felt when confronted with such agonizing suffering can be converted into power.

The opening sequence is followed by the presentation of an enormous number of martyrs. Over 140 men are shown either dead (mostly badly disfigured) or while alive on private photographs or ID cards.[38] The sequential arrangement, which places the martyrs after the civilian casualties, indicates the collective function accorded to the martyrs for the *umma*: victims are replaced by sacrifices, and these turn powerlessness into power. This is underscored by the narrative: it follows a series of excerpts of sermons by different preachers speaking about the plight of the Muslims in Bosnia and urging the Muslims to come to their help. Directly afterwards, those who responded to the call, the mujahidin, are shown undergoing training in Bosnia. The rest of the video tells the story of the mujahidin engagement in the Bosnian War, describing different operations and battles, while eulogizing the fallen mujahidin as martyrs.

Towards the end the scope of the video is broadened again: the last martyr presented, the Egyptian Waḥīd al-Dīn, commander of the mujahidin in Bosnia, is included in a row of outstanding religious scholars and Islamist activists who mostly died as martyrs, among them ʿAbdullāh ʿAzzām, Ḥasan al-Bannāʾ and Aḥmad Yāsīn.[39] After the story of Waḥīd al-Dīn, images from other centres of mujahidin activity are shown, namely Chechnya and Afghanistan (a lot of the material in this part stems from Western television channels like CNN and BBC), indicating that the jihad is ongoing. This is underlined by the following

---

[37] In the first bombing on 5 February 1994 a mortar shell landed in the centre of the crowded marketplace, killing 68 people and wounding another 144. In the second bombing on 28 August 1995 five mortar shells killed 37 people and wounded 90. Pictures of the massacres were broadcast in television news segments all over the world at the time of the bombings (the second leading to the NATO operation Deliberate Force, which had to be justified in Western public).

[38] The first is Sheikh Anwar Shaʿbān, a senior leader of the Egyptian Jamāʿa Islamiyya who was killed by Croatian Special Forces in 1995. His biography is given in the tape *Under the Shades of Swords*, for a transcript of his biography, see: http://forums.islamicawakening. com/f14/biography-of-shaheed-shaykh-anwar-shaban-13/see (retrieved 16.10.2012).

[39] Aḥmad Yāsīn was the spiritual leader of Hamas and was killed by an Israeli airstrike in 2004. At the time the video was produced he was in Israeli custody and released shortly afterwards at the end of 1997.

Hadith: "Jihad will be performed continuously since the day Allah sent me as a Prophet until the day the last member of my community will fight with the dajjal (Antichrist)."[40] The final sequences show leaders of the Chechen mujahidin, Shamil Basajev and the Saudi Ibn al-Ḥaṭṭab, as well as Usama bin Laden in Afghanistan. Here local Islamist resistance movements like Hamas and the defensive Bosnian and Chechen Wars are linked to al-Qaida, which at that time had already made the strategic shift to attack the "far enemy" on its own soil,[41] thereby lending it legitimacy.

III. Collective and Personal Salvation

Most of those who joined a war as foreign mujahidin – in Bosnia, as well as in Afghanistan before and Chechnya afterwards – expressed a feeling of responsibility or an obligation to fight on behalf of their oppressed fellow Muslims. This perceived responsibility is also considered to play an important role at the onset of radicalisation processes which may eventually lead to joining al-Qaida and other Islamist terrorist organisations (or to undertaking attacks without joining an organisation at all).[42]

The obligation to assist oppressed Muslims militarily was most prominently formulated in terms of *fiqh* (Islamic jurisprudence) by ʿAbdullāh ʿAzzām. The urgency with which he promoted martyrdom is linked to his concept of jihad as an individual duty of any (male and able) Muslim.[43] According to his view – which is in this respect in line with traditional concepts of jihad – jihad is a collective duty (*farḍ al-kifāya*) as long as the enemy has not reached Muslim lands. It

---

[40] Wording according to the video. The text is part of a longer Hadith: "Three belong to the roots of belief [*īmān*]; to refrain from [harming] whoever says: 'There is no god but God', and not to declare him a disbeliever because of a sin, and not to expel him from Islam because of an act, and jihad goes on since I was sent by God until my last community fights *al-dajjāl* [an eschatological figure in Islamic tradition], no despotic tyrant and no upright righteous will abolish it; and the belief in [God's] decrees." Abū Dāwūd, Sulaymān b. al-Ashʿath as-Sijistānī: *Ṣaḥīḥ sunan al-muṣṭafā*, 2 vols, ed. by Kamāl Yūsuf al-Ḥūt. Beirut [ca. 1980], No. 2532 [translation S.H.].

[41] For this strategic choice, see Fawaz Gerges, *The Far Enemy. Why Jihad Went Global*, Cambridge 2005.

[42] A spectacular case of self-radicalisation through the Internet was that of Arid Uka who killed two U.S. soldiers and injured two others in March 2011 at Frankfurt airport. He stated that the catalyst for his attack was a video on *YouTube* showing U.S. soldiers raping Muslim women. As it turned out, the rape scene was part of a film (*Redacted*, 2007) dealing with the massacre of Maḥmūdiyya in Iraq in March 2006, which he failed to recognise was a fictional dramatisation.

[43] For ʿAzzām's views on jihad with excerpts of major writings cf. Hegghammer, "Abdullah Azzām", 81-146, as well as Rüdiger Lohlker, *Dschihadismus*, 56-60; John C. M. Calvert, "The Striving Shaykh: Abdullah Azzām and the Revival of Jihad," in: *Journal of Religion and Society*, Supplement Series 2 (2007) 83-102; Andrew McGregor, "Jihad and the Rifle Alone': Abdullah Azzām and the Islamist Revolution", in: *Journal for Conflict Studies* 23 (2003) 92-113.

is the duty of the imam to ensure that jihad is undertaken by a group sufficient in numbers and strength (mostly the regular army). However, in case the enemy has entered Muslim lands jihad becomes an individual duty (*farḍ al-ʿayn*) of every Muslim, a duty incumbent as doing one's prayers and fasting. As a consequence, anyone who neglects this duty commits a sin, just as he who neglects prayers and fasting. Furthermore, ʿAzzām extends the duty of personal jihad from the inhabitants of the invaded area to the Muslim *umma* on a global scale, citing amongst others the Ḥanafī scholar Ibn ʿĀbidīn (1783-1836):

> [If] those nearby the attack cannot resist the enemy, or are indolent and do not fight jihad, then it becomes Farḍ ʿayn upon those behind them [...]. If they too are unable, then it becomes Farḍ ʿayn upon those behind them, and so on in the same manner until the jihad becomes Farḍ ʿayn upon the whole Ummah of Islam from East to West.[44]

In the lectures he delivered during his numerous trips around the globe to recruit men and raise money for the Afghan jihad, ʿAzzām even intensified this urgency by presenting martyrdom (not only fighting!) as the only way to reach forgiveness:

> O' sons of Islam! What will cleanse our sins? What will purify our mistakes? And what will cleanse our dirt? It will not be washed except with the blood of martyrdom, and know that there is no path except this Path.[45]

The deliverance of the *umma* is thus inextricably connected to the personal salvation of every Muslim. According to ʿAzzām's sacrificial rhetoric, only martyrs are able to bring about victory, achieve glory and secure the future:

> By the likes of these martyrs, nations are established, convictions are brought to life and ideologies are made victorious. [...] the clear-sighted eye and the enlightened heart knows [sic] that these sacrifices are the provisions of future generations for distant civilizations to come.[46]

---

[44] The translation follows the English translation of ʿAzzām's fatwa *Al-Difāʿ ʿan arāḍi l-muslimīn aḥammu furūḍ al-aʿyān* [Defence of the lands of the Muslims is the most important personal obligation]: *Defence of the Muslim Lands. The First Obligation after Iman*, Peshawar, 2nd edition, n.d., URL: http://www.religioscope.com/info/doc/jihad/Azzām_defence_5_chap3.htm (retrieved 11.07.2012).

[45] ʿAbdullāh ʿAzzām, "Martyrs. The building blocks of nations" n. d., originally from Azzam. com, available at Religioscope.com: http://www.religioscope.com/info/doc/jihad/Azzām_martyrs.htm (retrieved 21.02.2012). The translation is in large parts based on the Arabic lecture "Midād al-ʿulamāʾ wa dimāʾ al-shuhadāʾ" [The ink of the scholars and the blood of the martyrs], URL: http://aljoufreev.com/vb/showthread.php?t=9689 (retrieved 22.03.2012). ʿAzzām would probably not have made this point in a theological treatise on the Islamic concept of forgiveness, which is not based on a blood sacrifice (be it personal or vicarious) but on repentance (*tauba*) and good deeds on the side of men, and mercy (*raḥma*) on the side of God (see e.g. Koran 66:8, 9:104, 42:25, 40:3.). But on these occasions he was speaking to an audience of young men, seeking to convince them to risk their lives in Afghanistan.

[46] Ibid.

The modern myth of sacrifice as necessary for rejuvenating or keeping alive the nation, the community or the land is readily discernible in this mythical function assigned to martyrs. The idea of blood being necessary to ensure the well-being of further generations is familiar from both nationalist and communist propaganda. Both ideologies were imported into the Arabic world in the 19th century. In Palestine the national myth of the *fidāʾī* (literally: 'one who gives himself as a ransom') developed, where the fighter gives himself as a ransom for the (feminised) homeland and in a 'martyr wedding' (*ʿurs al-shahīd*) unites with it at his death. This myth draws on traditions as varied as nationalism, mystical love poetry (*ghazal*) and the recently re-discovered oriental myth of the vegetation god Adonis (or Tammūz), and was mainly articulated in the poetry of Mahmud Darwish.[47] It influenced a whole generation of Palestinians, including ʿAzzām, who himself took part in the Palestinian resistance for some 18 months, which at that time (the 1960s) was nationalistic and secular in orientation – much to ʿAzzām's dislike. ʿAzzām's emphasis on the classical figure of the *shahīd al-maʿraka* can therefore be seen as an 'Islamisation' of the nationalistic *fidāʾī*. 'Islamisation' however does not mean a simple recurrence of something old. In the effort to produce a counter-myth, elements of this modern myth are incorporated in what seems to be an old Islamic motif at first glance. Although of minor importance in early Islamic texts where no explicit sacrificial myth is elaborated, here the notion of sacrifice is stressed to such an extent due to its rivalry with the modern myth.

IV. Martyr Video Production in the Era of Digital Image Processing

Whereas the VHS video *The Martyrs of Bosnia* is composed only of recordings, and for this reason serves the illusion to "tell the story as it was" in the style of a documentation, the recently emerging possibilities of digital image processing have remarkably altered the character of martyr videos. The new technology enables or expands the possibility of converting mental and verbal images into graphic ones. This is often done in a very straightforward way: an example of how elements of ʿAzzām's sacrificial martyr myth are converted into images is the series *Winds of Paradise*[48] by *al-Sahab*. ʿAzzām stated that Islam itself is only

---

[47]   See Angelika Neuwirth, "From Sacrilege to Sacrifice: Observations on Violent Death in Classical and Modern Arabic Poetry," in: *Martyrdom in Literature: Visions of Death and Meaningful Suffering in Europe and the Middle East from Antiquity to Modernity*, ed. by Friederike Pannewick, Wiesbaden 2004, 259-281.

[48]   The series consists of five parts so far, the first released in July 2007 and the last in October 2010. The videos can be found at archive.org and elsewhere in the Internet. As the anonymous user who put the third part in archive.org wrote, al-Sahab follows with the series the model of *In the Hearts of Green Birds* and develops it further: "'The Winds of Paradise' series is the same thing, but takes on a much more personal approach as you actually get to see these Mujahideen and how they lived their lives as pious warriors." http://archive.org/details/winds-of-heaven-3 (retrieved 05.11.2012).

Fig. 1: Screen shot of the video *Winds of Paradise* (I)

provided for and safeguarded by the sacrifices of martyrs, describing their blood as the water that irrigates the tree of Islam,[49] the "water of life for this religion."[50] The first video in the series *Winds of Paradise* features, as way of introduction, a computer animation visualising this statement: a video recording of one of ʿAzzām's lectures is inserted into the animation of arid land with desiccated trees. The recording features the statement already mentioned at the beginning of our considerations: "Our words remain dead, like waxen dolls, unmoving and frozen, until when we die for them, they rise up, alive, to live among the living" (see fig. 1). Simultaneously the trees in the background once again flourish and the earth becomes green as the names of the seven martyrs to be presented appear in golden letters in the sky.[51]

The same iconography is used in the third part of *Winds of Paradise*, which is dedicated to Abū Laith al-Lībī, a senior leader of al-Qaida killed in January 2008 by an unmanned CIA Predator drone. In this case not only the name in golden letters appears, but something like a virtual shrine is erected for the martyr, with

---

[49] ʿAzzām, *ʿUshshaq al-hur*, n. p.

[50] ʿAzzām, "Midād al-ʿulamā' wa dimā' al-shuhadā'" [author's translation]

[51] Another statement of ʿAzzām alluding to this image: "The extent to which righteous convictions and correct beliefs spread within a nation, is the extent to which it plants its roots in the depths of the earth and sends forth orchards of trunks with their flourishing leaves so that Man can take shade by it from the troubles of life, its financial fever and from the flame of hatred, envy and competition for cheap thrills and temporary enjoyment. As for the Muslim Ummah, it does continue to exist in the course of history of humankind, except by a divine idology [sic] and the blood which flows as a result of spreading this divine ideology and implanting it into the real World." ʿAbdullāh ʿAzzām, "Martyrs. The Building Blocks of Nations".

Fig 2: Screen shot of the video Winds of Paradise (III) the golden letters give the name Abū
        Laith al-Lībī, the four cubic structures display video recordings of al-Lībī.

four cubic structures displaying videos of al-Lībī (see fig. 2). This is an especially
striking example for the all-out martyr cult of al-Qaida despite its severe reserva-
tions against hagiolatry stemming from their Wahhābī/Salafi doctrine.[52] Whereas
real Ṣūfi shrines are something to be detested, virtual shrines which visualise the
elevated status in the Hereafter may be erected.

The image of the flourishing land refers directly (if however probably unwill-
ingly) to one of the sources of the modern sacrificial myth of the *fidāʾī*: the myth
of the vegetational god Adonis (or Tammūz), who dies periodically and rejuve-
nates the land with his blood. Ironically, this myth was reintroduced to the
Middle East by the work of the European anthropologist James George Frazer
(1854-1941), whose book *The Golden Bough* was partly translated into Arabic.[53]

---

[52] The integration of hagiographic elements into Islamist discourse also goes back to ʿAzzām.
      As Cook writes: "Although radical Islam overall is hostile to Sufi mysticism, ʿAzzām essen-
      tially adopted its cult of holy men but changed it into a cult of martyrs." David Cook et
      al., *Understanding and Addressing Suicide Attacks. The Faith and Politics of Martyrdom Opera-
      tions*, Westport 2007, 48.

[53] Together with T. S. Eliot's *The Waste Land*, it influenced modern Arab poets in the 1950s
      and became a vital reference point in cultural criticism and the call for a renewal of society
      after the end of colonialism. See e.g. Terri De Young, *Placing the Poet: Badr Shakir Al-Sayyab
      and Postcolonial Iraq*, Albany 1998.

The animation is therefore a telling example of how ancient and modern sacrificial myths and the Islamic tradition come together to form a syncretic martyr
cult.

At the same time though, examples of images relating to the collective dimension of innerworldly salvation are rare. It is evident, as the rest of the video
shows, that the personal dimension of salvation is much easier to put into images. A number of motifs employed in visually presenting the martyrs are taken
from Hadiths: the golden letters are reminiscent of the golden lanterns in Paradise in which the green birds take their rest for the night. According to one tradition, these lanterns are hanging from the "throne" (*'arsh*) of God and therefore
indicate a particular nearness to God.[54] The *nashīd* in the background, of which
the English subtitles are given, makes these allusions explicit:

> Don't I only die once in my life? So why not make its finale martyrdom?
> When the soul of the Shaheed rises and approaches and God raises it up to a lofty status
> In the bodies of birds circling in Paradise and singing above the palaces and warbling.[55]

Each time the story of another martyr begins his name is shown in golden letters
emerging out of a glittering light streaming down above a larger band of green
light. Green is the colour of Islam, obviously the birds as well, and at the same
time indicates Paradise.[56] In the accompanying *nashīd* the martyr speaks from the
Hereafter and refers to the Koranic verse 3:169:

> I am in the Garden of Eternity, I did not die/ I have become a new creation in the Gar-
> dens
> So I am here, still alive, by my Lord/ And living happily in the care of God.

These lines, together with the images showing the martyr already in Paradise, an-
ticipate God's decision to accept the fallen as a martyr. Traditionally, the decision whether a person is considered to be a martyr or not is made by God, therefore after naming a martyr the words "we consider him (or her) so" are added.
While this wording is used in the videos, the images and the text of the *nashīd*
run contrary to it. Additionally – as in the other videos and in 'Azzām's marty-

---

[54]   See the Hadith mentioned in footnote 29.

[55]   The rest of the text relates to the well-known Hadith mentioned before which lists the
seven favours granted the martyr, who here speaks of himself:
> "Seven are won by the Shaheed to honor him/ If you have a heart, then tell me what
> they are
> The sin is forgiven with the first drop/ And I see my high place and abode
> And am [sic] secure from the horror and torment of the grave/ How delightful! And
> saved from the resurrection
> And crowned with the crown of dignity/ And given intercession for relatives, both near
> and distant
> And the houris [Paradise maidens] await my arrival longingly"

[56]   The green colour and light seem to be standard elements in martyr videos. It is also used
for example in the production by al-Malahim *And he may take martyrs from among you* (June
2010), accessible at archive.org (retrieved 15.10.2012). For more on this video see below.

rology –, miracles confirm the rank of a martyr, like the scent of musk emanating from the body or the blood, miracles which, according to the Hadiths, appear only in the Hereafter, when the martyrs stand before God.

The collective dimension is addressed almost only *verbally* by several al-Qaida-related preachers, e.g.: "Our beloved Ummah: your heroic sons and courageous knights went out to the land of Afghanistan [...]. They went out to lift from their Ummah the humiliation and weakness [...]."[57] Whereas the personal bliss of the martyrs is taken for granted and visualised in images of Paradise, the collective salvation of the *umma*, which is expected as an outcome from the martyrs' sacrifices, is only promised in an undefined future. The individual salvation of the martyrs thus compensates for the collective salvation which has failed to materialise.

Whereas in the case of the Afghan War it is plausible to claim that the mujahidin achieved a real success by forcing the Soviet Army to retreat,[58] it is much more difficult to find a similar success for al-Qaida. Al-Qaida can only claim 'victories' on a symbolic level and this is why the attacks on New York and Washington are so important. Because in the period after 2001 the attacks of al-Qaida targeted mainly Muslim civilians, the claim to be working for the deliverance of the *umma* is in fact cynical – a fact that is al-Qaida's weakest point when it comes to its reputation amongst Muslims and is of course not hidden to its propagandists.[59] This applies in particular to the majority of suicide attacks carried out by al-Qaida-related groups in Iraq, Afghanistan and elsewhere. It is therefore not surprising that the media representation of such attacks in propaganda videos concentrates on the attacker, not on the impact of his act.[60] Whereas the mujahidin in the defensive wars in Afghanistan, Bosnia and Chechnya at least earned a lot of sympathy amongst Muslims, even though only a few made their way to the battlefields, this is not the case with the terrorist attacks on civilians by al-Qaida and others. However, al-Qaida and similar groups still seem to consider martyrs as the most effective means to win the hearts of the Muslims and awaken the *umma*. One of the mujahidin in *Winds of Paradise* states: "The lamp of martyrdom has kindled in the Ummah."[61] Wishful thinking may be one

---

[57] Shaykh Muṣṭafā Abū al-Yazīd in al-Sahab, *Winds of Paradise*, Part 1, URL: http://archive.org/details/windsofparadise1_english (retrieved 05.11.2012). The text follows the English subtitles.

[58] The real impact of the Arab Afghans on the Afghan War is disputed.

[59] Cf. criticism of al-Qaida by non-Jihadist Salafists like Salmān al-ʿAwda in Jarret Brachman, *Global Jihadism. Theory and Practice*, New York 2009, 57. Within al-Qaida Abū Muṣʿab al-Zarqāwī was heavily criticised for his excessive violence against civilians in Iraq, especially by his own former mentor al-Maqdisī, see Jarret Brachman, *Global Jihadism*, 71.

[60] Cf. Akil N. Awan et al., *Radicalisation and Media: Connectivity and Terrorism in the New Media Ecology*, New York 2011, 39.

[61] Al-Sahab, *Winds of Paradise* Part 2, URL: http://archive.org/details/windsofparadise2_AMEF (retrieved 09.10.2012).

of the reasons why they present their martyrs over and over again, another being the need for compensation for the failure on the real battlefields.

V. Images of Death

Given that death is naturally the greatest taboo in war propaganda, it is at first striking how explicit death is shown in Jihadist media. The martyr cult converts the taboo into a site where the liminal space between life and death can be explored. As the martyr is taken to be not dead but living with God (according to Koran 3:169), the bodies and even more so the faces are searched for signs of this otherworldly life. The images of martyrs therefore are images of both death and eternal life. Again the mode in which these images are employed differs greatly in different phases.

A number of video clips feature a dying mujahidin. A "classic" amongst these is a sequence from a longer video series (*The Russian Hell*) dealing with the struggle of the Chechen rebels, which shows the fighter Abū Saʿīd al-Qurtashāʾī.[62] It first shows a group of wounded mujahidin who endure their injuries with composure, some of them even laughing to the camera. Others are already dead and one of the martyrs is buried with his blood-stained clothes and without the white shrouds which are otherwise used in Islamic ritual.[63] The last two minutes are devoted to Abū Saʿīd al-Qurtashāʾī, otherwise unknown and famous amongst Jihadists only for his death.[64] The camera follows the trail of his blood, flowing from a wound in his leg. It moves over his body to his arm, also severely injured, and then shows his face distorted in pain. As there is no original sound his screams are silent and only the accompanying *nashīd* can be heard. A green box with his name and the words *rahimalu 'llah* ("may God have mercy on him" – a wish for the dead) appears, indicating that he will soon die.

The next shot shows his face relaxed and even though the original sound is missing one can tell by the movements of his lips that he is uttering the words "Lā ilāha illā llāh" ("There is no God but God"), the first part of the Islamic statement of belief recommended to be said before one's death. The camera then

---

[62] The sequence, or parts of it, can be found in various versions on YouTube and elsewhere. The video considered here was uploaded on *YouTube* (Shaheed in Chechenya [sic]) and is about five minutes long. URL: http://www.youtube.com/watch?v=shfd5uPmOC0&feature =related (retrieved 09.10.2012).

[63] This practice goes back to traditions claiming that the Prophet buried the fallen Muslims after the battle of Uḥud in their clothes. For the discussions about the funeral rituals for martyrs see Etan Kohlberg, Art. Shahīd, *Encyclopedia of Islam²*, Vol. IX, 1997.

[64] It is not clear whether Abū Saʿīd al-Qurtashāʾī is his real name or a *nom de guerre* and where he comes from. A short text says that he had been in Bosnia. However, the source is unclear. (URL: http://ejabat.google.com/ejabat/thread?tid=1315cd3af0699749, retrieved 09.10.2012). The Combating Terrorism Center at West Point mistakenly uses his name for the Chechen leader Shamil Basayev in the description of several images, see e.g. here: http://www.ctc.usma.edu/posts/imagery/0146 (retrieved 09.10.2012).

Fig. 3: screen shot showing Abū Saʿīd al-Qurtashāʾī

zooms out and it becomes apparent that all his limbs are severely injured and he has lost an enormous amount of blood. The last 90 seconds concentrate mainly on his face. The cameraman obviously catches his very last breath and afterwards he lies calmly on the ground, a peaceful smile on his face. While the pain of dying is not hidden, it comes across as soothed without the original sound and with the consoling text of the *nashīd*. The peaceful last breath (or what is presented as such) recalls a Hadith, where death for a martyr is compared to the pinch of a gnat (see fig. 3).

These pictures are not only a documentation of the wounding and death of a fighter. They also tell a story and relate in many ways to the Islamic tradition surrounding martyrdom: the blood shown in the beginning refers to the forgiveness of sins, which according to the aforementioned Hadith takes place "with the first spurt of his blood", while the host of wounds and severed limbs stand for his readiness to make sacrifices. In accounts on the Muslim fighters engaged in the battles at the time of the Prophet, the number of injuries they suffered is often given and a high number indicates their braveness and fighting strength. In modern times, when fighting is no longer chivalric face-to-face combat and the enemy remains mostly unseen, sat in aircraft and behind other technical devices, injuries are no longer a sign of fighting strength but are imbued with a soteriological function for the community. According to ʿAzzām, blood, skulls and invalids are the requirements of glory:

> Glory does not build its lofty edifice except with skulls. Honour and respect cannot be established except on a foundation of cripples and corpses. [...] Indeed those who think that they can change reality, or change societies, without blood, sacrifices and invalids, without pure, innocent souls, then they do not understand the essence of this Deen [religion] [...].[65]

In shorter versions of the described sequence, often included in other video productions, it is mainly the peaceful face of the deceased that is shown, while the signs of pain are left out (for example, the sequence of al-Qurtashāʾī's last breath is included in the video testament of Aḥmad al-Ḥaznāwī mentioned at the beginning, when he speaks about the honour of dying as a martyr). A number of videos only feature martyrs with undamaged faces, giving the impression that a martyr's death is very easy. Series of pictures and clips, all of which last only a few seconds, join images from different places and times, showing one smiling dead man after another, including al-Qurtashāʾī.[66] As discussed, his death was originally part of a greater story, and the viewer here would know in which war he had fought, what his name was and what his injuries were. In such martyr series, however, one hardly gets to know who the men are, where they died and for what reason they fought, other than to attain martyrdom.

Another genre of martyr videos even more conceptual are those produced to accompany excerpts from ʿAzzām's lectures and sermons on martyrs. One of these, again to be found on *YouTube*, features the following English subtitles to the lecture held in Arabic:[67]

> Those are Martyrs. Makers of History. Building blocks of Nations. Makers of glory. Chanters of honour. Those are Building blocks of nations. Laying down for the Ummah (Muslim Nation), its honour. Their skulls – towers of honour. Their bodies – Buildings of dignity. Them – their blood – the water of life for this Deen [religion S.H.] till the Day of Resurrection. They – are martyrs. They bear witness that the principles are more valuable than life and also the morals, are more expensive than the souls and that the laws by which man lives to implement (laws of Allah) are more expensive than the bodies. And Nations, that do not sacrifice blood do not deserve to live – and do not live. "If you march not forth, He will punish you with a painful torment and will replace you by another people...". (Koran, 9:39)

In the background the viewer sees a seaside at sunset, waves breaking on the shore. Alluding to Paradise, this idyllic view is superimposed with pictures and video recordings of martyrs, shown in the upper left part of the screen. The name and country of origin of the martyr are given in Arabic. The multiple lay-

---

[65] ʿAbdullāh ʿAzzām, "Martyrs. The Building Blocks of Nations".

[66] There are numerous of such 'martyr series' produced by *YouTube* users, for an example see "Smiling martyrs", URL: http://www.youtube.com/watch?v=UMulYGQwWL0 (retrieved 06.11.2012).

[67] "The Station of the Shuhada (Martyrs) – Shaykh Abdullah Azzam", URL: http://www.youtube.com/watch?v=Nl0sJSduQ-Q (retrieved 14.09.2012). Translation, spelling, and punctuation of the subtitles are kept. Full stops or dashes are added before the beginning of a new subtitle, except when it is clear that a sentence continues.

ers of images (sometimes the image on the left is composed of up to three different smaller ones) are paralleled by a double audio track: the voice of ʿAzzām is accompanied by *anashīd* about Jihad and martyrdom. On the one hand, the viewer is hardly able to grasp the information presented in the multitude of images and voices; on the other hand though, there is hardly any specific information offered. At first the martyrs are shown while still alive, engaged in military action or training and posing with weapons; then the face of the dead man is blended in. All the viewer gets to know is that the fighter is dead; we do not learn where and when he died or how he fought before he died, since it is not even clear that the fighting scenes shown involved him. Whereas such details may be related in textual martyrologies like *Lovers of the Paradise Maidens* and in the longer video productions, these images are completely devoid of any information aside from the name and the country of origin.

This arrangement is highly conceptual and appears as a visualisation of a Koranic verse that ʿAzzām also cites in the lecture from which an excerpt is presented in this video clip ("Martyrs. The Building Blocks of Nations"): "God has bought from the believers their selves and their possessions against the gift of Paradise; they fight in the way of God; they kill, and are killed [...]" (9:111) In Jihadist discourse the verse serves to establish an exclusive connection between fighting, death and salvation.[68] The images of mujahidin fighting and dying, together with the indication that they get to enjoy Paradise, are a visualisation of this concept.

The abstract representation of death in battle as martyrdom matches the thoughts ʿAzzām sets out in his lecture: the martyrs are not making a sacrifice to a specific cause (like the liberation of Afghanistan), but are foremost witnesses to higher principles. Furthermore, they have the mythical function in preserving the *umma*: according to another of ʿAzzām's lectures, "their sacrifices are the provision for the future generations for long centuries".[69]

Whereas the earlier productions like *Martyrs in Bosnia* and the videos produced about the mujahidin in Chechnya feature disfigured corpses and faces as well as injured fighters (albeit never demoralised), the shorter martyr clips tend to avoid graphic pictures and show the martyr peaceful and smiling. Particular cases are suicide bombers and fighters struck by bombs, who, shredded into pieces, cannot be shown. In such cases only pictures taken when they are alive are used, as is the case with the al-Qaida's 9/11 martyrs, whose recorded last wills are presented while in the background pictures of the impact of the attacks are shown.[70]

---

[68] Verse 9:111, which is frequently cited in Jihadist circles, is an illustrative example for the arbitrary and reductionist way they treat the sources; for a discussion of this verse see Silvia Horsch, *Tod im Kampf*, 107ff.

[69] ʿAzzām, "Midād al-ʿulamāʾ wa dimāʾ al-shuhadāʾ" [author's translation].

[70] One has to note that these videos do not contribute to the still disputed question whether the men really were the attackers. Their statements do not include any hint to the attacks as they only speak generally of their intention to fight the Americans. Any connections to

Another option often deployed is to portray the "living martyrs" who are considered to have revealed signs of their future martyrdom. As is frequently related in the biographies of martyrs, those who went on to die as martyrs anticipated their martyrdom (e.g. in dreams) and were in particular high spirits, so that signs of their coming martyrdom were noticeable in their voices or faces. One attempt to put these signs into images is to show the martyrs to-be smiling. A striking example is a more recent martyr video produced by the al-Malahim Foundation, the media arm of AQAP, the Yemen-based group al-Qaida on the Arabian Peninsula. *And He May Take Martyrs From You*, as the video is entitled (referring to the Koran verse 3:140), was made in 2010.[71] It is about five members of AQAP killed on 15 September 2009.[72] Pictures showing the martyrs-to-be in high spirits are standard, but here the producers of this video have made especially heavy use of such material. The men are shown smiling with a fey look, as if there were already no longer part of this world, an impression underscored by the green background from which lights moving like falling stars emerge and take their way into their photos. Their voices, reinforced with artificial reverberations, create the impression that they already speaking from the after world. Several times the men are shown smiling in slow motion, in particular Abū Yaqīn – a handsome looking young man with a charming smile, at one instance presented for a full minute. This manipulation creates the weird impression that one is watching an advertising spot, for example for toothpaste,[73] were it not for the stern voice in the background talking about jihad and martyrdom. The analogy to advertisement is by no means arbitrary, since these pictures aim to entice the viewer to act in a certain way. The pictures thus belong to "sorts of direct expressions of pictorial desire [which] are [...] generally associated with 'vulgar' modes of imaging–commercial advertising and political or religious propaganda."[74] It is therefore unsurprising that they not only rely on Western technology but also on Western pictorial language.

---

   the attacks of September 11 (like the pictures of the destroyed towers, etc.) are added at a later stage in producing the video.

[71] Al-Malahim, *And He May Take Martyrs From You* (June 2010), accessible at archive.org, URL: http://archive.org/details/TheEnglishTranslationOfAl-malahimsReleaseAndMayHeTake MartyrsFromYou (retrieved 16.10.2012). One of the martyrs, Abū Yaqīn, was detained in Guantanamo and included in an anti-radicalisation programme – obviously to no avail. The video also contains two excerpts from recorded lectures by ʿAzzām.

[72] From the video it neither becomes clear where exactly this happened (whether in Saudi Arabia or Yemen, as only the Arabian Peninsula is mentioned) nor who dropped the bomb (local authorities or the Americans).

[73] Actually *kitsch* is an integral part of martyr videos (cf. computer animated campfire and motifs like horsemen etc). This applies likewise to the sound, e.g. to the "acoustic icons", as Philipp Holtman puts it aptly (Philipp Holtman, "Virtual Leadership: How Jihadists guide each other in cyberspace", in Lohlker, *New Approaches to the Analysis of Jihadism: Online and Offline*, Göttingen 2012, 77f.). These are e.g. sound of swords drawn out of the sheaths (used several times in *And He May Take Martyrs From You*), or the chirping sound of birds, referring to the green birds in Paradise (for this example see Holtmann, 77f.).

[74] W.J.T: Mitchell, *What do pictures want? The lives and loves of images*, Chicago 2005, 39.

Fig. 4: Advertising image for the video *And He May Take Martyrs From You*

In the same way an advertising image for the video was created for the second is-sue of *Inspire* (see fig. 4), an English-language magazine apparently linked to AQAP which with its colloquial language and numerous pictures and graphics seemed to be designed to appeal to young (male) Muslims living in the West.[75] Imitating Hollywood film posters, the image is a very explicit example for the function of Western media as a role model, not only for Jihadist media but also for Jihadist action, as remarked on earlier.[76] This feature becomes increasingly

---

[75] This magazine received a lot of attention in Western media, however, with regard to the contents there is hardly anything new, see Thomas Hegghammer, "Un-Inspired" in: *Ji-hadica*, 6 June 2010, URL: http://www.jihadica.com/un-inspired/ (retrieved 06.11.2012).

[76] "From spectacular attacks to sundry communiqués and beheadings, the jihad's world of reference is far more connected to the dreams and nightmares of the media, than it is to

visible as Jihadism is presented as "Jihad Cool", as a youth subculture, a trend which intensifies with the on-going Web 2.0 stage of Cyberjihad.[77]

Once again, in this video the personal dimension of salvation is translated into images and pictures, while the collective dimension is only verbally addressed. With the insistent misjudgement of reality typical for Jihadists when it comes to the effects of martyrdom, the narrator states: "Their lives came to an end after many hopes of Muslims had come true. [...] Their lives came to an end after the jihad issue had become a case of all Muslims after it used to be that of the elites."

It is easy to criticise such images as "unreal", especially when one considers the real situation "on the ground", the overall failure of the Jihadist organisations to reach their goals. This becomes especially evident in the last example: the planned attack failed completely as the men were killed by a bomb during their preparations. However, such a critique is misguided in two ways: firstly, the (expected) individual salvation of the martyrs compensates for the failure of any operations (and the greater goals in general); secondly, these images gain their power precisely by not showing reality. As W.J.T. Mitchell puts it: "It is never enough to simply point out the error of a metaphor, or the lack of reality in an image. It is equally important to trace the process by which the metaphoric becomes literal, and the image becomes actual."[78] Images may gain an "operational reality"[79] and this is obviously the case with the martyr images of al-Qaida and the like, which draw on Islamic symbols and motifs as well as modern sacrificial myths. Jihadist media has been very effective in creating and perpetuating a martyr cult, even though recruit numbers remain small and the media production of Jihadist organisations primarily addresses their immediate followers:

> The creation of a martyr cult is probably the most worrying 'success' of more than thirty years of Jihadi propaganda, which gained interpretative dominance over numerous Islamic symbols and ideas. Today martyrdom in Islam is equated with suicide attacks not only by Jihadists but the broader public as well.[80]

However – and this point is equally important – the operational reality of images may change according to different historic and political circumstances. This can be observed in Arabic countries with regard to martyr pictures in the recent years.

VI. Latest Developments and Future Prospects

The equation mentioned above seems to disintegrate with the events of the so-called Arab Spring, which has brought forth numerous martyrs and continues to

---

any traditional school of Islamic jurisprudence or political thought." Faisal Devji, *Landscapes of the Jihad. Militancy, Morality, Modernity*, London 2007, 90.

[77] Asiem Defraoui, *jihad.de*, 12.

[78] Mitchell, *Cloning terror. The war of images. 9/11 to the present*, Chicago 2011, XVIII.

[79] Ibid.

[80] Asiem Defraoui, *jihad.de*, 16 [author's translation].

do so. The non-violent martyrs of Egypt and Tunisia turned out to be much more 'effective' according to the martyr logic (even though it turned out that the struggle for freedom is by far not over with the downfall of the respective presidents and that the old powers may return, as recent events in Egypt since summer 2013 have shown). The stories of the martyrs on Tahrir Square in Cairo and elsewhere are told in various media and especially in the Internet the martyrs are commemorated. Islamist groups, namely the Muslim Brotherhood, also have their martyrs of the revolutions. The commemoration of these martyrs shows that there is another model in Islamist discourse available besides the Jihadi fighter and suicide bomber. One example is the story of the student and member of the Muslim Brotherhood ʿAbd al-Karīm, who was shot during a demonstration on Tahrir Square. His story was told several times by Ṣafwat Hijāzī, one of the Muslim Brotherhood's organisers of the protests on Tahrir Square, on Arabic television channels.[81] ʿAbd al-Karīm is also connected to the Islamic martyr tradition, however in a significantly different way: the martyr on the battlefield is not the model, but the person taking a stand against injustice. His martyrdom is related to the prophetical Hadith: "The master of martyrs is Hamza [one of the Prophet's uncles killed in one of the first battles of the Muslims] and the one who stands up before the unjust ruler and advises him so that he [the ruler] kills him."[82]

A video on *YouTube* commemorating ʿAbd al-Karīm shows elements of the Islamist rhetoric and iconography familiar from Jihadist discourse,[83] such as the citing of the Koranic verse 3:169: "Count not those who were slain in God's way as dead, but rather living with their Lord, by Him provided, rejoicing in the bounty that God has given them [...]". This verse is generally understood to relate to those killed in military jihad, and has been almost monopolised in the martyr media production of those organisations deploying suicide bombings. In the aforementioned story jihad is used in a broader sense, one that nonetheless refers to roots in the tradition as a prophetical Hadith indicates: "The best jihad is to speak a word of truth to a tyrant".[84] Also included in this video is the quotation from ʿAzzām cited at the beginning, which is part of so many video productions on martyrs: "Our words remain dead, like waxen dolls, unmoving and frozen, until when we die for them, they rise up, alive, to live among the living." Formally, this video very much resembles the martyr videos discussed above: ʿAbd al-Karīm is shown talking and smiling (again in slow motion), *nashīd* can be heard in the background, the viewer is told that the smell of musk emanated

---

[81] For a more detailed account of his story see my article in this volume "Global martyr practices and discourses".

[82] The actual text reads not "ruler" but "imām". Al-Ḥākim, *Al-Mustadrak ʿalā al-ṣaḥīḥayn*, Vol. 2, Book 31, No 4884/482.

[83] "Shahīd al-thaura ʿAbd al-Karīm Aḥmad Rajab" (Martyr of the revolution ʿAbd al-Karīm Aḥmad Rajab) URL: http://www.youtube.com/watch?v=gmE2ssqDW_Y (retrieved 20.05.2012).

[84] Related in several Hadith collections as Abū Dāwūd, *Sunan* II, No. 4344, Ibn Māja, *Sunan* II, No. 4011, al-Tirmidhī, *Sunan*, No. 2174.

from his blood and pictures of him dead show the peaceful smile. However, elements adopted by the radical martyr discourse are now used to commemorate those who died during civil demonstrations, a transformation which (re-)claims these elements from al-Qaida's discourse and its focus on the exclusive connection of martyrdom and violence.

It is arguably not possible to predict whether the non-violent model of martyrdom will become more potent than the violent version. Most probably they will exist side by side, with one model preferred to the other depending on the respective circumstances. As the case of Syria (and Libya earlier) has shown, non-violent resistance can turn to violent insurgency when the regime fails to respond in a positive way, increasing repression instead. What is certain is that in the Arab (and the Muslim) public the martyrs of the 'Arab Revolutions' are of far greater significance than the martyrs of al-Qaida and the like.

IV.
Political Action and Ideological Discourse

Martyrdom in Light of the Arab Spring

Farhad Khosrokhavar (Paris)

Martyrdom is an issue that needs qualification within the religious and social realms in the contemporary Muslim world.[1] In the popular view martyrdom was traditionally associated with dying for Islam, an act defying non-Islamic invaders. According to the views of Muslim commentators on the Koran, there are only a few cases where *shahīd* means not only witness but also martyr, while according to some Hadiths, those killed in the first violent encounters with the Meccans were known as such.[2] The notion of *shahīd* as equating to martyr seems to have become widespread in the Hadith literature after the first century of Islam, thereafter gaining even further in currency during the Christian Crusades. It was revived, along with jihad, in the 19th century, vis-à-vis imperialist invaders. Martyrdom has a long history in Shiism, its keystone the martyrdom of Ḥusayn, the third imam, while fighting against the Umayyad caliph Yazīd in the year 61/680. His sacred death became a paragon for the fight against imperialists (in Iraq against British rule in the 1920s and 1930s), while in the 1970s it was focused against the pro-Western authoritarian Shah regime in Iran. The major ideological contribution of the Islamic Revolution of 1979 was a reshaping of martyrdom, claiming that to die as a martyr was an accomplishment promoting the worldwide Islamic Revolution.

The modernisation of the Muslim world has thus changed the relevance of martyrdom, in both the Shiite and Sunnite worlds. Against the backdrop of revolutionary tendencies in Islam in the second half of the 20th century, the notion of martyrdom is closely associated with jihad in a new way. Martyrdom can be a "mass phenomenon" related to the mobilisation of the people, mainly youths, by governments (in Iran the revolutionary government), as a means to accomplish their goals in their struggle against the enemy (the Iraqi Army in the long war between 1980 and 1988); it can also mean "suicide bombers" who enter the fray against an enemy who is technologically and economically far superior (usually within non-state networks, be they transnational, as in the case of al-Qaida, or national like the Chechen and Palestinian attacks against the Russian and the Israeli governments, respectively). "Suicide bombers" decide to die in advance; they do not succumb to a probable death in the battlefield but choose and embrace almost certain death by detonating bombs; secondly, in many cases they even long to die and their "love of martyrdom" sometimes even trumps the

---

[1]   For a general outline see David Cook, *Martyrdom in Islam*, Cambridge 2007.
[2]   For the notion of martyrdom in early Sunni Islam see Silvia Horsch-Al Saad, *Tod im Kampf. Figurationen des Märtyrers in frühen sunnitischen Schriften*, Würzburg 2011.

wider goal of spreading or defending Islam (the specific case of "martyropaths"[3]); and last but not least, even though influenced by Jihadist organisations, they decide to die as an "individual", constructing a personal relationship to this and the next world. In this way they promote what we might call a decisionist "death-ridden individualism" (or "individualism through death"),[4] which is quite distinct from the two dual categories developed by Louis Dumont, namely "individual in-the-world" and "individual out-of-the-world". The new type of martyrdom reshapes secularisation within enraged groups and individuals.[5] While the framework of "jihad and martyrdom" remains formally identical in the traditional view, the actual anthropological content and, particularly, the relationship to individualisation and secularisation are revolutionised in this new type of martyrdom.

Martyrdom in its new anthropological cast first found expression in the Shiite world, mainly in the Islamic Revolution of Iran in 1979; it then spread to the Sunni world, particularly amongst the Palestinian and Lebanese in their struggle against Israeli forces since the 1980s through to the first years of the current century. A major change occurred with the advent of movements calling for greater democratisation in Iran (first the student movement repressed by the regime in 1999, then the intellectual and feminist movement after 2005, and finally the Green Movement in 2009), which has since been followed by a wave of Arab Revolutions since the end of 2010. In these movements new forms of martyrdom have emerged which neither followed the traditional pattern of martyrdom, nor its new revolutionary forms as practised by Shiite martyrs in the Islamic Revolution (1979) and during the Iran/Iraq War (1980-1988) as well as, in the Sunni realm, amongst the Palestinians, mainly in the Second Intifada (2000-2005), and the Chechens (The Islamic Brigade of *shuhadā'* since 1999) and other Islamist groups. The self-proclaimed martyrdom that emerged with the Iranian Green Movement and the Arab Revolutions was not officially recognised by the Shiite clergy or the Sunni *ʿulamā'*. To briefly clarify the notions, we may distinguish between the traditional, the radical Islamist and the "democratising", nonviolent forms of martyrdom in the Muslim and, particularly, the Arab world.

The Islamist period, from the 1970s onward, witnessed the Islamic Revolution in Iran (1979), the beginning of the Afghan insurgency against the Soviet invasion (1979), and the attacks on the *al-ḥaram* mosque in Mecca by a group of political and religious dissidents led by Juhaymān al-ʿUtaybī (November 1979). The spread of the revolutionary movements in the Arab world, first throughout the

---

[3]   See Louis Dumont, *Essais sur l'individualisme. Une perspective anthropologique sur l'idéologie moderne*, Paris 1983.

[4]   See Farhad Khosrokhavar, *L'Islamisme et la Mort*, Paris 1995.

[5]   There is no room to develop in this article the notion of martyrdom in Shiite, Sunnite and other Islamic "sectarian" trends within the framework of secularisation and modernisation. See Farhad Khosrokhavar, *Suicide Bombers. The New Martyrs of Allah*, London 2005; id., *Inside Jihadism:Understanding Jihadi Movements Worldwide*, London 2009.

Shiite and then the Sunni realm, was based on a new and close association between martyrdom and jihad, differing from both the origins of Islam as well as the 19th century and the first half of the 20th century, the anti-imperialist period of jihad and martyrdom. Muslims now had to fight against the heretic rulers in the Islamic world (who were characterised as 'false gods', *ṭāghūt*) and the "new crusaders" (the Christian world, mainly America and the Zionists) who attack the Muslims in their homeland. The "arrogance" (*istikbār*) of the illegitimate rulers and the "crusaders" (the Americans and to a lesser extent Europeans) towards Muslims triggers their jihad, which seeks to put an end to this attitude. Through the influence of communism, *istikbār* has become synonymous with imperialism and neo-colonialism, while sometimes the expression *world arrogance* is used. Martyrdom for the Jihadists (adherents of the radical Islamic tenets of a worldwide caliphate) is violent in the sense that one has to defend Islam by relentlessly fighting the enemy, giving absolute privilege to jihad and rejecting any kind of peaceful compromise. Killing or getting killed, sacrificing one's life and inflicting death on a maximum number of enemies of Islam are the prerequisites of this type of martyrdom. The aim is to put an end to the rule of the idolatrous regimes (*ṭāghūt*) and restore the reign of genuine Islam by declaring a merciless war to the enemy. In this perspective, violence is not only legitimate but also more than desirable, meaning that killing the enemy or dying when fighting for this cause (martyrdom) are unavoidable. This paradigm, summarily sketched, reigns supreme in the minds of many Jihadist actors willing to take their fierce fighting resolve to the impious world of disbelievers (the West but also the Muslim world ruled by fake Muslim rulers), denouncing peacefulness and calling for a globalised violence on a worldwide scale. This pattern of martyrdom closely follows the concept of global jihad. It is also fascinated by the global media and the notion of an "Apocalypse Now", that is a large and bloody event largely publicised by the media (foremost television and internet) that prefigures the "apocalypse" to come in the jihad against the unbelievers: without the sight of the Twin Towers in flames and collapsing live on television screens around the word, the meaning of this new jihad and martyrdom would have been different on the social and anthropological levels. The new pair martyrdom/jihad is inseparable from the "exhibitionist" dimension of global death accomplished through the spectacle of "Apocalypse Now". Its foretaste is given by the apocalyptic pictures of the September 11, 2001 attacks that promoted "spectacular" jihad and martyrdom. This was not an unintended consequence of this new type of jihad/martyrdom; rather, it was intentionally calculated as a fundamental aspect of this type of experience by those who promoted it, believing that it would induce worldwide awe and lend new impetus to their promotion of martyrdom and gain massive support amongst Muslims.[6]

---

[6]   These dimensions are developed further in Farhad Khosrokhavar, *Inside Jihadism* and *Suicide Bombers*.

Preceded by the Iranian Green Movement (July 2009), the new wave of Arab Revolutions mark a break with this violent, exhibitionist martyrdom. They usher in a new era of "peaceful" martyrdom that is anthropologically distinct from the Jihadist trend in many respects. In sharp contrast to the jihadist martyrs, who pledge to fight godless regimes and the secular West in the name of Islam, the new "democratic martyrs" did not embrace sacred death in direct reference to any radical version of religion. Only after their deaths were they glorified as martyrs, more by public opinion than by Islamic scholars (they should also be distinguished from the "bread martyrs", those who died in demonstrations for better living conditions in social protests throughout the 20th century and did not ask for democratic reform). For the Islamist martyr, violence is an inalienable part of the strategy, directed as much towards the self as towards the enemy. The martyrs of the Arab Spring did also not sacrifice themselves for a nation dominated by a father-like figurehead such as Gamal Abdel Nasser in Egypt, Habib Bourguiba in Tunisia, Muammar Gaddafi in Libya, Hafiz Assad in Syria or Ali Abdullah Saleh in Yemen. Furthermore, the nationalist hero and martyr of the 1950s and 1960s sacrificed himself for the society as a whole, without reference to democracy, in an anti-imperialist fight aiming at realising national unity. The "democratic martyrs" aim to implement pluralist rule and this sets them apart from the martyrs of previous generations, be they the Jihadist or "bread" martyrs.

The Arab Revolutions begin with a type of "martyrdom" that is at the antipode of the religiously supported one, namely the self-immolation of Muḥammad Bū ʿAzīzī, the young Tunisian who set fire to himself publicly in protest against the social injustice he felt, in particular in order to denounce Ben Ali's regime and its security forces. Still, this "martyrdom" signalled the beginning of the Arab Revolutions (the so-called Tunisian "Jasmine" Revolution) without being the only type of "sacred death" in the long series of the deaths taking place in the succeeding protest movements that spread through the Arab world during 2011 and 2012.[7] The best way to understand the new type of martyrdom is to closely follow those who engaged in it. Analyzing their cases, one can distinguish many subcategories of martyrdom in the 2011-2012 Arab Revolutions.

I. The Self-Immolation Paradigm

In the Arab world self-immolation is a daring act, denoting a rupture with Islamist rhetoric and a high level of secularisation. Muḥammad Bū ʿAzīzī's setting himself ablaze on 17 December, 2010 and his ultimate death on 4 January, 2011 from the injuries set the tone for this new style of "sacred death". People called it martyrdom, but among the *ulamāʾ* (Islamic scholars) the act was regarded as an infringement of God's commandment that no one should take their

---

[7]   See Farhad Khosrokhavar, *The Arab Revolutions that Shook the World*, London 2012.

own life, and death can only be willed by God – with the exception of a few, among them Yūsuf al-Qaraḍāwī, the head of the World Union of Islamic Scholars (*ra'īs al-ittiḥād al-ʿālamī li l-ʿulamā' al-muslimīn*) and one of the most prominent scholars in the Sunni world (he is known for his contribution to *Islamonline* and his broadcast on Al Jazeera, *Sharia and Life*, which attracts tens of millions of Muslims), who found extenuating circumstances. From an orthodox Islamic perspective Bū ʿAzīzī's act was not only no martyrdom but indeed a desecration of God's rule stipulated in the Koran: "No person can ever die except by Allah's leave at an appointed term" (Koran 3:145), or more explicitly: "Don't kill yourself" (Koran 4:29) or "Don't throw yourself into destruction" (Koran 2:195). Still, people celebrated his heroic death, and songs and videos were created in his honour, calling him a martyr. One can observe a widening disconnection between the religious meaning of martyrdom and its secular, popular signification, the latter becoming largely autonomous of the religious idiom.

Even Yūsuf al-Qaraḍāwī said in an interview with Al Jazeera that he would not produce a fatwa (religious opinion) but simply content himself with a commentary in his programme *Sharia and Life* on the subject of the young Tunisian Muḥammad Bū ʿAzīzī: "I implore Allah the Almighty, and pray Him to pardon this young man and forgive him and go over his action that was against the religious law, which forbids killing oneself."[8] Under the pressure of the Arab public opinion, al-Qaraḍāwī softened his position, explaining on his website that Bū ʿAzīzī's self-immolation was justifiable since it was an act expressing rejection of humiliation and hunger.[9] Still, the scholars of al-Azhar, the most prestigious Sunni university in the world, issued a fatwa condemning self-immolation.[10] The Saudi grand mufti ʿAbd al-ʿAzīz al-Shaykh condemned suicide even when committed in response to harsh living conditions.[11]

Killing oneself is not traditionally regarded as martyrdom, all the more so as the act in Bū ʿAzīzī's case did not entail any notion of jihad or fight against disbelievers or un-Islamic rulers. Even those "suicide bombers" who kill themselves while killing their proclaimed foes in reference to jihad are considered by many *ʿulamā'* as infringing upon the tenets of Islam, for their death occurs before that of the enemies and is not induced by them but by himself; in addition, many innocent women, children and elderly are killed, some of them Muslims, which

---

[8] See for the Arabic text: "Qaradawi explique sa position sur Bouazizi", URL: http://www. radiojektiss.com/qaradawi-explique-sa-position-sur-bouazizi/ (retrieved 13.04.2012).

[9] Cf. Jalal Ghazi, "Tunisian Uprising: The Other Martyrs", in: *New American Media* 22.01.2011, URL: http://newamericamedia.org/2011/01/tunisian-uprising-the-other-martyrs.php (retrieved 13.04.2012).

[10] Cf. "Al-Azhar: Self-immolation is a 'sin'", in: *Al-Ahram Online*, 19.01.2011, URL: http:// english.ahram.org.eg/News/4310.aspx (retrieved 13.04.2012).

[11] Cf. "Man Dies after Setting Himself on Fire", in: *Gulf News*, 23.01.2011, URL: http://gulf news.com/news/gulf/saudi-arabia/man-dies-after-setting-himself-on-fire-1.750642 (retrieved 13.04.2012).

they justify through the notion of "shielding" (that is the fact that they *nolens volens* shield enemies of Islam and their death is therefore deemed necessary to defend Islam). On the other hand though, many radical clerics consider their act to be martyrdom for it targets the enemies of Islam. In the case of Bū ʿAzīzī there was no reference to Islam in his act, which was a pure protest against social injustice and humiliation, with no hint of any religious background or justification. Secularisation was obvious in his act of protest. Two decades earlier the trend had been towards adherence to the religious meaning of martyrdom, and Islamist would-be martyrs were proud to claim the title and show their willingness to be categorised as Islamic heroes by sacrificing their lives for the sake of their religion. Now, what is regarded by public opinion as "martyrdom" has become totally secular, an act of protest, wrapped up afterwards as martyrdom by others, not by its actor.

Bū ʿAzīzī's self-immolation triggered a series of imitators in Arab countries and even in Europe. In all these cases the reference point was the individual's desperate situation and despondency, not the will to die for Islam (which should be, theoretically, the necessary condition for martyrdom). In Sīdī Bū Zīd, Tunisia, after Bū ʿAzīzī's death, a second young unemployed man, Ḥusayn Nājī, committed suicide by jumping from an electricity pylon on 22 December, 2010. A young Moroccan set himself on fire during a teachers' sit-in in front of the Ministry of Education in Rabat. The demonstration was being held to demand secure jobs for teachers with precarious contracts. The police intervened and saved his and a bystander's life.

A young, unmarried woman, Fadwā al-ʿUrwī, a 25-year-old mother of two, set herself on fire after being refused social accommodation, a flat for her and her children to live in, by the authorities. Her house made of dried mud in which she lived with her parents and children had been demolished by the authorities. She burned herself before the municipality office of Sūq al-Sabt in the centre of Morocco and died of her injuries in a Casablanca hospital. She was the first woman to commit suicide by fire since the wave of suicides triggered by Bū ʿAzīzī's self-immolation.[12] Here, too, the act had no religious content and since the movement did not succeed in Morocco it was not widely characterised as martyrdom. The success or failure of the protest, its generalisation into larger segments of the society, plays a role in it being designated as martyrdom or not by the public at large. The model can be copied from one country in another one, as was the case in Mauritania. There a 43-year-old man tried to burn himself on 17 January. In Egypt, ʿAbd al-Munʿim Jaʿfar, a 49 year-old owner of a small restaurant in the town of Qanṭara close to Ismāʿīliyya, attempted to take his own

---

12   Cf. "Une jeune mère célibataire s'immole par le feu", France 24, 23.02.2011, URL: http://
     www.france24.com/fr/20110223-maroc-jeune-femme-celibataire-immole-feu-suicide-loge
     ment-social-souk-sebt-fadoua-laroui (retrieved 13.04.2012).

life by fire in front of the Egyptian parliament in Cairo on 17 January.[13] Apparently he had not received vouchers to buy bread for his restaurant.[14] Two others attempted suicide, a 25-year-old jobless man with mental problems in Alexandria and another, in Cairo, can also be mentioned.[15]

On 15 January in Algiers a 34-year-old jobless man attempted to commit suicide in front of the city's security building. Another man, Muḥsin Bū Ṭarfif, a 37-year-old father of two, committed suicide by fire in response to a challenge by the authorities: "The mayor told Mohcin Bouterfif: if you are courageous, do as did Bouazizi, kill yourself by fire!"[16] He died on 24 January. Maʿāmir Luṭfi, a 36-year-old unemployed father of six who was denied a meeting with the governor, burned himself in front of the al-Wādī town hall on 17 January. He died on 12 February.[17] There have been a number of other incidents of self-immolation in Algeria.[18]

In Saudi Arabia, perhaps for the first time in the history of the country, a 65-year-old man died on 21 January after setting himself on fire in the town of Ṣāmiṭa, Jāzān.[19] Europe did not remain immune to the wave of copycat suicides by fire. On 11 February Nūr al-Dīn ʿAdnān, a 27-year-old Moroccan street vendor, burned himself in Palermo, Sicily, in protest against the confiscation of his wares and harassment by municipal officials. He died five days later.[20]

Bū ʿAzīzī's act had a tremendous effect in the Arab world, but also beyond. It made a horrendous suicide an accessible model for others who probably thought it might initiate a social protest. Consideration of the pain to be endured before death almost disappeared before the earthshaking consequences of the act, bringing post-mortem fame to insignificant individuals who became national heroes

---

[13] Cf. "In Egypt, Man Sets Himself on Fire, Driven by Economic Woes", in: *Al-Ahram Online*, 17.01.2011, URL: http://english.ahram.org.eg/NewsContent/1/2/4115/Egypt/Society/In-Egypt,-man-sets-himself-on-fire,-driven-by-econ.aspx (retrieved 13.04.2012).

[14] Cf. "Trois hommes se sont immolés par le feu", in: *France 2*, January 18, 2011, URL: http://info.france2.fr/monde/trois-hommes-se-sont-immoles-par-le-feu-66885754.html (retrieved 13.04.2012).

[15] Ibid.

[16] Mehdi Benslimane et al., "Le maire à Mohcin Bouterfif: 'Si tu as du courage, fais comme Bouazizi, immole-toi par le feu'", *DNA-Algérie*, 24.01.2011, URL: www.dna-algerie.com/interieure/le-maire-a-mohcin-bouterfif-si-tu-as-du-courage-fais-comme-bouazizi-immole-toi-par-le-feu (retrieved 13.04.2012).

[17] Cf. "Quatrième décès par immolation en Algérie, à la veille de la marche du 12 février", in: *Jeune Afrique*, 12.02.2011, URL: www.jeuneafrique.com/Article/ARTJAWEB 2.00110212 105526 (retrieved 25.04.2012).

[18] Cf. the list of self-immolations in 2011 in Algeria in Wikipedia, URL: http://en.wikipedia.org/wiki/2011_Algerian_self-immolations (retrieved 25.04.2012).

[19] Cf. "Man Dies in Possible First Self-Immolation in Saudi", in: *Sunday Times* (Sri Lanka), 22.01.2011, URL: http://sundaytimes.lk/world-news/4231-man-dies-in-possible-first-self-immolation-in-saudi (retrieved 12.10.2011).

[20] Cf. "Palermo, Moroccan Street Vendor Dies after Setting Himself on Fire", in: *Ahora Italia*, 22.02.2011, URL: www.ahoraitalia.com/giornale//117595/palermo-dies-after-setting-himself-fire.htm (retrieved 12.10.2011).

and thereby wreaked revenge on repressive power holders. The copycat effect did not have the same results in other countries. The element of surprise had waned, police forces were now ready to confront demonstrators, and the "trigger element" of the protest movement had to change in order to succeed. In Egypt protestors came up with the innovation of tying the project to a place, Tahrir Square. Notwithstanding, Egyptians had their own "martyrs" (the equivalent of Bū ʿAzīzī was the Egyptian restaurateur ʿAbdū ʿAbd al-Munʿim, who died after suicide by fire on 17 January, 2011).

Bū ʿAzīzī's act made him a national hero in Tunisia, and a hero for many in Arab countries where demonstrators followed suit in their protest movement against their rulers. One *YouTube* declaration in French called him "the hero of the Tunisian nation and the founder of democracy in Tunisia".[21] In this post the chanting of a man in the Arab dialect of Tunisia set to traditional guitar accompanies Bū ʿAzīzī's photo, together with a French translation of the song and words attributed to Bū ʿAzīzī. Then the statement follows:

> The uproar spreads: with a long clamor, the warships of the barbarous soldiers are thrust. Everywhere floats death. And the homicidal sword pierces at the threshold of the altars the bold hero. Mohamed Bouazizi, the eagle who carries fire, the benefactor of humanity, the bird whose omen is happiness!

II. The Unintentional Martyr

Contrary to the category of martyrs who announce their probable death, there are others who suffer violent death without this expectation and are venerated afterwards by the society or their community as such. In Egypt on 9 October, 2011, the worst violence since the January Revolution broke out, with more than 26 Christians killed and as many as 300 injured. They did not expect to die during their demonstration, mainly due to the fact that they did it after the Egyptian Revolution, which seemed to have freed them from the fear of arbitrary harassment, let alone killing. The Coptic Church declared three days of fasting and prayer for them. Hundreds of mourners gathered at the Coptic cathedral in al-ʿAbbāsiyya, a Cairo neighbourhood, chanting anti-military and anti-Ṭanṭāwī (the head of the military government) slogans. Many distressed Coptic women carried wooden crosses and were dressed in black, mourning over the death of their "martyrs". For them as Christians, martyrdom points to those Christians who were killed by the military in their confrontation with the Salafi fanatics.

Another case of this type is when security forces kill someone who intended to protest against the prevailing social situation. Their death is regarded by many

---

[21] Cf. "Mohamed Bouazizi Héros Tunisian Révolution Tunisie Túnez", *YouTube*, URL: www.youtube.com/watch?v=5Nir6FcXDM8&feature=related (retrieved 13.04.2012).

as "martyrdom" due to its social significance. The secular meaning of martyrdom is obvious in this type as well.

One example is Muḥammad Nabbūs from Libya. Born in Benghazi in 1983, he graduated from Qāryūnis University with a degree in mathematics and computing. He completed his education in networking and computing, including postgraduate studies in Benghazi.[22] His wife, Perdita, was pregnant with the couple's first child at the time of his death. Nabbūs was the primary contact of many international journalists looking for information about Libya. He had founded an internet television station, Libya Alhurra TV, which broadcasted on Livestream. com. Libya Alhurra TV was the only broadcast coming from Benghazi when Gaddafi shut down the internet at the beginning of the February 2011 uprising. Nabbūs had managed to bypass government blocks on the web to broadcast live images from Benghazi across the world. On 10 March, 2011, the *Washington Post* reported that the U.S. Broadcasting Board of Governors (which includes Hillary Clinton) and the U.S. State Department were funding tech firms that helped political dissidents in Libya, Egypt, and Tunisia to communicate through the internet under the noses of government censors.[23]

Libya Alhurra TV included nine cameras streaming 24 hours a day after the channel's creation on 17 February. As Libya Alhurra TV's communications became more sophisticated, Nabbūs was able to take cameras with him to different parts of Benghazi to capture up close the destruction and carnage caused by mortars and shelling. During the last few days and hours of his life Nabbūs continued reporting. Streaming over Libya Alhurra TV, he shared live video and provided commentary regarding the bombing of the Benghazi power station and fuel tank explosion on 17 March, the firing of missiles on Benghazi from the nearby of city Sultan on 18 March and the death of two young children killed by a missile launched on the morning of 19 March. These images and reports provided an eyewitness account of the events on the ground relevant to UN Security Council Resolution 1973 regarding the situation in Libya. Adopted on 17 March, 2011, it formed the legal basis for military intervention in the Libyan Civil War.

Nabbūs was in all likelihood shot in the head by a sniper soon after exposing the Gaddafi regime's false reports of a ceasefire declaration. His death was announced by his wife in a video on Libya Alhurra TV.[24]

---

[22] Cyril Washbrook, "Online Journalist Mohammed Nabbous Killed in Libya", in: *Media Spy*, 20.03.2011, URL: www.mediaspy.org/report/2011/03/20/online-journalist-mohammed-nabbous-killed-in-libya (retrieved 13.04.2012).

[23] Ian Shapira, "US Funding Tech Firms That Help Dissidents Evade Government Censors", in: *Washington Post*, 10.03.2011, URL: www.washingtonpost.com/wp-dyn/content/article/2011/03/09/AR2011030905716.html (retrieved 13.04.2012).

[24] "Live Show Sat Mar 19 2011", *Libya Alhurra TV* 19.03.2011, URL: www.livestream.com/libya17feb/video?clipId=pla_9745ec21-c64d-440f-abe7-a412e7db456d? (retrieved 13.04.2012).

III. The Almost Nonviolent Martyr

The new type of martyrdom does not imply absolutely renouncing violence. The main goal of "nonviolence" is to protect human life and violence can be exercised over property or other goods. Violence can even be used for self-defence against those repressive forces that unhesitatingly deploy it against peaceful demonstrators. The major difference between the "nonviolent martyr" and "violent martyr" is that the latter involves violence as the major ingredient of his action in an intentional manner, whereas the nonviolent martyr does not glorify violence, indeed would like to shun it and possibly renounce it openly and directly. But in the heat of action (public demonstration), sometimes defending one's life can involve some violence against the forces of repression. At any rate, the distinction between the two categories, pertinent though it is, should not mean that avoiding violence means totally renouncing it, exerting it occasionally for the sake of self-defence. The case of Al-Mahdī Zīwi points to violence against the garrison in Libya, but not directly against the people in it. At the age of 49, Al-Mahdī Zīwi became a revolutionary hero in Benghazi at the beginning of the Libyan revolt against Gaddafi, in February 2011. For many, his killing ignited Benghazi's protest movement.

Zīwi, who worked for an oil company for 30 years, joined the protest movement against Gaddafi on its first day. He was shocked by the violence of the Gaddafi regime against its own people during the demonstrations. Late at night, three days after the bloody protest, Zīwi loaded cylinders of propane gas into his car. The next day, the corpses of those killed the day before obstructed his approach to the notorious Kātib garrison in the city of Benghazi. He drove his car at high speed toward the gates of the garrison. The car skipped over the first barricade, and the gas cylinders exploded when the vehicle knocked against the second barricade, creating a huge hole in the garrison's defences. This became a turning point in the battle of Benghazi. A friend of Zīwi's from work said he was astonished by this courageous act, induced by Zīwi's indignation at the regime's killing of Libyans.

The security forces arrested a brother of Zīwi's intimate friend, beat him and used him as a human shield against the handcrafted grenades protesters were throwing at the garrison. He later said that Zīwi's act had saved his life since the blowing up of the barricades allowed the people to conquer the garrison later on, freeing him from there.[25]

---

[25] "Al-shahīd alladhī ḥasama maʿraka Binghāzī" [The Martyr Who Settled the Battle in Benghazi"], in: *Al Jazeera* 01.03.2011, URL: http://www.aljazeera.net/news/pages/fbc610d7-45 50-4d44-bc67-8aa09bd4870a (retrieved 02.05.2012).

IV. Martyrdom Legitimising a Corporate Structure (Al Jazeera)

The death of one of Al Jazeera's journalists became an occasion to extol not only his but also Al Jazeera's role in the Arab Revolution. On 14 March, in the capital of Qatar, Doha, the special "collective prayer of the dead" (*salāt al-janāza*) was recited over the corpse of the martyr ʿAlī Ḥasan al-Jābir, a Qatari national, Al Jazeera's cameraman, killed in an ambush near Benghazi, the first journalist slain in the Libyan conflict. The crew's car came under fire from the rear. He was shot three times in the back and a fourth bullet hit the correspondent near the ear.

He died as a martyr in Libya on Saturday, 12 March, while covering the Libyan Revolution. A large protest was organised later in Benghazi in solidarity with the slain cameraman. Some banners read: "Targeting journalists reveals the criminal regime of the tyrant."[26] The night before the ceremony, al-Jābir's body was sent to Doha airport where many of his colleagues waited with his family. His coffin was covered with the national flag of Qatar and Libya's liberation flag (the old tricolour flag instead of the green flag imposed by Gaddafi). Among the people at the airport were the crown prince of Qatar, al-Shaykh Tamīm b. Ḥamd b. Khalīfa al-Thānī, and Al Jazeera's general director, Waddāḥ Khanfar. In Benghazi, before his departure, thousands of people took part in the mourning ceremony and recited the prayer of the dead over his corpse.

The leader of the World Alliance of Islamic ʿulamāʾ, Doctor Yūsuf al-Qaraḍāwī, recited the prayer over al-Jābir's corpse wrapped up in a burial garment, while the political elite prayed for the commemoration of the martyr, whose body was to be sent to the Abū Ḥamūr cemetery in the region of Musaymīr. An important avenue in Doha was named for him. Al-Jābir thus became not only Al Jazeera's martyr but also Libya's and Qatar's.

V. Martyrs with Premeditation

People "martyred" because they demonstrated and were shot at or mortally wounded by the security forces are legion in the Arab Spring. Aḥmad Basyūnī and Muṣṭafā al-Ṣāwī, two martyrs of the Egyptian Revolution, are immortalised on a highway overpass in Zamālik. Aḥmad Basyūnī, a musician, became a symbol of defiance after he was killed by security forces on 28 January. Born in Cairo in 1978, he was an assistant teacher in the Faculty of Arts, Ḥilwān University. The father of two joined his fellow Egyptians in chanting for the toppling of

---

[26] "Al Jazeera: Cameraman Ali Hassan Al-Jaber Killed In Libya Ambush", in: *Huffington Post*, 30.10.2011, URL: http://www.huffingtonpost.com/2011/03/12/al-jazeera-cameraman-ali-hassan-al-jaber-killed-libya_n_834947.html (retrieved 02.05.2012).

Mubarak's regime. As he raised up his hands in a victory sign, he was shot dead by police.[27]

In sharp contrast to unintentional martyrdom (as the case of Aḥmad Basyūnī, who did not expose himself to very high risks but was killed all the same), there are cases of people who know almost for sure that they are exposing themselves to death. This is true in highly repressive regimes like the Syrian. Some even foretell their death and declare their victory over the forces of evil that killed them, the sense of calling exceeding their self-preservation instinct.

In the Syrian town Darāyā, a 26-year-old activist, Ghayāth Maṭar, was detained at the beginning of September in a trap and tortured. Four days later he was dead, having suffered from burns, lashes and bullet wounds. Maṭar was re-nowned in Darāyā for his peaceful behaviour towards the security forces. He urged colleagues to confront the security forces by presenting them with a rose and a bottle of fresh water. The government told Maṭar's family that he had been shot by "armed gangs", a euphemism that the government uses to describe the opposition.

As the uprising persists and the numbers of deaths and arrests mount, a new trend has emerged among activists. Many of them have started writing wills should they be killed. Ghayāth Maṭar said in his will, read on a new online radio broadcast called One Plus One run by activists:

> I announce to you the news of my martyrdom, and I want you to know that now I gained happiness and freedom. Don't think they triumphed over me with the bullet they shot me with. No, I won and my case won every time I went to the street.[28]

Seven ambassadors attended Mr. Maṭar's funeral, including the American ambassador, Robert S. Ford.[29]

VI. Vicarious Martyrs

In Tunisia, after the overthrow of Ben Ali on 14 January, sit-ins, demonstrations and even hunger strikes continued in protest against unemployment and social injustice. In the towns of Al-Qaṣrayn, Tāla and Sīdī Bū Zīd, the jobless youth, or *diplômés chômeurs*, gathered in the city centre in improvised tents displaying photos of the martyrs of the revolution.[30] This reference was essential as they

---

[27] Susan Yasin, "Egypt Revolution Martyrs... Ahmad Bassouni", in: *@onislam*, 13.02.2011, URL: http://www.onislam.net/english/news/africa/450994-egypt-revolution-martyrs-ahmed-bassiouni.html (retrieved 02.05.2012).

[28] Nada Bakri, "In Syrian Town, Uprising Turns Into Grim Standoff", in: *New York Times*, 15.09. 2011, URL: http://www.nytimes.com/2011/09/16/world/middleeast/in-syrian-town-uprising-turns-into-grim-standoff.html?pagewanted=all (retrieved 02.05.2012).

[29] Ibid.

[30] "Soulevements populaires en Afrique du Nord et au Moyen-Orient (IV): La voie tunisi-enne", in: *Middle East/North Africa Report* No. 106. International Crisis Group, 28.04.2011,

claimed that the martyrs had died for the cause of the jobless, the poorly paid workers and all those who endure social injustice. Martyrdom was thus claimed in a vicarious manner as belonging to a social group in conflict with the governing elites, insensitive to the plights of the cast-off youth.

Martyrdom, generally speaking, is referred to the "general interest" of the society and claimed to go beyond corporatist interests. But in this case, martyrdom is brandished for the sake of the betterment of the lot of a social category, the *diplômés chômeurs*, who demand the improvement of their situation because they offered martyrs to the society, contributing thus to the overthrow of the authoritarian regime. This, in their view, induces a "debt" of the society towards them, entitling them to ask for social advantages. Martyrs assume a "vicarious function" in this specific case.

VII. The Ambiguous Martyr

Sally Zahrān, a 23-year-old woman, died in Egypt on 28 January, the "black Friday" of repression on Tahrir Square. In subsequent days her face appeared on walls across Cairo and on the sun visors of taxis. In the cafés close to Tahrir Square people said that she had been beaten to death by a police henchman. NASA reportedly put Zahrān's name on one of its Mars exploration spacecrafts. But when a journalist from the Swiss newspaper *Le Temps* investigated Zahrān's death, she could find no evidence of it and was met with embarrassed silence. The story was enveloped in mystery. On 23 February Sally Zahrān's mother announced on TV that her daughter had fallen from the balcony of a flat in her hometown Sūhāj, in southern Egypt. In Cairo people believed that Zahrān's mother had been coerced to make this statement by the new military regime so as to conceal the killing of her daughter. Martyrdom and rumour are thus inextricably interwoven, illustrating the generally febrile and unstable atmosphere in revolutionary societies, which are rather prone to over-interpreting facts in a polarised fashion.

Since martyrdom has become a symbolic stake in the struggle between the government and the opposition, the former manipulates it to discredit the latter and to defame the international organisations, in particular the human rights institutions. The case of Zaynab al-Ḥusnī is symptomatic of the manipulation found mainly in Syria and Iran in cases related to the killing of opponents. The young woman, aged 18, was found beheaded and badly disfigured, most probably by the Syrian security services. She had been arrested by the Syrian forces to force her brother, an opponent to Bashar al-Assad, to put an end to his activities. Her brother was arrested in September. On 13 September the security services

---

URL: www.crisisgroup.org/fr/regions/moyen-orient-afrique-du-nord/afrique-du-nord/
Tunisia/106-popular-protests-in-north-africa-and-the-middle-east-iv-tunisias-way.aspx
(retrieved 02.05.2012).

summoned her mother to take charge of the corpse, marked by bruises and gun-shots. According to Amnesty International, once at the morgue the mother found her daughter's corpse mutilated and beheaded as well. She was buried and a protest in Homs was organised the next weekend, greeted as "the flower of Syria".[31] Then a coup de théâtre was staged by the Syrian government and on Wednesday, 8 October a young woman called Zaynab al-Ḥusnī was presented on Syrian TV, denying having been kidnapped and killed. Amnesty International had reported her case on 23 September to denounce the execution of the civil population by the Syrian regime. Her parents had identified the mutilated body shown to them by the authorities as being hers. On TV the young girl said during her interview that she had fled from home because her brothers beat her frequently. Her family recognised her on TV and realised their mistake.[32] Probably the Syrian regime manipulated the whole story to discredit Amnesty International by monitoring the whole affair, defaming at the same time the family, whose son had been killed by the security forces.

Martyrdom, killing and the manipulative utilisation of the death cases are intermingled in a way that leaves a great deal of scope for "instrumentalisation" and antagonistic interpretations of death, simulated or real, by different protagonists.

VIII. Martyrs of Hunger Strikes and Peaceful Resistance

Against the repressive regimes killing peaceful demonstrators and arbitrarily arresting those who seem to oppose their denial of civil rights, one can detect the emergence of a new type of martyr, one who is willing to die by opposing the regime peacefully, through a hunger strike or other nonviolent means, gradually endangering their health, bit by bit, allowing the media to continually follow the unfolding story. This type of martyrdom is not formally recognised by the religious authorities but is proclaimed as such by public opinion, forcing some ʿulamāʾ to belatedly recognise them. In some cases, the potential death through hunger strike entitles the person to be given the title of martyr. This is the case of the Bahraini ʿAbd al-Hādī al-Khawāja, whose condition in prison continued to deteriorate up to 13 April, according to his lawyer, Muḥammad al-Jīshī.[33] According to Amnesty International, al-Khawāja and thirteen other prominent op-

---

[31]   Bassem Mroue et al., "Syria: Zainab Al Hosni Believed To Be Killed In Custody", in: *Huffington Post*, 23.09.2011, URL: http://www.huffingtonpost.com/2011/09/23/syria-zainab-al-hosni-died-custody_n_977550.html (retrieved 02.05.2012).

[32]   See "Zeinab Al-Hosni, victime de la répression syrienne, réapparait à la télévision", in: *Le Monde* 05.10.2011, URL: http://www.lemonde.fr/proche-orient/article/2011/10/05/zeinab-al-hosni-victime-de-la-repression-syrienne-reapparait-a-la-television_1582771_3218.html (retrieved 02.05.2012).

[33]   Bahrain Freedom Movement, 13.04.2012, URL: http://www.vob.org/en/index.php?show=news&action=article&id=1437 (retrieved 02.05.2012).

position activists held with him in Bahrain are prisoners of conscience, held solely for peacefully exercising their rights to freedom of expression and assembly; they have not advocated violence in any way, shape or form.[34]

More and more, those who struggle for human rights by resorting to nonviolent means, be it in prison or in street demonstrations or through new communication channels (internet), once they are killed by or die in the hands of the security forces the public by and large regards them as "martyrs". Hunger strikers play a new role among them, all the more so as their death is gradual, extending over many days or weeks and can be documented at length by the media, presenting an opportunity to initiate pathos-charged discourses and dramatise the story into a crescendo.

VIII. Jihadist Versus Civil Sphere Martyrdom

In comparison to the Jihadist type of martyrdom, the new sacred deaths resulting from the Arab Spring have many distinct features. The Jihadist martyrdom is violence-prone: it is not only violent but also praises violence as the sole way of dealing with political and cultural problems in a globalised world. The al-Qaida martyr sees no way of resolving the problem of the "world disbelief" other than through waging all-out war with the disbelievers. This martyrdom is also approved, even glorified by the Jihadist *ʿulamā* (like Abū Muḥammad al-Maqdisī, Abū Baṣīr al-Ṭarṭūsī, Abū Muṣʿab al-Sūrī, Abū Qatāda and many others) and they feel that their acts are utterly "religious" in content. Moreover, their action is politicised in the sense of including politics in the realm of religion. Their fourth characteristic is that, from their perspective, the individual does not exist as such: he is entirely subordinated to the religious community, the *umma*. The only way for the individual to assert himself is to act as a would-be martyr, accepting and embracing the need to make the supreme sacrifice for the sake of his version of Islam. Otherwise, individual's rights are non-existent towards God's and the former has only duties, no rights where the Godly order that has to be promoted against the heretics and seculars is concerned.

The new type of martyrdom can be qualified as a "civil sphere sacred death". The notion of civil sphere[35] gives its meaning to this martyrdom, based on two related topics: the notion of the citizen's dignity (*karāma*) and their right to social justice and solidarity. These characteristics distinguish this martyrdom from the Jihadist version: nonviolent (the refusal to exert violence against the others), promoting the dignity of the citizen as an individual (against the backdrop of the Jihadist anti-individualist credo), and asking for the recognition of the fundamental rights of citizens, who happen to wield rights and have not only duties

---

[34] Ibid.
[35] See Jeffrey Alexander, *The Civil Sphere*, Oxford 2006.

towards the community. This type of martyrdom is "secular" in the sense that the act of putting an end to their lives (the Bū ʿAzīzī model) or being killed by police or security services or government thugs (*balṭajiyya*) is not framed within a religious mould and takes on a social meaning, autonomous from the religious garb. It is only its "sacralisation" by the society that gives a religious sense to it and makes a martyr's act out of a social protest death. In this respect, the new martyrdom denotes the secularisation of the society and deep-seated tendencies towards democratisation from below. The Jihadist martyrdom enrols its recruits within the framework of "antisocial movements" (antidemocratic social movements),[36] whereas Arab Spring martyrdom develops within the "civil sphere movements", where the claim to democracy, the autonomy of the civil sphere and the dignity of the citizen are its major ingredients.

In the case of a prolonged civil war as in Syria, nonviolence can give way to violent action, as is the case with the Free Syrian Army that uses names like *katība shuhadāʾ Talkalakh* (Martyrs' Brigade Tal Kalakh). This type of martyrdom joins the traditional or revolutionary ones, and is close to the Iranian, Palestinian or other national cases.

X. Conclusion

The notion of martyrdom has undergone a number of changes over the course of the Modern period: during the imperialist period, jihad was revitalised for the fight against imperialism and martyrdom was associated with it as the sacred death necessary for the defence of Islam against non-Islamic intruders (the notion of defensive jihad).

The Islamist period puts martyrdom at the centre of the ideological agenda. Waging a holy war against the godless imperialists was not possible without the ultimate sacrifice of one's life in a violent manner: dying, and in so doing, causing the death of the maximum number of the enemies of Islam, defined in very broad terms (all those who were, Muslims and non-Muslims alike, against the project of the Jihadist version of Islam). The association of martyrdom as an informal protest against injustice and oppression was toned down and a violent, militant view of sacred death surfaced that intended to systematically use violence against the enemy, with no regard to the killing and suffering caused by the Jihadists' action. This was the last outcome of martyrdom in its regressive form within a framework where violence became an end in itself, rather than a means to achieve the global end of jihad.[37]

With the new Arab Revolutions beginning with the Tunisian Jasmine Revolution and the ousting of President Ben Ali on 14 January 2011, a new period for

---

[36] See Michel Wieviorka, *Sociétés et terrorisme*, Paris 1988.
[37] This dimension is elaborated further in my works *L'Islamisme et la Mort* and *Inside Jihadism*.

martyrdom begins in which nonviolence towards others (including the enemy) is the rule. Two models of martyrdom are evident: the martyr dies not through killing opponents, but either by intentionally killing themselves in a display of public protest (Bū ʿAzīzī's model), or by being put to death by the regime's violence (those killed by the security forces or thugs, the so-called *balṭajiyya*, of authoritarian regime; in those cases like Syria, Yemen and Libya, where a protracted civil war partially brings nonviolent action to an end and military defence is proclaimed as the only means of ousting the authoritarian rulers, we witness the return of the revolutionary pattern of martyrdom: violent death against the oppressor, loosely connected with Jihad). This type of martyrdom denotes the democratic secularisation of Muslims in Arab and Iranian societies. The new martyr no longer seeks to kill the "enemy" but to discredit him by highlighting his own trampled dignity (*karāma*) and demanding social justice and an open political system.[38]

---

[38] Cf. Farhad Khosrokhavar, "Les révolutions arabes: révolutions de justice sociale et de liberté", in *Cultures & Conflicts*, no. 83 (2011).

The Discursive Construction of Palestinian *istishhādiyyāt* within the Frame of Martyrdom

Lisa Franke (Leipzig)

On 27 January, 2002 Wafāʾ Idrīs committed an act of self-sacrifice, or in other words a suicide bombing in Jerusalem. She was the first female *istishhādī* ('one who brings about martyrdom on him/herself', a neologism used in the parlance of the Palestinian groups which support those acts)[1] in the Israeli-Palestinian conflict. A couple of other women followed her example, attracting from then on the attention of the media. The period of the Second Intifada (2001–2005) was characterised by severe political unrest and extreme insecurity. Clashes between Israeli troops and Palestinians increased in their intensity. Both sides resorted to extreme forms of force, the Israelis employing air attacks on civilians, while the Palestinian militant resistance organisations launched attacks on settlers and Israeli military bases within the occupied Palestinian territories.[2] In addition, martyrdom operations were now used frequently as a method to fight the occupation. Nonetheless, suicide bombings or acts of self-sacrifice are territorially or geographically not bound to Palestine or the region of the Middle East and North Africa, indeed they are not even an entirely new phenomenon in political conflicts around the world.[3]

I intend to show how Palestinians deal with the *istishhādiyyāt*, how it is possible that they are glorified within the realm of martyrdom and resistance, and how ideological or manipulative practices are employed. Although modern discourses[4] (esp. nationalism) play a decisive role in the construction of the *istishhādiyyāt*, the figure of the modern martyr has its roots in religious tradition. How

---

[1] The term *ʿamaliyyat istishhādiyya* ("Martyrdom Operation") was first used by the Hizbullah in Lebanon during the Lebanon War (1975-1990). See Christoph Reuter, *Mein Leben ist eine Waffe. Selbstmordattentäter. Psychogramm eines Phänomens.* Munich 2002, 107.

[2] This term is used to refer to the Gaza Strip (Gaza), the West Bank and East Jerusalem. It was first introduced at the Oslo Accords (Oslo I). Even though Gaza is technically no longer occupied by Israeli settlers, Israeli military incursions still take place regularly. Moreover, Israel controls the airspace, the territorial waters and the borders, which is just another form of occupation. Thus, throughout this paper the term "(occupied) Palestinian territories" or "Palestine" is used synonymously for the three areas.

[3] Such attacks have been used by organisations elsewhere, such as the PKK in Turkey (Kurdistan), the LTTE in Sri Lanka, Hizbullah in Lebanon, and by various organisations and individuals in places such as Iraq and Afghanistan, the Black Widows in Chechnya or the Kamikaze fighters in Japan. These are examples from other geographical areas with different socio-political and religious backgrounds.

[4] I use the plural discourses since it is not one single discourse that deals with the *istishhādiyyāt*. Some of these discourses are overlapping, some complementary, while others are opposed and conflicting.

can the relationship between the religious and the nationalist element be described? What are the processes that glorify the *istishhādiyyāt* as martyrs? What is the impact of these modern discourses on the changing role of women?

I. Contexts of Modern Palestinian Resistance: Religious Nationalism and the Status of Women

Women not only fought in the rebellion of 1834[5] – during the Ottoman period – against the Egyptian occupation by the ruler Muḥammad ʿAlī, but also in the Arab Revolt of 1936–1939, the struggles for independence since 1967 and the First and the Second Intifada. Yet, "the inclusion of women in the public sphere [was] to a large extent utilitarian (because conservative gender norms were viewed as barriers to national liberation)."[6] The nationalist discourse dominated all parts of the Palestinian social milieu: nationalism was (and still is) the unifying factor that transformed society into an active resisting and dynamic project. All of these developments can be summarised in what Joseph Massad calls "nation first, women after".[7] Women's issues were again subjected to the national goal of regaining the homeland.

The central importance given to nationalism in the resistance struggle is also perceptible in the context of martyrdom operations and women's involvement therein. However, as far as the martyrdom discourse of the *istishhādiyyāt* is concerned, a religious language has been adopted that was absent with regard to the women previously actively involved in the resistance. Women were thus included in the discourse of "religious nationalism" which the Islamists and the nationalists mutually employ in their language and to describe their actions.[8] In the

---

[5]   This was already the third rebellion against Ottoman rule in which women participated. Two uprisings (primarily directed at the tax collection policies, perceived as unjustifiable, of the ruling system) took place in Jerusalem in 1703-1705 (the rebellion of Naqīb al-Ashrāf) and in 1825-1826, both lasting for about two years, whereas the third revolt was put down after a couple of months. The latter is of special significance though, because large parts of the Palestinian population, both urban and rural from throughout the area, took part, while the first two revolts were geographically concentrated. Cf. the article by the Palestinian historian Adel Manna, "Eighteenth- and Nineteenth-Century Rebellions in Palestine", in: *Journal of Palestine Studies* 24 (1994), 51-66 and Gudrun Krämer, *Geschichte Palästinas. Von der osmanischen Eroberung bis zur Gründung des Staates Israel*, Munich 2006, 53ff.

[6]   Frances S. Hasso, "Modernity and Gender in Arab Accounts of the 1948 and 1967 Defeats", in: *International Journal of Middle East Studies* 32 (2000), 491-510.

[7]   Joseph Massad, "Conceiving the masculine: Gender and Palestinian nationalism", in: *The Middle East Journal* 49 (1995), 469.

[8]   Nationalism and its meaning have to be defined in order for to use the combined term "religious nationalism". According to Friedland, "[n]ationalism is not ideology. It is a discursive practice by which the territorial identity of a state and the cultural identity of a people whose collective representation it claims are constituted as a singular institutional fact. [...] Nationalism offers a form of representation – the joining of state, territoriality, and culture. It has nothing to say about the content of representation, the identity of that

words of Roger Friedland, the marriage between religion and nationalism is represented as follows: "religion partakes of the symbolic order of the nation-state and [...] contemporary nationalisms are suffused with the religious."[9]

Religious nationalism is a discursive process that employs narratives, rituals, symbols and myths to strengthen identities and fulfil societal needs for solace. The amalgamation of religious and nationalist motives in militant resistance is important to keep the resistance kindled and to alleviate society's feelings of despair and worry. Religious narratives are woven around the web of nationalist intentions and both the nationalist and the Islamic movement "make politicized use of ritual spaces and religious ritual practices as devices for mobilization."[10] This elevates the struggle for independence from a merely territorial dimension onto a higher transcendental domain.

II. Gendered Martyrdom

The analytical concept of gender and the notion of martyrdom can be brought together in the term *gendered martyrdom*. This concept links a certain form of death or dying – which is perceived as martyrdom – with the social category of gender, thus focussing on the specificity of male or female martyrdom and the question whether male martyrdom is different from (or similar to) female martyrdom. In either case this difference of meaning (i.e. male vs. female) is noteworthy and makes *gendered martyrdom* a binary-termed concept.

Martyrdom (including martyrdom operations) in the Palestinian context takes place as sacrifice within the scope of the notion *fī sabīli 'llāh* (i.e. in the way of God) and/or in the context of the homeland.[11] In order to uphold the struggle for independence (i.e. Palestinian resistance), relevant symbols and icons are produced and used.[12] The social construction and transformation of reality is thus a creative, culturally communicative and communicated process. The term 'martyr' (*shahīd*) or 'self-sacrificer' (*istishhādī*) for a suicide bomber is one such symbol and

---

collective subject, or its values. Religion offers an institutionally specific way to organize this modern form of collective representation, how a collectivity represents itself to itself, the symbols, signs, and practices through which it is and knows itself to be." Cf. Roger Friedland, "Religious Nationalism and the Problem of Collective Representation", in: *Annual Review of Sociology* 27 (2001), 138.

[9] Ibid. 126.

[10] Ibid. 140.

[11] It is also linked to other notions like resistance, trauma, narratives of suffering and objects of commemoration, collective mourning and the celebration of funerals (which can however not be further elaborated on due to the limited scope of this article).

[12] In this context, the notions of 'culture of death', 'new social movement' or 'rite de passage' (for instance in relation to resistance) play a decisive role with respect to Palestinian self-sacrificers. Cf. for these concepts Julie Peteet, "Male gender and rituals of resistance in the Palestinian intifada: A cultural politics of violence", in: *Imagined Masculinities: Male Identity and Culture in the Middle East*, ed. by Mai Ghoussoub et al., London 2000, 103-126 and Kevin Hetherington, *Expressions of Identity. Space, Performance, Politics*, London 1998.

his or her death combines religious and nationalistic connotations. The same applies to the myths, of which the best example is the myth of the "Palestinian wedding", re-contextualised in texts glorifying the martyrs. Instead of referring to it as an event of sadness, death is considered to be a wedding ceremony in which the dead is wedded to the land Palestine. As a symbolic act, this wedding represents the suffering of the Palestinian people, a suffering enriched with new meaning through the transformation of the (upcoming) funeral into a wedding ceremony.[13]

The myth of the "Palestinian wedding" is also referred to in the glorifying text on Ayāt al-Akhras, irrespective of the fact that she is a woman.[14] While Palestine was formerly connoted to be feminine, in this case the land is depicted to be a male bridegroom:

> For today is her wedding, even though she does not wear the white dress and even though no bridal procession to her groom takes place ... she was adorned with her red and proud blood which transformed her into a Palestinian wedding ... she wanted to be wedded to her ["]bridegroom["] [the earth Palestine] exclusively in the 'blood-suit', with ["]which["] only the likes of her consummate the marriage – in order to create the pride of her people by means of her success in killing and injuring dozens of Zionist occupiers in a successful and heroic operation.[15]

Moreover, this passage creates a mythical reference to blood: the blood of the *shuhadā'* and the *istishhādiyyūn* is a recurring theme alluded to in various texts, songs and poetry glorifying the heroic death. The transformative power said to be characteristic of blood can be seen in the image of the blood spilled over the land. Thanks to this act the earth is invigorated with new life – as if the blood was water nourishing nature.[16] This is highlighted with regard to the context of the *istishhādiyyāt* in an encomium on Wafā' Idrīs:

---

[13] Cf. Angelika Neuwirth who discusses the "Palestinian wedding" in the context of works by the poet Mahmud Darwish; Neuwirth, "Opfer, Gewalt, Genealogie und Erinnerung. Biblische und koranische Erinnerungsfiguren im vorderorientalischen Märtyrerdiskurs", in: *Die Künste im Dialog der Kulturen. Europa und seine muslimischen Nachbarn*, ed. by Christoph Wulf et al., Berlin 2007, 53-54.

[14] Ayāt al-Akhras carried out a martyrdom operation on 29 March, 2002. Born in Jerusalem, she was the third *istishhādiyya* and the youngest, having joined the active militant resistance at the age of 16. The operation took place under the auspices of the al-Aqsa Brigades at the Kiryat HaYovel supermarket in Jerusalem and killed two people, a 17 year-old Israeli girl and a 55 year-old Israeli security guard.

[15] Cf. the glorifying text on Ayāt al-Akhras published by the Katā'ib shuhadā' al-Aqṣā, "Al-Akhras, Ayāt", URL: http://kataebaqsa.org/arabic/modules.php?name=News&file=article&sid=20 (retrieved 15.06.2010).

[16] Cf. *Mythen des Blutes*, ed. by Christina Braun et al., Frankfurt et al. 2007. Cf. also the mourning ceremonies in Babylonia for the deity Tammūz (Adonis), who died and was buried and reborn according to seasonal cycles: Joseph Campbell, *Oriental Mythology: The Masks of God*, New York 1962.

She said that spring only blossoms if one waters it with blood. For Palestine is the only country of the world, in which the olives, the oranges and roses grow without water [but with blood] [...]. Further on she said that the seeds of the earth would breed spikes if they are watered with blood.[17]

In the case of women a connotation of blood and motherhood can be found, namely that the female martyrs nourish Palestine through their blood as if it was milk for their offspring.

Especially the image of the Palestinian wedding is regularly repeated and does not only remain in the text-based sphere but has entered the social realm, leaving its mark on death processions and burial rites. The myth of spilled blood is one example for the hybrid topoi and images which endorse martyrdom and are taken from political, religious and cultural discourse.

III. Discourses and Documents of Glorification[18]

In order to heroise martyrs, or rather to produce them in the first place – to transcend and mythologise the individual –, a collective in the form of a community or society is necessary. Only within the collective, texts (encomiums, poetry) and discourses are produced that glorify the martyrs. In turn, these texts and oral accounts have to be received and accepted by the individual and by society with the intention of commemorating the fallen combatant.[19]

The source of the discourse lies in the interest of the respective dispatching organisations, who on the strength of their official position utilise propagandistic means to present a collective opinion. I have identified ideological elements which stem from these organisations, are disseminated and exploited by them, as the major source of the discourses on the *istishhādiyyāt*. Amongst these are references to martyrdom and Islam, a highlighting of the activities of the dispatching organisations, and a focusing on the role of women in Palestinian society.

Some of the ideological elements are national aspects that are accordingly magnified so as to act as a trigger for carrying out martyrdom operations and militant resistance activities. Here, religious, political and cultural/social elements are drawn upon in order to make the struggle meaningful, to better justify the position of the organisation by corroborating it with widely known and powerful discursive elements derived from language, symbols, and myths. Other discourses – such as those initiated and shaped by journalists or university lecturers or other 'ordinary'

---

¹⁷ Cf. the glorifying text on Wafā' Idrīs published on the website of the al-Aqsa Brigades. The links are unstable due to the Brigades frequently changing their domains in order to remain anonymous. Katā'ib shuhadā' al-Aqṣā: "Idrīs, Wafā'". URL: http://www.kataebaqsa.org/arabic/modules.php?name=News&file=article&sid= 72 (retrieved 15.06.2010).

¹⁸ The findings in this section are based on the interviews I conducted in Gaza and the West Bank.

¹⁹ Lori A. Allen, "The Polyvalent Politics of Martyr Commemorations in the Palestinian *Intifada*", in: *History & Memory* 18 (2006), 107-138.

people – on the *istishhādiyyāt* do not focus on religious aspects but place more emphasis on nationalist elements. Again they are substantiated with religious, political and cultural/social aspects. The nationalist factor is likewise highlighted in predominantly religious discourses which support martyrdom operations.[20]

The processes of negotiation, re-negotiation, production and re-production informing the discourses on the Palestinian *istishhādiyyāt* are rather complex and do not occur in any streamlined manner.[21] Audio, visual and print media and especially the Internet play an essential role in the re-production of those discourses spread by the dispatching organisations, particularly in the public space. In the private and the domestic realm narratives and conversations are more important.[22] However, glorification (oral, visual and written), commemoration, funerals and demonstrations as well as public depictions and (re-)presentations in the form of posters and portraits are both part of the public and the private sphere: all of them constitute a public context that can trigger personal emotions. These emotions are then very private expressions of – for instance – grief and suffering. In other words, the public forms of the commemorated martyrdom operations have an effect on sentiments that are articulated in private.

The sheer occurrence of female self-sacrificing martyrs in the Israeli-Palestinian conflict serves as multiplier for the reproduction of martyr discourses – be they glorifying or demonising. This shows the extraordinarily diverse ways of addressing the *istishhādiyyāt* who are part of so many representations and debates.

With the emergence of the *istishhādiyyāt*, the participants in the established *shuhadā'* discourses had to deal with the fact that suddenly women were now part of the issue.[23] Temporarily they even dominated the discourse, provoking heated discussion amongst religious scholars and political leaders as to whether martyrdom operations in general, and those carried out by women in particular, can be justified.[24]

Gender-specific references constitute one part of these discourses.[25] Gender is mentioned in comparative ways when *istishhādiyyāt* and *istishhādiyyūn* are evaluated. The context here is the traditional patriarchal social order, an order that

---

[20] Cf. Meir Hatina, "The 'Ulama' and the Cult of Death in Palestine", in: *Israel Affairs* 12 (2006), 29-51.

[21] Cf. Amnesty International: "Middle East" (2002).

[22] Allen, "The Polyvalent Politics of Martyr Commemoration", 107-138.

[23] Cf. David Cook, *Martyrdom in Islam*, New York 2007, 135-172.

[24] Cf. Haim Malka, "Must Innocents Die? The Islamic Debate over Suicide Attacks", in: *Middle East Quarterly* 2 (2002), 19-28.

[25] For instance the notion of the wedding, where the martyr is wedded to the land through the act of spilling his blood over the soil; because female Palestinian self-sacrificing, intentional martyrs are a quite recent phenomenon, opinions regarding their status 'in the garden' vary greatly. Even though it is mostly assumed that they enter the garden as martyrs, it is not clear what will await them in the afterlife: if they are going to enter the garden as brides ready to be married off to someone they know, or if they turn themselves into one of the *ḥūr*. The issue of this modern phenomenon of female martyrs has not been treated in the

usually prevents women from taking part in active militant resistance. The transfiguration of the female martyrs, the *istishhādiyyāt*, the act of being highlighted by means of the role of the organisations, takes place on the basis of patriarchal clichés. These stereotypes are thus confirmed, enforced and reproduced by the organisations, which produce and spread material on the glorified *istishhādiyyāt*. Instead of solely portraying the women's uniqueness and effectiveness, the higher aim is to maintain current structures, which reflect patriarchal dominance and decision-making: the glorifying media is produced by men and they decide how the women are portrayed and what is published about them. The women's religiosity, their "good behaviour" within their families and societies are highlighted to reflect images of these women which are deemed to be society-compliant values. Yet, the 'gendered' discourse has to also be situated in the wider geopolitical frame of Palestinians living under occupation, since this is the real-life setting which has brought forward resistance activity and which legitimises means of resistance. Gender is then primarily referred to in two ways, either in terms of the legitimisation of *istishhādiyyāt* or with regards to the *de*legitimisation of *istishhādiyyāt*. In both, the traditional role of women, their religious background, social possibilities and behavioural guidelines, their position in culture, society, religion, and politics, family structures, domestic obligations, as well as nationalist concerns are part of the particular discourse. As to the legitimisation of *istishhādiyyāt*, their femininity is not classified as a disadvantage but as an appreciated asset, useful in the resistance struggle, since women can often meander more inconspicuously through the streets and checkpoints than men. Religious references are then consulted to strengthen the position that men and women are equal before God. Historical examples serve as valid proof that fighting women are not a new phenomenon but that they had already taken up arms during the times of the Prophet Muhammad. Furthermore, it is said that the occupation concerns men and women mutually and consequently requires the active commitment of both sexes.[26]

---

classical written sources and is thus subject to vigorous debate. Cf. Lisa Franke, *In front of the doors of paradise: discourses of female self-sacrifice, martyrdom and resistance in Palestine*, University of Leipzig, 2011 (unpublished).
Another notion is that of blood through which the earth is invigorated with new life. For instance it is said in the glorifying text or encomium about Ayāt al-Akhras that she was wedded in her military blood suit instead of a white bridal gown (she was supposed to get married in summer 2002), cf. note 14.

[26] During my field research the approving position was taken by the dispatching organisations, such as the military leader of the al-Quds Brigades in Gaza and Fawzy Barhoum, the (then) spokesperson of Hamas (see an analysis of these interviews in my dissertation *In front of the doors of paradise*. See also Shannon Dunn, "The Female Martyr and the Politics of Death: An Examination of the Martyr Discourses of Vibia Perpetua and Wafa Idris", in: *Journal of the American Academy of Religion* 1 (2010), 1-24.

When it comes to the *de*-legitimisation of *istishhādiyyāt* things look a bit different.[27] In this case women are depicted as weaker than men and their femininity is considered to be the reason why they cannot participate in the armed resistance struggle. The traditional social and cultural role of women as guardians of the domestic space, responsible for the birth and education of children, is highlighted. It is considered to be more important to deliver children than to jeopardise or let alone sacrifice the precious, fertile female life. Other positions, according to my interviewees, argue that it is indecorous for women to carry weapons and to be present in a male-dominated space where the men are not relatives. In the *de*-legitimisation argument women are not necessarily degraded to worthless beings, but their role is clearly and strictly separated from the duties and responsibilities of men and actions considered acceptable for men. However, in this context it should also be mentioned that the discourse can take another quite different direction, namely to be entirely reluctant to accept martyrdom operations in general, regardless of whether men or women are the perpetrators.[28] Representatives of this position fear the complete exclusion and isolation of Palestine in (international) politics and see martyrdom operations as threatening Palestinian societal structures. In short, martyrdom operations would cause more harm than good.[29]

IV. The media depiction of the istishhādiyyāt

Support for and the popularity of martyrdom operations and martyrdom *per se* also depend on how efficiently the propaganda machine of the respective organisations deploying martyrdom operations functions.[30] The glorification of the death of male and female *istishhādiyyūn*, apparent in some parts of Palestinian society, results *inter alia* from media manipulations (which are one form of communicative processes) – particularly with regard to militant resistance organisations such as the al-Aqsa Martyrs Brigades which support martyrdom operations as a *modus operandi*.[31] The organisations deliberately construct the *istishhādiyyāt* and their heroine identities by publishing their testaments and glorifying texts on the Internet. Post-

---

[27]   Cf. Hatina, "The ʿUlamaʾ and the Cult of Death in Palestine", 37.

[28]   Amira Hass, "Hamas activist: most Gazans now object to suicide bombings", in: *Haʾaretz* (2002).

[29]   Mostly young university students and journalists have advanced this view, especially my female research assistants. Moreover, the father of Mīrfat Masʿūd told me that he was absolutely opposed to such actions, regardless of the gender of the perpetrator (cf. my dissertation for more details of the interviews and group discussions). See also Hatina, "The ʿUlamaʾ and the Cult of Death in Palestine".

[30]   Muhammad Sayyid al-Tantawi, "Wer Unschuldige tötet ist kein Märtyrer. Nach den Attentaten: Eine Erklärung zur Menschlichkeit des Islam", in: *Frankfurter Allgemeine Zeitung* (30.11.2002), 33.

[31]   Cf. David Cook, *Martyrdom in Islam*, New York 2007, 135-172.

ers and other visual (or audio) material portraying the self-sacrificing martyr also function as media for their glorification, and this material is produced, distributed and exploited by these organisations to reach and influence public and private opinions.[32] Moreover, these media, as well as the martyrdom operations themselves, are important in raising the profile of the respective organisation within the contentious rivalry between the different armed groups during the Second Intifada.[33]

The Palestinian *istishhādiyyāt* are part of the media sphere, which consists not only of television and broadcasting programmes or newspapers but also grey literature, Internet publications (i.e. the encomiums) and leaflets – one can also include posters, videos and songs in this category. The latter are mostly produced and distributed by the dispatching organisations. Thus, the media itself and those making use of it, such as the dispatching organisations or the Palestinian Authority (PA), are involved in the creation of discourses on the *istishhādiyyāt* and utilise these women as propagandist objects.[34]

Depending on the intention behind the media depiction of the *istishhādiyyāt*, the women are constructed either as heroic resistance fighters and glorious martyrs, or as obstacles to a prospective peace agreement – yet still considered to be martyrs, or suicidal figures illegitimately attributed the status of martyrs.[35] The gender aspect plays an important role in this context, for Palestine's patriarchal society (the media and the dispatching organisations, both part of this society, are male-dominated and usually male-led) needs to furnish an explanation for those women who, seemingly all of a sudden, became independent and determined their own course of action. Often intertwined with the various explanations are arguments for justification or disapproval. On the one hand, the identity and responsibility of the *istishhādiyyāt* as fearless mothers of the nation and beautiful, pious women sacrificing their lives for society and the Palestinian cause is then accentuated in media depictions: often for the purpose of influencing society at large. On the other hand – also with the intention to direct society's perceptions and opinions – the *istishhādiyyāt* are *de*-legitimised on religious

---

[32] Cf. Helena Lindholm Schulz and Juliane Hammer, *The Palestinian diaspora: Formation of identities and politics of homeland*, London 2003, 121-122 and *The Road to Martyrs' Square. A Journey into the World of the Suicide Bomber*, ed. by Anne Maria Oliver et al., Oxford et al. 2005. This material consists of posters, videos, songs, glorifying texts, photographs as well as social practices such as funerals and funeral processions.

[33] Cf. Joseph Croitoru, *Der Märtyrer als Waffe. Die historischen Wurzeln des Selbstmordattentats*, Munich 2006, 190-192.

[34] Lori Allen, "Martyr bodies in the media: Human rights, aesthetics, and the politics of immediation in the Palestinian intifada", in: *American Ethnologist* 1, 161-180. For the motif of the green birds see also the contribution of Silvia Horsch "Making salvation visible".

[35] The first construction is usually made by the media related to the dispatching organisations, the second construction is often made by the media related to the Palestinian Authority (PA) and the latter construction by newspaper journalists such as al-Quds. See the interviews with journalists in Lisa Franke, *In front of the doors of paradise*, 149-154.

and moral grounds: they cannot be attributed the status of a martyr for the operation is considered to be an act of suicide and, moreover, their action has no moral basis because such attacks only result in even greater oppression by the occupiers.[36]

V. Martyr Posters as Quotidian Icons for Society

Common images that form the background for songs in video clips, illustrations of lyrics and decorating the martyrs' posters are loaded with "classical, religious and national references".[37] This includes direct visual links to the Israeli occupation, such as the footage of Palestinians killed by Israeli soldiers, resisting the occupation and house demolitions. Other images are geographical or of religious sites and edifices – including places which were Palestinian prior to the creation of the state of Israel in 1948 – such as the al-Aqsa Mosque and the Dome of the Rock at the *haram al-sharif* in Jerusalem, which play a decisive role as unifying symbols in past and current political negotiations as well as in the collective memory of the Palestinian people. In addition, maps with the borders of historical Palestine (pre-1948) are featured in the posters. The holy Koran is also pictured on posters and in video clips, often in combination with an illuminating frame or emblazed with a ray of light. The national Palestinian flag, together with flags and symbols of the political faction which has produced the song, video tape, or poster, are also common elements of visual decoration. Furthermore, the posters usually present the photograph of a self-sacrificing martyr in front of a rifle and/or the al-Aqsa Mosque in Jerusalem. Verses from the Koran and other words of praise in Arabic surround the pictures. Green birds are often included, a symbol based on a statement by the Prophet Muḥammad that the martyr's soul is taken to Allāh in the bosom of the green birds of Paradise.[38] Despite this vast visual repertory, the information given in the posters is quite limited – apart from the name of the martyr, the date and place of his/her death/operation, no further details about the portrayed person are included. Moreover, the dead are not termed as being dead but referred to as martyrs who have been martyred by the Israeli occupation or who have committed a martyrdom operation – suicide or death are never mentioned.[39] As for the gendered aspect of the posters, there are no major differences between the portrayal of men and women. They are very similar: both are depicted in civilian or in military

---

[36]　See also Amnesty International, "Middle East" (2002), esp. 22-26.

[37]　Mahmoud Abu Hashhash, "On the Visual Representation of Martyrdom in Palestine", in: *Third Text* 20 (2006), 392.

[38]　Cf. Nasra Hassan, "An Arsenal of Believers: Talking to the Human Bombs", in: *New Yorker* (22.11.2001), 5.

[39]　Abu Hashhash, "On the Visual Representation", 400-401.

uniform, usually with, or even carrying, weapons. The most striking variation for the female figures is whether they wear a headscarf or not.

Visual representations like posters are important because they furnish meaning for a society and the object – hence, iconography is another facet of (public) discourses. The posters are a form of cultural production during a sustained political conflict because they express support for the attacks and the resistance against the Israeli occupation (developed within the particular space of suppression).[40]

After having interviewed the father of Mīrfat Masʿūd,[41] he gave me the glorifying poster of his daughter as a present, which I shall describe here as an example for this category of poster (see fig. 1). Already in the headline the poster clearly claims the martyrdom operation of Mīrfat to have happened under the auspices of Sarāyā al-Quds, the military wing of the movement of Islamic Jihad in Palestine. It is even stated that she, the fighting *istishhādiyya*, is the daughter of Sarāyā al-Quds and that her martyrdom operation will be acknowledged and rewarded by God. Not only her full name – Mīrfat Amīn Masʿūd – is highlighted and written in prominent letters, she is also identified as the perpetrator of the "heroic martyrdom operation" carried out at an Israeli army checkpoint in Bait Ḥānūn on 6 November, 2006. The religious salutation – "peace be upon you" – is positioned next to the salient photograph of Mīrfat. This salutation is on the picture's background, comprising a yellow-orange surface interspersed with rays of light. While this design is probably intended to invoke heaven, when viewed together with the exploding tank this background seems more like a poster advertising an action movie. In the lower transparent part of Mīrfat's photograph, destroyed houses, probably of Bait Ḥānūn, are identifiable. With this picture the poster also communicates the reasons for the operation: the destruction of Bait Ḥānūn, which shall be revenged by attacking the Zionist enemy, a vengeance Sarāyā al-Quds accomplished in form of this martyrdom operation. The impression generated with this arrangement is that the martyr arises directly out of the debris of her destroyed hometown.

The three male hooded and armed fighters are wearing a headband with the emblem and the name of Sarāyā al-Quds in the organisation's colours: yellow letters on black background. One of them is placed behind exploding tanks, out of which military helmets with the Star of David are flying, indicating of course that the tanks belong to the Israeli army. The four smaller sequentially arranged photographs of Mīrfat give the impression of a flipbook or slide show. The topmost and the last portray the *istishhādiyya* with a Kalashnikov directly looking at

---

[40]   This is comparable to some extent to the graffiti of the First Intifada. Cf. Julie Peteet, "The Writing on the Walls: The Graffiti of the Intifada", in: *Cultural Anthropology* 11 (1996), 139-159 and Julie Peteet, "Words as interventions: naming in the Palestine - Israel conflict", in: *Third World Quarterly* 26 (2005), 153-172.

[41]   Mīrfat Masʿūd, an 18 year-old woman from Jabāliyya refugee camp in northern Gaza, carried out her martyrdom operation in Bait Ḥānūn on 6 November, 2006. The al-Quds Brigades claimed responsibility for the attack in which six people were killed.

Fig. 1: glorifying poster of Mirfat Amīn Masʿūd

the viewer (or photographer). In all of these four photos she is wearing a black baseball cap with the name and emblem of the dispatching organisation, together with her black *jilbāb* and black *ḥijāb*, and she is standing in front of a black banner, embroidered with the Islamic statement of belief – *al-shahāda* – written in yellow or golden letters. In the second sequence, Mīrfat is taking aim at someone or something outside of the picture. The third photograph shows her sitting in a chair in front of a desk with the Koran placed on it, holding the weapon in her right hand. Her mouth is open and she is obviously reading from her testament, which was released as a video tape. These scenes and posed moments belong to the standard elements of the glorification of *istishhādiyyūn* and the self-glorification of their dispatching organisations. She shall be honoured, immortalised and remembered by means of this poster. At the same time though, the serious, almost sad, outlook of the young woman stands in stark contrast to the pictorial language of this poster, which has her appear as the female hero of an action movie produced by the organisation in whose name she died.

> Martyrs are the public figures through which the process of legitimisation [of martyrdom operations] takes place and which allows the makers and hangers of posters to act on behalf of the public with unchallenged authority. A sense of collective recognition arises from the political nature of the martyr's death, which gives him or her the new identity of a public figure.[42]

Posters are thus part of visual discourses and are used as a medium by militant resistance organisations to spread their ideologies. Through posters they gain public support, for the posters clearly demonstrate that these organisations are keeping the resistance struggle alive, proven by those who have died under their auspices. Posters help the organisations to announce recurring anniversaries and remind the community of an annual commemoration, which often culminates in a public procession or demonstration (with the majority gathered members of the particular organisation the dead had been affiliated to). Every year on the anniversary of the death of Wafā' Idrīs – 27 January – posters of her are hung on the doors of houses, shops and walls to honour and remember her death which shall not be forgotten.[43] The Palestinian *istishhādiyyāt* are even known beyond Palestine and visual reminders have ensured that these women have entered the collective memory – regardless of the ambivalence they stand for. Public announcements and processions for the *istishhādiyyāt* and *shuhadā'* have another level of meaning:

---

[42] Abu Hashhash, "On the Visual Representation", 399.

[43] "Although one might have the impression that these are exclusively public spaces, it has to be kept in mind, that the shops and walls are often owned by private people. This space is then used as propagandist institution for the purposes of the organisations the portrayed person on the poster was affiliated with. The owners are not asked for permission but their approval is taken for granted. Moreover, spatial divisions as in the public-private dichotomy become blurred – everything is politicised and made use of in the name of the resistance for the Palestinian cause (regardless of the single person's opinion, agreement or disagreement)." Ibid.

they also portray the Israelis, who apparently caused these deaths, as a dominant and cruel force – either directly killing or resulting in the death of the innocent. The symbolic and ritual act of commemorating the dead, who seem to have ascended to the status of national heroes, unites the Palestinians. Gender and factional boundaries are softened as men and women, children and elderly, *Ḥamsāwiyyūn* (members of the Hamas) and *Fatḥāwiyyūn* (members of the Fatah), all participate and mourn the dead.[44]

Moreover, "martyr posters [create] a visual continuity between public and domestic space, mirroring the dual nature of martyrs as social beings. Martyrs [die] because of a collective political situation affecting everyone, but they [are] always also mourned as someone's dear relative or friend."[45] Although the martyr posters are part of the glorification in public space, they also refer to the private realm of personal loss and suffering. Simultaneously, the posters transport the message "that this was a victim of the occupation, who is now remembered and revered by the nation for which his or her life was sacrificed."[46] Again, the nationalist aspect cannot be ignored, bringing politics to the homes, especially because the militant resistance organisations publish their names on the posters claiming the dead to be 'theirs'. At the same time, the personal story of the dead and/or his/her family is spread and dealt with in public through the media – resulting in strangers feeling as if they personally knew the dead. The repetitive visualisation of the faces contributes and reinforces this feeling of personal connection, since the posters are produced in large numbers and remain visible until pasted over by others. The cases of the *istishhādiyyāt* clearly demonstrate how the public is involved in these deaths. Firstly because the *istishhādiyyāt* – according to their testaments and the way they are portrayed – have died for the collective that is Palestinian society; secondly, they are remembered in public and so almost every Palestinian knows their name and personal story.

What is particularly interesting about the way visual commemoration is staged is how the public reacts to these presentations, which are not portraying simply persons (who were alive at the time when the picture was taken) but figures who have been elevated into a transcendent state of glorified heroes/heroines simply through medium of the poster: "[t]hus the posters capture what, in religious terms, is the kind of eternal life of the martyr who is not believed to be dead (in a literal sense)"[47] but to be still alive in Paradise and in memory.

---

[44] Factional boundaries are only crossed if the death has nothing to do with inter-factional rivalries and if the dead person was an important public figure for all Palestinians, regardless of political differences. Cf. Laleh Khalili, *Heroes and Martyrs of Palestine. The Politics of National Commemoration*, Cambridge 2007, 187-190.

[45] Allen, "The Polyvalent Politics of Martyr Commemoration", 115.

[46] Ibid., 114.

[47] Ibid., 117.

The production and consumption of imagery gives an insight into social structures and the ways martyrdom, death and loss have entered everyday life. The disastrous death of the martyr or self-sacrificing martyr with his/her mournful victims is transformed thanks to societal dynamics into a heroic death resulting from a glorious act. The commemoration and re-enactment of the respective death in form of posters, video clips and songs keep the dead alive and memorable for society. As far as this visual material is concerned, we need to keep in mind that images can also be manipulated (as in the photo collages created for the glorifying posters) and/or have a manipulative effect, for instance to encourage support for martyrdom operations or the dispatching organisation, which is blatantly represented with its name and symbol on the posters and photos of the martyrs. Nonetheless, the image itself does not produce relevant information without someone verbalising and giving meaning to the portrayed content and an audience who receives this narration. Again, it is not the photographs, posters or videos *per se* that transfigure the dead into martyrs, but society and social practice, which do so through discursive interaction with the visual material, turning the imagery into a symbol for the struggle and martyrdom.[48] The story is thus the picture in combination with words circling around it, or to put it differently, it is a question of "narrative picturing".[49]

Parts of Palestinian society are thus not content to acquiesce to the banality of the death of the *istishhādiyyāt*. Instead, these women are glorified by all means and trigger public, political, nationalist resistance, factional as well as personal and familial sentiments. The way they died has nothing to do with an ordinary death, nor shall their act fall into oblivion. Hence the women's characters are elevated and glorified, their acts and commitment abstracted beyond mundane death. The visual and audio immortalisation of the *istishhādiyyāt* is present in many places in the West Bank and Gaza, and the business done with *istishhādiyyāt* and other martyr-related documents and indeed products (their pictures are not only featured in videos and on posters but are used on labels and decoration for everyday items) appears to be a form of commercialisation of social and emotional capital.

VI. Conclusion

The *istishhādiyyāt* can be seen as a continuity of the participation of Palestinian women in resistance activities, which has taken place since the earliest struggles against Ottoman rule. However, this participation does not seem to fundamen-

---

48 Cf. Roland Barthes, *Camera lucida: reflections on photography*, New York 1981, where he discusses the relation between photographs/photography and the spectator.

49 Barbara Harrison, "Photographic visions and narrative inquiry", in: *Considering Counter-Narratives. Narrating, resisting, making sense*, ed. by Michael Bamberg et al., Amsterdam et al. 2004, 121.

tally change patriarchal gender relations in Palestinian society. Despite this, the depiction of the *istishhādiyyāt* as female martyrs is unique and their gender and special position is highlighted, especially in those discourses legitimising the acts and commitment of these women. Compared to male martyrs, the femininity of the *istishhādiyyāt* is accentuated. They are elevated into heroic mothers of the nation, lauded as young, beautiful and respected combatants who fight side-by-side with their male companions, brave martyrs who take up arms to fight the occupation instead of remaining passive, a contrast to some of the male political leaders. On the discursive level shifts in gender can be accounted for: namely, when women are declared to actively contribute to the resistance struggle instead of passively remaining in the background. But it is still yet to be proven that these (discursive) developments, initiated by the emergence of the *istishhādiyyāt*, have had a permanent impact on the social sphere – in particular it is not always the case that discourses evoke changes in or influence social realities. The impression one might get from the intensive discussion on the *istishhādiyyāt*, namely that the militant revolution against the occupation deploying martyrdom operations is headed primarily by women, as well as the assumption that this female resistance is being transported from the national and political realm to the more private and/or public space of social interaction, is untenable given my findings and field research. First of all, the small number of *istishhādiyyāt* can by no means indicate the gender of the resistance, let alone make it feminine. Secondly, similar to the First Intifada where the participation of women was much stronger, comprehensive, pronounced and distinct – the women's revolutionary actions and power did not permeate existing social structures. However that may be, it is clear that the awareness and perception of the abilities of women has changed. Indeed, women as active resistance fighters have entered the discursive level, leading to various interpretations. And although the positions taken on this issue vary from vehemently opposed to being in favour, women are talked about and therefore the actions of the *istishhādiyyāt* have had an effect on discourses, debates and perceptions.

As I hope to have shown, the various ways in which the *istishhādiyyāt* have been dealt with depend on the opinion of the respective individual or on the image the particular media tries to transmit. Ideological and manipulative practices on the side of PA-related media as well as those affiliated to the dispatching organisations influence the formation of opinion. Here, religious elements of martyrdom are highlighted and mixed with nationalist elements of resistance. The merging of these notions is essential and frames the background for the glorification of the *istishhādiyyāt*. Other such processes are the posters that portray these women, plastered all over walls and shops. The repeated confrontation with the subject in the form of private discussions, songs, media reports, newspaper articles etc., in sum, to repeatedly see and hear (about) the *istishhādiyyāt*, created an atmosphere of glorification and veneration. Especially the dispatching organisations aimed at controlling society at large by dominantly spreading their opinion on the *istishhādiyyāt*, seeking to garner support and attract followers. Consequently, the *istishhādiyyāt* have been instrumentalised for the resistance struggle as heroic fighters, while for society they are pious martyrs whose death shall not have been in vain.

Global Martyr Practices and Discourses

Entanglements between East and West

Silvia Horsch (Osnabrück)

The so-called "Arab Spring" started with an act of martyrdom that was unexpected to a world public that, for the most part, had grown accustomed to equating "martyrdom" in the context of the Islamic world with suicide bombings. The street vendor Muḥammad Bū ʿAzīzī, who set himself on fire as an act of protest, triggered the first demonstrations that ultimately led to the resign of the Tunisian president. His act was highly acknowledged in Europe where the remembrance of Jan Palach was immediately aroused and is at least partly responsible for the labelling of the events as "spring" (which is somehow ambiguous, since Palach's death marked the end of the Prague Spring).[1] This appreciation is indicated by the wide media coverage as well as the bestowal of the Sakharov Prize for Freedom of Thought by the European Parliament in 2011 to Bū ʿAzīzī, posthumously, along with four activists of the Arab uprisings.

The discourse on martyrdom which accompanies the Arab uprisings – not only in the region but also in the West – provides insights into the mechanisms of "martyr-making" and the significance martyrs may gain not only for their respective societies and movements but on a global scale. The global martyr discourse which emerged is revealing with regard to the relation between "East and West," especially when comparing the current discourse with that of another martyr-type, this time one explicitly marked as "Islamic:" the suicide bomber. This article will scrutinise the circulation and transformation of these two extreme martyrdom practices – self-immolation and suicide bombing – and the discourse about them as well as about the non-violent martyrs of the Iranian (2009) and Arab (2010/2011) uprisings. The focus lies in determining how the relation of religion and the secular can be described in both of the practices and their evolving discourses. There is a tendency, in scientific as well as in popular discourse, to associate self-immolators and non-violent martyrs with the secular while suicide bombers are connected to religion (i.e. Islam). This article will not only try to deconstruct this assumption, but, furthermore, show that martyr figures tend to question the distinction of the secular and the religious. While the martyrs blur the lines, the emerging discourse often aims for a re-arrangement of the order which upholds the central conceptions of religion and the secular.

---

[1] In the Arab public and media the term "Arab revolutions" is mostly used, the term "Arab Spring" was albeit taken over from Western media. For the difficulties of both terms, which include an assessment of the events, see Tariq Ramadan, *The Arab Awakening. Islam and the New Middle East*, London 2012, 2-4.

I. "Global" Martyr Practices and "Local" Martyr Discourses

One aspect shared by the two extreme martyr practices of self-immolation and suicide bombing is that they both have found global diffusion. The "success" of these practices in certain historical situations paved the way for their adoption in other contexts and places. This raises the question of what happens when a practice emerging in a specific socio-political and cultural context is taken up elsewhere and how it is adapted to different local and temporal circumstances.

1. Self-immolation

The already-mentioned death of Jan Palach is an example for a "proliferation" of martyr practices. Ritual self-immolation has been practiced for many centuries in some strands of Mahayana Buddhism and Hinduism, and the practice is also known from the Old Believers during the Great Schism of the Russian Church, when entire villages burned themselves to death in an act considered to be a baptism by fire. In this case, there was already a notion of public protest involved as the Old Believers reacted with the self-immolations to death threats made by the authorities.[2] The most famous incidents of self-immolation in modern times occurred during the Vietnam War in the 1960s when Buddhist monks set themselves on fire to protest against discrimination of Buddhists by the Roman Catholic administration in South Vietnam. Due to this extreme form of protest their cause was noticed on a global level, especially after the death of the monk Thich Quang Duc in 1963. The monk's death was captured in photographs by an American journalist whose record of the event circulated in the world's media. This incident of martyrdom was well-planned and took place at a highly visible location at a busy Saigon intersection. Thich Quang Duc was accompanied by other monks who immediately commented on his death using terms of martyrdom. Using a microphone, one of the monks shouted in Vietnamese and English: "A Buddhist priest burns himself to death. A Buddhist priest becomes a martyr."[3] The act, of which American journalists were informed of in advance, was designed to appeal to the Western public, and politicians in particular, and was highly effective in this respect. As a statement of U.S. Senator Frank Church, a member of the Senate Foreign Relations Committee, shows, it even raised the remembrance of the martyrs of the Christian tradition: "such grisly scenes have not been witnessed since the Christian martyrs marched hand-in-hand into the Roman arenas."[4] The self-immolation of Thich Quang Duc was later considered to be a turning point in the Buddhist crisis and a critical point

---

[2]   Cf. Robert O. Crummey, "Belief and Practice in Russia", in: *Religion and the Early Modern State: Views from China, Russia and the West*, ed. by James D. Tracy et al., Cambridge 2004, 73.

[3]   Howard Jones, *Death of a Generation*, Oxford 2003, 269.

[4]   Ellen J. Hammer, *A Death in November. America in Vietnam 1963*, New York 1987, 145.

in the collapse of the South Vietnamese regime.[5] The great success of this action was partly due to the fact that self-immolation was something new to the Western public. Self-immolations had repeatedly taken place in Vietnam since the 1920s, but no such case has become known in the United States or Europe.[6]

In the following years six American citizens burned themselves in acts of protest against the Vietnam War. The self-immolations of these peace activists were simultaneously a denunciation of the cruel military strategies of the United States which included the use of Napalm.[7] Three of the self-immolators were active members of Christian groups or movements and as such transferred the martyr technique of self-immolation from a Buddhist setting to a Christian one. Among them was 82-year-old Alice Herz, who referred to the self-immolations of the Buddhists monks in her final message. Being a German with Jewish heritage, she was active in Christian-socialists circles, joined the Quakers after immigrating to America[8] and became a member of the Unitarian Church in the last years of her life.[9] Her death is described by fellow Christian-socialist authors and pacifists as martyrdom, a self-sacrifice for the sake of peace and international understanding.[10] Norman Morrison, also a Quaker,[11] and Roger Allan LaPorte, a member of the Catholic Worker Movement, also burned themselves.[12] The latter asked for his reasons before his death answered: "I'm a Catholic Worker. I'm against war, all wars. I did this as a religious action."[13] Just as in the case of Thich Quang Duc, these incidents show how difficult it is to separate religion from politics since political aims and convictions may at the same time be religiously motivated. These martyrs stood at the beginning of the growing anti-war movement in the United States, but their actions obviously failed to have a greater impact since media coverage was scarce due to a political climate that considered such acts unpatriotic. One of Alice Herz's friends complained in a letter: "[...] Alice Herz, whose life was given for the cause of PEACE, was given hardly any space

---

[5]   Seth Jacobs, *Cold War Mandarin. Ngo Dinh Diem and the Origins of America's War in Vietnam, 1950-1963*, Oxford 2006, 149.

[6]   Hammer, *A Death in November*, 146.

[7]   This is explicitly stated in the title of a biography of one of the activists: "Get off your apathy! a biography of Florence Beaumont, who burned herself instead of others! – like phony politicians!" Thomas Michael Dunphy. Hollywood 1968.

[8]   Shingo Shibata, "The life and thought of Alice Herz – for united action between Marxists and Christians", in: *Phoenix. Letters and Documents of Alice Herz. The Thought and Practice of a Modern-day Martyr*, ed. by Shingo Shibata, Amsterdam 1976, 163.

[9]   Hayes B. Jacobs, "The martyrdom of Alice Herz", in: *Phoenix. Letters and Documents of Alice Herz*, 155.

[10] Cf. Shibata, *Phoenix. Letters and Documents of Alice Herz*.

[11] "The Pacifists", in: *Time Magazine*, November 12, 1965. URL: http://www.time.com/time/magazine/article/0,9171,834576,00.html (retrieved 02.05.2012).

[12] A third, George Winne, student of history, had apparently no religious affiliation. The same applies for Florence Beaumont, a mother of two, who burned herself in 1967.

[13] Barbara Tischler, "The Antiwar Movement", in: *A Companion to the Vietnam War*, ed. by Marilyn B. Young et al., Oxford 2002, 386.

at all [in newspapers] and no TV coverage, so that comparatively few people will know of her sacrifice."[14]

Jan Palach, the Czechoslovakian student who burned himself in 1969 to protest against the violent crushing of the Prague Spring, was also aware of the example set by the Vietnamese monks[15] and told one of the physicians who treated him in the days before his death, "In Vietnam it helped."[16] Just as in the case of Bū ʿAzīzī, Palach's act triggered a number of copycat incidents and attempts – even outside Czechoslovakia and Eastern Europe in places like Austria and Argentina –[17] but the political motivations were not always as clear as they were for Palach.[18] In 2003, there was a new series of self-immolations in the Czech Republic, and the first person to self-immolate made an explicit reference to Palach in his farewell letter.[19]

In Asia as well as other parts of the world, self-immolations are still regarded as a means of extreme public protest. This occurs mainly in the context of the Tibetan struggle and endeavours aiming at the foundation of an independent state of Telangana in India,[20] but it can also be observed in Europe and America. From the 1960s to the 2000s, a number of self-immolations occurred for a variety of reasons, including protest against the treatment of homosexuals by the Catholic Church (Alfredo Ormando on January 13, 1998 in Italy) and protest against the U.S. invasion of Iraq (Mark David Ritscher on November 3, 2006 in Chicago). Self-immolations occurred as well in the Middle East prior to 2010: Humā Dārābī protested with her death against the oppression of women by the Iranian regime on February 21, 1994 in Tehran. That time the transgression of the religious verdict against suicide was part of the protest against how the Iranian regime imposed Islamic rules on women.[21] A number of activists of the Kurdistan Workers' Party (PKK), a leftist group fighting for an independent Kurdistan, set fire to themselves in Turkey as well as in different places in Europe from the 1980s to the 2000s. The "successful" death of Muḥammad Bū ʿAzīzī has seemed to trigger a new wave of self-immolation not only in the Arab coun-

---

[14]   Mary Phillips to Shingo Shibata on 28 March 1965, in: *Phoenix. Letters and Documents of Alice Herz*, 8.

[15]   His biographer Jiri Lederer found a number of articles about the self-immolations of the Vietnamese monks in Palachs collection of cuttings from newspapers, Jiri Lederer, *Jan Palach. Ein biographischer Bericht*, Zürich 1982, 60.

[16]   Ibid., 122.

[17]   Levy, *Rowboat to Prague*, New York 1972, 484.

[18]   Lederer, *Jan Palach*, 151-157.

[19]   Rob Cameron, „Seventh self-immolation in less than two months?", in: *Radio Prague*, 29.04.2003. URL: http://www.radio.cz/en/section/curraffrs/seventh-self-immolation-in-less-than-two-months (retrieved 25.04.2012).

[20]   A. R., "Frighteningly common. Self-immolation in India", *The Economist* 26 March 2012, URL: http://www.economist.com/blogs/banyan/2012/03/self-immolation-india (retrieved 29.04.2012).

[21]   For her biography see Parvin Darabi and Romin P. Thomson, *Rage against the veil: the courageous life and death of an Islamic dissident*, New York 1999.

tries but on a global level:[22] In March 2012 there have been reports of a series of more than 26 self-burnings of Tibetans, and in Europe two Italians, including one of Moroccan-descent;[23] and a Greek[24] set themselves on fire in the context of the debt crisis. All three could be rescued. Not all of them have been acknowledged by a community as martyrs, as this necessitates the recognition of a common cause by a significant number of people, and the cases in Europe during the debt crisis are especially ambiguous since these incidents are difficult to differentiate from "ordinary" suicide attempts. However, those who choose this highly visible and spectacular form of suicide often combine it with a message of protest.

As seen, self-immolations take place in different places in diverse cultural and religious settings. Though the act itself may not be affected let alone triggered by religious convictions on the side of its protagonists, as it seems to be the case with both Palach and Bū ʿAzīzī, religion plays a role in the emerging discourse concerning the acts. In both cases martyrdom was clearly acknowledged in the respective societies by the broader public and the (post-revolutionary) political authorities: A square was named after Jan Palach in 1990 as well as several streets not only in the Czech Republic but throughout Europe, the Tunisian post-revolutionary government issued a stamp showing a portrait of Bū ʿAzīzī,[25] and there is a significant number of pop and other cultural references in songs, videos and paintings to both men. A common characteristic of both cases is the blending of religious and national motives. In his eulogy at the funeral of Jan Palach the rector of the Charles University said: "Jan Palach brought to the altar of his home the highest possible sacrifice."[26] But from the religious point of view, from both the Christian and the Islamic perspectives, the difficult question of how to differentiate martyrdom from suicide requires an answer. Religious actors and authorities deal with the question how to react to an act that because of its aims and – in the case of Bū ʿAzīzī – its results is highly appreciable but which also violates certain religious tenets.

---

[22] For self-immolations during the Arab uprisings see the contribution of Farhad Khosrokhavar in this volume. Cf. also the (incomplete) list of political self-immolations in Wikipedia which shows a rise after 2010, URL: http://en.wikipedia.org/wiki/List_of_political_self-immolations (retrieved 14.05.2012).

[23] Palash R. Gosh, "Two Men in Italy Commit Self-Immolation to Protest Financial Pressures," in: *International Business Times*, 30.03.2012, URL: http://www.ibtimes.com/articles/321951/20120330/italy-economic-crisis-self-immolation-austerity.htm (retrieved 01.06.2012).

[24] Teo Kermeliotis, "Austerity drives up suicide rate in debt-ridden Greece," in: *CNN World*, 6. April 2012, URL http://articles.cnn.com/2012-04-06/world/world_europe_greece-austerity-suicide_1_pharmacist-dimitris-christoulas-shot-suicide-note-anti-austerity?_s=PM:EUROPE (retrieved 01.06.2012).

[25] Cf. *International Stamp News*, 16.04.2011, URL: http://www.stampnews.com/stamps/stamps_2011/stamp_1302943586_624352.html (retrieved 04.05.2012).

[26] Levy, *Rowboat to Prague*, 481.

In the case of Jan Palach, there have been symbolic as well as rhetorical gestures, which associated his act with Christian martyrs of the past, both Protestant and Catholic. His body was laid out in the Karolinum next to a statue of Jan Hus, the Czech Catholic Church reformer and national hero who was burned at the stake in 1415.[27] According to one of the physicians who treated him in the days before his death, Palach saw himself as "another Jan Hus, as the second Czech in our history to burn for truth."[28] The Czech Cardinal Josef Beran said in a widely acknowledged speech on Radio Vatican:

> To kill oneself is not human and no one shall follow them in doing it. However, all people shall rather keep in view the great ideal that these people laid their young lives for. This ideal is good and noble in its core – to sacrifice oneself for the benefit of all. […] This shining ideal is like a banner that is handed over.[29]

Pope Paul VI clarified as well that the form of his protest could not be endorsed, but "we can uphold the values that put self-sacrifice and love of others to the supreme test."[30] In a Radio Vatican broadcast two days earlier on January 24, Palach and the Czechoslovak youths who had attempted burning themselves after him were compared to the early Christian martyrs.[31] In a desire to express support for the Czechoslovakian resistance against their common foe of communism, the Vatican rendered affirmation on a rhetorical level although the act itself goes against religious rulings. The appreciation of a martyr's cause, however, is not the same as offering substantial support for it, since the Vatican's Ostpolitik was in fact rather reserved.[32] This epitomises one of the ambiguities of martyr commemoration: The martyrs may sometimes be given honour in order to distract from the fact that the issue itself is not addressed.[33]

---

[27] Cf. Levy, *Rowboat to Prague*, 478. Jan Palach himself entertained great admiration for Jan Hus and Jan Žižka, the general and follower of Jan Hus, as his father did as well. As it seems this admiration has been more for nationalist as for religious reasons, cf. Lederer, *Jan Palach*, 8, 12, 81 f.

[28] Cf. Levy, *Rowboat to Prague*, 478.

[29] "40th anniversary of Jan Palach's self-immolation for freedom", Press Office of the Czech Bishops' Conference, 15 January 2009, URL: http://tisk.cirkev.cz/en/czech-republic/40th-anniversary-of-jan-palach-s-self-immolation-for-freedom/ (retrieved 18.05.2012).

[30] Cf. Levy, *Rowboat to Prague*, 484.

[31] Vatican sources had confirmed that the broadcast "had been directed by the pope's Secretary of State", Vojtech Mastny, *Czechoslovakia: Crisis in World Communism*, New York 1972, 192.

[32] Walter M. Iber, "Die Ostpolitik des Vatikan und der 'Prager Frühling'", in: *Prager Frühling. Das internationale Krisenjahr 1968*, ed. by Stefan Karner et al., Cologne 2008, 515-530.

[33] An example for this is the commemoration of a young Palestinian martyr of the Second Intifada, Muḥammad al-Durra, in a number of Arab countries (with the naming of streets, stamps etc.) all of which keep low profile in the Israeli-Palestinian conflict. Cf. Silvia Horsch, "Muhammad al-Durrah – die Generation der zweiten Intifada", in: *Märtyrer-Porträts. Von Opfertod, Blutzeugen und Heiligen Kriegern*, ed. by Sigrid Weigel, Munich 2007, 294-298.

In the case of Bū ʿAzīzī, the Islamic institutions tried as well to contain the "Werther Effect" as the series of copycat incidents was frequently described. The most important Sunni institution, Al-Azhar-University, issued a fatwa in January 2011 saying that "suicide violates Islam even when it is carried out as a social or political protest."[34] However, some ʿulamāʾ (Islamic scholars), among them the well-known Qatar-based Egyptian scholar Yūsuf al-Qaraḍāwī, found mitigating circumstances. In a statement in his TV talk show *Al-sharīʿa wa-l ḥayāt*, he compared Bū ʿAzīzī to a companion of the prophet who is known for his piety and strong sense of justice: "It's like our master Abū Darr said, 'I wonder why someone who finds no food in his home does not go out and draw his sword [in rebellion] against the people.'"[35] This comparison is as reserved as the one of Jan Palach to the early Christian martyrs, and it only makes apparent the need for religious figures to respond to feelings of the people. It also shows the difficulties of condemning an act which testifies to an absolute readiness to sacrifice for the good of others – at least it is perceived as such. Al-Qaraḍāwī even considered God's forgiveness possible because of the outcome of this act: He called on Muslims "to ask God to forgive this youth for he is the reason for the good in awakening this *umma* [community of believers as well as nation] and in the ignition of this revolution".[36] But al-Qaraḍāwī's stance is an exception, and the ʿulamāʾ were largely univocal in the clear condemnation of such an act. Bū ʿAzīzī and those who followed him are nevertheless hailed as heroes and regarded as *shuhadāʾ* (martyrs) by large parts of the population. His family, however, do not see him in this light and, in fact insisted that it was not deliberate death, but an accident.[37] Even this, however, could make him a "martyr of the next world", *shahīd al-ākhira*: according to a prophetical hadith, which counts the victims of fire, as well as of falling debris, drowning and certain diseases as martyrs.[38]

The number of copycat incidents in the Arabic world declined, however, and there have been no further incidents of self-immolation reported after February 2012. A number of elements account for this, including the missing effect of surprise and the changing nature of protest,[39] but it seems plausible that the public debate on the religious permissibility of such an act and the by and large ex-

---

34   Robert F. Worth, "How a single Match Can Ignite a Revolution", in: *The New York Times*, 21.01.2011, URL: http://www.nytimes.com/2011/01/23/weekinreview/23worth.html?_r=1 &src=twrhp (retrieved 29.04.2012).

35   For a transcript of the program see: *Al-sharīʿa wa-l ḥayāt: jihād al-ẓulm wa wasāʾiluhu* [Shariʿa and live: Jihad against injustice and its means] (16.01.2011), URL: http://www.aljazeera.net/ programs/pages/845aaae4-f6a3-480e-83f9-a81beefdad47 (retrieved 14.05.2012)

36   Ibid.

37   Ulrike Putz, „Was vor Mohammeds Martyrium geschah", *Spiegel online* 23.01.2011, URL: http://www.spiegel.de/politik/ausland/0,1518,740901,00.html (retrieved 14.05. 2012).

38   For the difference between martyrs of this and next world and martyrs of the next world see Kohlberg, Art. "Shahīd", *Encyclopedia of Islam²*, Vol. IX, Leiden 1997, 203-207.

39   As argues Farhad Khosrokhavar in this volume.

plicit opinion of Muslim scholars to the effect that self-immolation is forbidden have had an impact as well.[40]

2. Suicide bombing

If this is true, it poses the question of whether the acceptance of another form of suicide – suicide bombing – contributed in paving the way for the widespread public acknowledgement of self-immolation. Interestingly, Shaykh al-Qaraḍāwī, who found mitigating circumstances for Bū ʿAzīzī, also allows an exception for suicide bombings. *ʿAmaliyāt istishhādiyya,* martyrdom operations as they are called, are vindicated by him and others in the case of the Palestinians as the only option given the military superiority of the Israeli army. According to this strategic argument, there is a justification both the killing of the self and the killing of non-combatants, prohibited in the sharia. Both self-immolation and suicide bombing are in stark conflict with the religious verdict against suicide. The vindication of the latter in terms of military strategy as part of an incumbent jihad cannot conceal the fact, that the protagonists of suicide bombings are not killed by their enemies – as is the case with the classical *shahīd al-maʿraka,* martyr on the battlefield[41] – but kill themselves, although they would not consider this act to be suicide. The affirmation offered for this form of taking one's own life by a number of acknowledged scholars, whom do not rank among the radicals who also affirm the suicide bombings of al-Qaida and similar groups, may well have blurred the Islamic verdict against suicide in other contexts as it implies that suicide *for a cause* may be acceptable.

Suicide bombing is another practice of martyrdom that can be found around the world.[42] As Joseph Croituro has shown, it spread in the 20th century first from the Japanese Kamikaze to secular and later to religiously oriented armed groups in Palestine and Lebanon, to Sri Lanka, where the LTTE first used the explosive belt, and to Turkey as well as other places.[43] The political circumstances

---

[40] E.g. Moroccan students asked about the self-immolation of two fellow country men, emphasised the religious verdict against suicide and considered the hailing of self-immolators as martyrs by the society as wrong. Cf. Laura Pannasch, „Selbstverbrennung als Heldentat?" in: *Zenith online,* 01.02.2012, URL: http://www.zenithonline.de/deutsch/gesellschaft// artikel/selbstverbrennung-als-heldentat-002533/ (retrieved 19.04.2012).

[41] For this figure cf. Silvia Horsch, *Tod im Kampf. Figurationen des Märtyrers in frühen sunnitischen Schriften,* Würzburg 2011.

[42] Suicide bombings and suicide attacks have to be differentiated from one another. The suicide bomber (using an explosive belt, a car carrying explosives or similar devises) causes his or her own death, therefore those who cause the crash of an airplane are considered as suicide bombers, even though they don't use explosives. Suicide attackers undertake attacks which result with almost certainty in themselves being killed, however by others and not by themselves.

[43] Cf. Joseph Croitoru, *Der Märtyrer als Waffe. Die historischen Wurzeln des Selbstmordattentates,* Wien 2003, for the international dissemination of suicide attacks see 209-224.

and the discursive background in the course of this spreading have been very different: The Japanese emperor cult backed by strands of both Shintoism and Buddhism was vital for the Kamikaze pilots.[44] Communist rhetoric accompanied the first suicide attacks of leftist groups in Palestine, the first being the attack of the Japanese Red Army Faction in Lod in 1972, followed in 1974 by attacks of the Popular Front for the Liberation of Palestine-General Command (PFLP-GC), which they claim was the first suicide bombing,[45] and of the Democratic Front for the Liberation of Palestine (DFLP); as well as attacks of the Syrian Social Nationalist Party (SSNP) in Lebanon. Islamist rhetoric began to accompany suicide bombings first with Hizbullah in Lebanon beginning in 1982 and later Hamas and Islamic Jihad in Palestine, which took up the practice in the mid-90s. In the Second Intifada (2001 – 2005) all involved armed wings of Palestinian groups – of the nationalist PLO, the Islamist Hamas and Islamic Jihad, as well as the communist Popular Front for the Liberation of Palestine (PFLP) – carried out suicide bombings, which were not only a means of resistance but also a means for each group to distinguish itself in a rivalry for the most spectacular attack. The LTTE in Sri Lanka, which began using suicide bombings in 1987, is a Marxist-Leninist, nationalist-orientated group fighting for an independent Tamil state. The PKK, again a Marxist-Leninist nationalist-orientated group fighting for an independent Kurdish state, began engaging in suicide bombings in the in the mid-90s. Interestingly, at the same time self-immolations by members of the PKK as forms of public protest took place between the 1980s and the 2000s. After the spectacular suicide attacks of September 11, 2001 and with the rise of Salafi-Jihadist groups, suicide bombings occurred in high numbers in places like Iraq, Pakistan, Afghanistan and elsewhere.[46]

This short overview shows how different the religious and cultural settings are in which suicide attacks and suicide bombings have been and are being used. Not only the suicide techniques themselves but also the modes of its representation and mediation afterwards, which include a martyr's testament, have a long history that started with the Kamikaze of whom pictures, letters and short films were produced.[47] The Palestinian PFLP-GC was the first to call their attackers "suicide squadrons" (*majmuᶜat intiḥāriyya*),[48] a term which was soon established and later changed to "martyrdom operations" (*ᶜamaliyāt istishhādiyya*), when the

---

[44] Cf. Croitoru, *Der Märtyrer als Waffe*, 23-38; as to whether the Kamikaze pilots opted voluntarily for this actions, see 45-49.

[45] Members of the PFLP-GC attacked Kirjiat Schmnona and are said to have blown themselves up together with the hostages. The Israelis deny this claim. Cf. Croitoru, *Der Märtyrer als Waffe*, 81.

[46] For the spread of suicide missions with the rise of Salafi Jihadi ideology see Assaf Moghadam, *The Globalization of Martyrdom. Al Qaeda, Salafi Jihad, and the Diffusion of Suicide Attacks*, Baltimore 2008.

[47] Croitoru, *Der Märtyrer als Waffe*, 83.

[48] Ibid., 82.

Islamist military wings appeared on the scene, which had to bypass the term suicide given the religious verdict against it. In view of the complexity of the contexts, the ubiquitous linking of suicide bombings to Islam requires explanation and will be addressed in the second part of this article.

On one hand, varying religious and cultural backgrounds are relevant for the acceptance or rejection of a certain practice. On the other hand, religious dogma can easily be overridden by the subversive dynamic of martyr events and the martyr cult, which is true for both the self-immolator and the suicide bomber. For the latter the availability of the Islamic concept of the "martyr" who is rewarded in the afterlife and especially the figure of the "martyr on the battlefield" (*shahīd al-maʿraka*) helped frame the act of suicide bombing in the context of jihad and thus rendered it legitimate. There are also strong religious arguments against this device: the tenets against suicide as well as against the killings of non-combatants. The function of religion in the martyr cult is, therefore, twofold: it provides concepts, images and ritual forms on which the martyr cult draws, and at the same time religious arguments can be used for a critique of illegitimate martyrdom.

There are other decisive factors regarding the effect of "martyr events" which are connected to the specific historical time and place in which they occurred. There have been, for example, several other incidents of self-immolation in history, which failed to garner lasting global attention.[49] This poses the question of what exactly makes some deaths "successful" in the sense that they are considered to be martyrdom by a larger part of society and able to trigger certain effects while other incidents prove futile insofar as they are not recognised as martyrdom – even in some cases where achieving this recognition was the explicit intention of the person who chose to commit suicide. One the most important factors is, arguably, to attract the public's attention, which in modern times means attracting media coverage.

II. Global Martyr Discourses

1. Global media and global reactions

The most recent incidents of martyrdom initially were not perceived by a greater public via mass media but via social media on the Internet. Facebook and Twitter not only played a crucial role in the Arab uprisings but were also involved in the Iranian election protests in 2009/2010. The most prominent martyr of these protests was Nidā Āqā-Sulṭān. Her death took place in the first days of the Ira-

---

[49]   Cf. e.g. the case of Ryszard Siwiec, who set himself alight in Warsaw during a national festival on September 8, 1968 at a stadium just four months before Jan Palach. He protested with his act against Poland's participation in the invasion of Czechoslovakia. The authorities were able to keep this incident unknown until 1989.

nian demonstrations and became a focal point of protests. She was shot in the chest during a demonstration in Tehran in June 2009. Her death was captured on video and broadcasted over the internet. It was described as "probably the most widely witnessed death in human history,"[50] – though this seems to be exaggerated considering the assassination of then U.S. President John Kennedy, which was also captured on film and could be seen on television.

Another victim of security forces was Khālid Saʿīd in Egypt, who was beaten to death by plainclothes security officers in June 2010 in Alexandria. His family released a photo of his disfigured face on the internet, and it circulated widely online. Later the well-known Facebook site "We are all Khalid Said" was established, which played an important role in organizing the demonstrations since January 2011. The process of identification and the unifying force of such martyrs is best expressed in the slogan "We are all Khalid Said" and "We are all Neda," which is the name of one of the websites created for Nidā Āqā-Sulṭān.[51] Pictures of the martyrs play a crucial role in the function of a martyr as a unifying symbol. The urgent need for photographs has problematic aspects as shown by the Nidā case: The picture of another woman, Nidā Sulṭānī, was initially published worldwide as the picture of the martyr Nidā. All attempts to regain power over her own image were to no avail as mass media used the incorrect picture even after the mistaken identity was known.[52]

There have been many deaths resulting from attacks on demonstrators both in Iran and Egypt, but these two became symbols of the uprisings not only in Iran and Egypt but also on a global level. Contrary to the suicide bombers, this type of martyr, the victim of persecution by authoritarian states, also appeals to a Western audience. This includes not only the worldwide Facebook and Twitter communities, but institutions like the Queens College in Oxford, which established a Neda Agha-Soltan Graduate Scholarship, the newspaper *The Times,* which nominated Nidā as "Person of the Year 2009", and Germany's Friedrich-Ebert-Stiftung which posthumously awarded Khālid Saʿīd its human rights award.[53] There is an even greater number of artistic references to Nidā and Khālid, of which one example is connected to the bestowal of the human rights

---

[50] Krista Mahr, "Neda Agha-Soltan," in: *The Time,* 08.12.2009 URL: http://www.time.com/time/specials/packages/article/0,28804,1945379_1944701_1944705,00.html (retrieved 29.05.2012).

[51] http://weareallneda.com/ (retrieved 15.04.2012).

[52] Nidā Sulṭānī ultimately had to leave Iran and seek asylum in Germany due to pressure from Iranian authorities who wanted to use her in order to present Nidā's martyrdom as a fictitious event. Cf. David Schraven, "Die falsche Tote. Das zweite Leben der Neda Soltani," in: *Sueddeutsche Zeitung* 05.02.2010, URL: http://www.sueddeutsche.de/politik/das-zweite-leben-der-neda-soltani-die-falsche-tote-1.68172 (retrieved 03.05.2012).

[53] Daniel Roters: "Khaled Saeed: Wenn die Welt zusammenrückt," Goethe Institut: *Blog Transit* 27.09.2011, URL: http://blog.goethe.de/transit/archives/277-Khaled-Saeed-Wenn-die-Welt-zusammenrueckt.html (retrieved 02.05.2012).

Fig. 1: Andreas von Chrzanowski's mural of Khālid Saʿīd

award: a martyr mural by the German artist Andreas von Chrzanowski was presented on parts of the Berlin Wall [fig. 1]. The commemoration of the Egyptian
martyr is thus linked to the recollection of Germany's own recent history.

Gregg Chadwick, an American artist, painted a portrait of Nidā [54] as did German artist and actor Armin Müller-Stahl,[55] the American sculptor Paula Slater
made two bronze sculptures of Nidā naming them the "angel of freedom",[56] an
epithet which was used for Nidā in Iran during the demonstrations (*fereshteh
āzādī*). Another American artist, Tim O'Brien, made a portrait of Nidā, around
which her family assembled during a mourning ceremony in Tehran.[57]

---

[54] The picture can be seen in the internet: "Arts showcase for Iran", URL: http://speak4iran.
wordpress.com/category/art/gregg-chadwick/ (retrieved 02.05.2012).

[55] Mathias Raabe, "Bilder eines Schauspielers. Ausstellung von Armin Mueller-Stahl," in: *Berli-
ner Zeitung* 09.03.2012, URL: http://www.berliner-zeitung.de/berlin/ausstellung-von-armin-
mueller-stahl-bilder-eines-schauspielers,10809148,11803806.html (retrieved 02.05.2012).

[56] The sculpture can be seen on Paula Slater's website, URL: http://www.paulaslater.com/
NedaPortraitSculpture.htm (retrieved 02.05.2012).

[57] On O'Brien's website one can find a video of this scene as well as the painting, URL: http://
www.drawger.com/tonka/index.php?section=articles&article_id=8147 (retrieved 02.05.2012).

Fig. 2: Mural of the martyr Tāriq ʿAbd al-Laṭīf by the artist Ganzeer in Cairo

Khālid and Nidā met many requirements of an ideal martyr. They were both young and attractive and in both cases photos clearly depicted the sharp contrast between the beautiful living and the disfigured dead, thereby underlining their innocence and denouncing the cruelty of the respective regimes. The artistic paintings of them – mostly portraits based on the published photos – shown both in the East and in the West and even wandering from America to Iran – evoke the impression of a unitary, global commemoration of martyrs. The picture of Khālid Saʿīd on the Berlin Wall could well have been taken from a Palestinian wall showing the portrait of a victim of an Israeli military attack.[58] Furthermore, the commemoration of the martyrs of the Arab uprisings has at times taken on deliberately global forms. In Egypt, a pop-art form of martyr commemoration has evolved and resulted in an increase in street arts accompanying the uprisings [see fig. 2]. Mural graffities of Khālid Saʿīd can be found throughout Egyptian cities, and on public buildings they are frequently removed. The form of martyr graffiti is perhaps best known from the ubiquitous Che Guevara graffiti, which can also be found in the Arab world.

Are these global forms of martyr commemoration a sign of humankind coming together under a set of shared values that transcend religious and cultural barriers? One commentator remarking on the Friedrich-Ebert-Stiftung's bestowal of the human rights award to Khālid Saʿīd perceived this event as the world

---

[58]   Consider e.g. fig. 3 in the article by Angelika Neuwirth in this volume.

Fig. 3: Tim O'Brien: "Eyes" (2009, detail);   Fig. 4: Follower of Perugino: "Saint Sebas-
                                                             tian" (around 1500, detail)

"closing ranks".[59] However the universal martyr cult – if it exists – at times shows a distinctive Christian grounding: Rhetoric and iconographic forms are involved in the commemoration and veneration of these martyrs that are familiar to the Christian tradition. This becomes visible when comparing one slightly altered portrait of Nidā to well-known paintings of the martyr Sebastian and the Ecce Homo Motive (see fig 3 and 4).[60] The similar head posture and the line of sight appear only after rotating and mirroring the painting, but the faint halo may indicate that Nidā is included in "our" martyr tradition. The allusion to the Christian martyr culture is therefore not an interpretation of the event in terms of a Christian martyrology, but a gesture of Nidā's affiliation to the Western tradition whose values – for which Nidā apparently died – are often held to be secularised Christian principles.

Perhaps this comparison of images visualises a line of thought that underlies much of the Western assessment of Iranian and Arab martyrs. They are non-violent, they are modern – and therefore they are less Islamic and more like "us".

The deliberately modern forms of protests, namely the non-violent resistance tactics inspired by the American political scientist Gene Sharp, the use of social media and global forms of (pop) art, and – most importantly – the fact that demonstrators related to "our" values, including freedom and democracy, are behind

---

[59] Daniel Roters, "Khaled Saeed: Wenn die Welt zusammenrückt," Goethe Institut: *Blog Transit* 27.092011, URL: http://blog.goethe.de/transit/archives/277-Khaled-Saeed-Wenn-die-Welt-zu sammenrueckt.html (retrieved 02.05.2012).

[60] The painting of Nidā has been rotated and mirrored, for the original see the artist's website: http://www.drawger.com/tonka/index.php?section=articles&article_id=8147 (retrieved 02.05.2012).

the public Western approval of both of the Iranian protests and the Arab uprisings. This is particularly applicable to the seemingly non-violent uprisings as there has been considerably less sympathy for revolutionaries in Libya and Syria, despite the fact that protesters in those two countries had similar concerns as those that led to uprisings in Egypt and Tunisia. The mentioned observations led many to the conclusion that both movements were "secular" and Western commentators on the Arab and the Iranian uprisings mostly insisted on a framework of secularists against Islamists. The veneration of "secular" martyrs fits into the narrative of a secular revolution. The fact that Nidā studied Islamic theology as well as philosophy was often omitted in favour of descriptions of her as a student only of philosophy,[61] her interest in music and classical instruments like violin and piano was stressed, as well as – somewhat surprisingly – her lack of interest in politics. Described in this way she appears similar to any Western youth – non-political, interested in music and travelling. This view – regardless of its veracity – matches the general perception of the Iranian protests as secular, despite the fact that major protagonists of the so-called Green Revolution were religious leaders.

Politics is deeply involved in the commemoration of martyrs, especially when official institutions take part. This becomes abundantly clear when considering the martyrs who failed to gain acknowledgement on a wider level. The afore mentioned six American self-immolators during the Vietnam War, as well as the one who protested the US invasion of Iraq are seen as martyrs only in the eyes of the peace movement. There has failed to be a wider acknowledgement of their sacrifice, and one of the reasons for this was the scarce media coverage they received (v.s.). The same is true for Rachel Corrie, an American peace activist and member of the International Solidarity Movement, who was killed in Gaza in 2003 while trying to block an armoured Israeli bulldozer, which ultimately ran over her. She was and still is hailed as a martyr (*shahīda*) in Palestine and globally in circles that engage on behalf of the Palestinians. Many songs have been dedicated to her – mostly by leftist and activist singers – and she has been the subject of a theatre play, a film and several books.[62] But there has not been coverage of her in Western mainstream media to a degree comparable with the attention paid to Bū ʿAzīzī or Nidā, let alone institutional acknowledgement of her act. Again, she is young, pictures showing her living and dead circulate on the internet, she acted non-violently and promoted freedom and justice – but her commemoration in the West remains restricted to a narrow part of the society. She is one of "us" but she died for "them". This incident shows that a martyr's commemoration need not only share a high degree of the often political aims for which the martyr died

---

[61] E.g. in the *Time's* naming her one of the ten most important people of the year 2009: Krista Mahr, "Neda Agha-Soltan," in: *Time*, 08.12.2009 URL: http://www.time.com/time/specials/packages/article/0,28804,1945379_1944701_1944705,00.html (retrieved 29.05.2012).

[62] For all these examples see the Wikipedia page on Rachel Corrie: URL: http://en.wikipedia.org/wiki/Rachel_Corrie (retrieved 19.05.2012).

or is supposed to have died but must also receive an influential amount of media coverage. Given the interdependence of mass media and politics, this critical amount of media attention will only be reached if the martyr fits into a particular political agenda. Not only was the Western non-acknowledgement of Rachel Corrie politically motivated due to the nature of the Israeli-Palestinian conflict and the possible negative impact on relations with Israel, but her being hailed as a martyr by the Palestinians was also politically motivated as they were keenly aware that the death of an American citizen could attract the world's attention to the deaths of Palestinians.[63] The decision of whether martyrs are to be given coverage and awarded titles and prizes or will receive only short and superficial international attention – if they receive any at all – is a form of necropolitics. A comparison of the reactions to martyrs like Nidā Āqā-Sulṭān and Khālid Saʿīd to those like Rachel Corrie reveals the fact that the features of the martyr, such as courage, non-violence and adherence to certain values, are only part of the reasons why he or she is commemorated.

2. Our martyrs and theirs: self-immolators and suicide bombers

The self-immolation of Bū ʿAzīzī – perceived as a reprise of Jan Palach's death and thereby connected to European history – was immediately intelligible for the "Western mind". The supposed reasons for his act – poverty, desperation, and humiliation among them – were discussed at length and made his act understandable on a global scale. Reports relating that parts of the story were exaggerated or even invented are mostly neglected.[64] Exactly the opposite is the case with suicide bombers. Although they may address at least partly similar grievances, such as humiliation and injustice, and express political issues, these aspects are not seriously considered. Instead, "Islamic" motives, the reward for martyrs in paradise and most prominently the virgins awaiting them therein, are mainly considered to form the basis of their motivation. It is therefore revealing to see the prominent role played by the legend of the Assassins even in scholarly studies on suicide bombings.[65] The legend is cited and linked to the acts of suicide bombings in order to create an "Islamic tradition" of suicidal attacks. Not

---

[63] "'Her death serves me more than it served her,' said one activist at a Hamas funeral [...]. 'Going in front of the tanks was heroic. Her death will bring more attention than the other 2,000 martyrs.'", Sandra Jordan, "Making of a martyr", in: *The Observer*, 23.03.2003, URL: http://www.guardian.co.uk/world/2003/mar/23/internationaleducationnews.students (retrieved 19.05.2012).

[64] For such a report see Mary Boland, "Death of Arab Spring 'martyr' which led to uprisings may not be all it seems", in: *The Irish Times* 25.11.2011, URL: http://www.irishtimes.com/newspaper/world/2011/1125/1224308109672.html (retrieved 19.05.2012).

[65] Cf. Claudia Brunner, "Assassins, Virgins, Scholars. Epistemologies and Geopolitics in Scholarly Knowledge on Suicide", in: *Gender, Agency and Political Violence* ed. by Linda Ahåll et al., Houndmills 2012, 132-147.

only is this legend by far not as prominent in the Middle East as it is in Europe, where it was invented, the Nizārīs, the historical name for those who figure as Assassins in European literature, as a Shiite sect are the detested enemies of true Islam in the eyes of the Sunni jihadists. Nevertheless, in order to understand the events this legend is preferred by many commentators to anything the protagonists themselves may say or have said. Suicide bombings by Muslim protagonists are thus linked to Islam as the *cause*, detached from any political, social or other factors that require scrutinisation.

As Brunner has shown, the historicisation of suicide attacks underwent a shift especially after the events of September 11, 2001.[66] Some historic examples, like the Japanese Kamikaze, disappeared from comparative works on suicide attacks while others were generalised: "We can identify an increasing trend of culturalisation based on privileged interest in one category that experienced a renaissance which it had almost lost during the Cold War: 'Islam'."[67] Furthermore, it is not only the missing Islam-factor that is responsible for the marginalisation of the Japanese Kamikaze, but also the fact that they constituted part of a regular army, which makes the category of suicide attackers much more comparable to European history as there were intentions by some Nazis to co-opt the Japanese military's suicide tactics and weapons-technology experiments at the end of the Second World War.[68] To include such examples in the consideration of suicide bombings shifts the line of comparison, so that it no longer runs along the line rational vs. irrational or religious but along one acting in the framework and with the legitimisation of a nation-state vs. the other acting as partisans and therefore without legitimisation.[69]

Whereas the martyrdom of Bū ʿAzīzī and his followers is considered to be secular because no religious discourse accompanies it – at least not on the part of the self-immolators themselves – the martyrdom of the suicide bombers is considered to be religious because the most obvious religious imaginary, especially

---

[66] Brunner identifies historicisation as one of the modi of occidental self-reassurance in the construction of the epistemic object "suicide bombing" the others being pathologisation, (ir-)rationalisation and sexualisation, cf. Claudia Brunner, *Wissensobjekt Selbstmordattentat. Epistemische Gewalt und okzidentalistische Selbstvergewisserung in der Terrorismusforschung*, Wiesbaden 2011, 220-340.

[67] Claudia Brunner, "Assassins, Virgins, Scholars", 143. This assessment is for the scholarly knowledge production in terrorism research, in general discourse it might well be even more unidimensional.

[68] Cf. Croitoru, *Der Märtyrer als Waffe*, 55-70.

[69] As Talal Asad has argued with respect to the notion of suicide bombings as terrorism, there is no qualitative difference on the side of the victims between the terror caused by a suicide bomber and the terror caused by the bombing of civilian areas, as it is regularly the case in modern warfare. The two different categories of "warfare" and "terrorism", which legitimate the first and de-legitimate the latter, "are constituted according to different logical criteria, the one taking it primary sense from the question of legality and the other from feelings of vulnerability and fear of social disorder, and [...] they are not therefore mutually exclusive." Talal Asad, *On Suicide Bombing*, New York 2007, 39.

aspects that relate to the hereafter, is given precedence over the very earthly, political arguments which are also presented. When, for example, the case of al-Qaida politics is considered, attention is restricted to phrases of the "worldwide caliphate" – which remains very nebulous – and assessed as illegitimate mingling of politics and religion, whereas concrete accusations, such as those of the American backing of the Saudi regime and the United Nations sanctions on Iraq that resulted in the death of more than a million children, are most often ignored.

Upon closer inspection, the reason for the Western admiration of Bū ʿAzīzī and peaceful protesters in general is only partly due to their non-violence. By the same token, the Western detestation of the suicide bombers is only partly due to their violence. Part of the difference is also that al-Qaida addressed the West, "us", as its enemy whereas the protests of the Arab and Iranian uprisings were not directed against the West as a geopolitical (post)colonial power, but against the protesters' own regimes and at the same time allowed the admirers of the protests to support a popular movement while often remaining silent about previous Western backing of the dictators. Another reason for the discrepancy in perception is the filter of media coverage: Whereas in the case of al-Qaida the public mainly hears those arguments that can most clearly identified as "religious" and thereby irrational, the peaceful protesters in the Middle East are represented as secular insofar as most of the many references to Islam are omitted.

One of the martyr stories popular in Egypt and the Arab world, which is not told in the West, is the story of the student ʿAbd al-Karīm. Ṣafwat Ḥijāzī, one of the Muslim Brotherhood's organisers of the protests on Tahrir Square, told this story several times in Arabic television channels, including Al-Jazeera:[70] During one of the clashes with security forces who shot the demonstrators with live ammunition while they answered with stones, he spoke with a young man, ʿAbd al-Karīm, whom he met only the day before. ʿAbd al-Karīm asked him whether those killed in these clashes would be martyrs and Ḥijāzī replied that would be the case. Asked for evidence in the sources Ḥijāzī cited a prophetical hadith: "The master of martyrs is Ḥamza [one of the prophet's uncles who was killed in one of the first battles of the Muslims] and the one who stands up before the unjust ruler and advises him so that he [the ruler] kills him."[71] ʿAbd al-Karīm asked him to greet Ḥamza for him in case he should be killed first, and Ḥijāzī said the same to him. Immediately afterwards ʿAbd al-Karīm was shot and killed by a bullet to the head shot by one of the snipers. After wiping away the blood from his face, Ḥijāzī realised the smell of musk emanating from the blood, which was

---

[70]   An extract of the interview with Ṣafwat Ḥijāzī can be seen on *YouTube*: http://www.youtube.com/watch?v=O5ECx90Ir1k&feature=related (retrieved 20.05.2012). For glorifying videos of his death see my article in this volume "Making salvation visible".

[71]   The actual text reads not "ruler" but "*imām*". Al-Ḥākim, *Al-Mustadrak ʿalā al-ṣaḥīḥain*, Vol. 2, No 4884/482.

also noticed by a Christian demonstrator, who was part of a group of Christian youth who had protected the Muslims' prayer earlier in the day. It was only afterwards that Ḥijāzī came to learn that ʿAbd al-Karīm was also a member of the Muslim Brotherhood.[72]

As any martyr story from the Tahrir Square – and elsewhere – this account aims at the commemoration of those who died for the fight against injustice and who shall not be forgotten and betrayed with a failing of the revolutions. Furthermore, it serves the image of the Muslim Brotherhood by stressing the sacrifices of its members and their engagement for the Egyptian people, which, of course, is designed to increase their influence among the public.

Narratives like these are also part of the story of the Arab uprisings which have to be considered in order to get a more complete image of events. The fact that they are omitted in Western observation illustrates how the West wants to see the East to develop: as an honest follower on the path of progress which means to leave behind "unenlightened" forms of religion. Whereas in the case of suicide bombers the emphasis on Islamic references is part of the abhorrence which they evoke, the downplaying of a connection to Islam is a precondition for sympathy for this new kind of martyr. They are like "us" now because they learned the lessons of Western democracy and Western values. If this is the assumption that underlies most of the Western commentaries on the events of the uprisings, the rejoicing about the coming-together of the world, of which the shared commemoration of martyr figures can be seen as an expression, is to be put into question. It seems that it is only for this prize that the other "ceased to be Muslim",[73] or in more general terms ceased to be religious, that the martyr is no longer the other. In her article "The Martyrs of the Revolution" journalist Charlotte Wiedemann stated: "When they attempt to grasp the role of religion in the Arab uprisings, non-Muslim observers often fail because of their tendency to see things in black and white: if religion does not show itself to be a protagonist, then the movement must be secular."[74]

Caught in the dichotomy between religious and secular, the fact that Islamic organisations did not play a role – at least not at the beginning – is seen as a proof of the "secularness" of the revolts. But the established secular political parties and organisations, such as the Wafd party, did not play a role either, a fact which was not in turn seen as a proof for the "religiousness" of the protests. The Egyptian blogosphere, which stood at the beginning of the uprisings, however was able to engender "a political language free from the problematic of seculari-

---

[72] A transcript of the account of Ṣafwat Ḥijāzī can be found at the website of the Muslim Scholar Ḥusayn ʿĀmir: http://housseinamer.net/index.php/2010-01-22-19-38-31/792-2011-05-18-10-12-42 (retrieved 20.05.2012).

[73] Tariq Ramadan, *The Arab Awakening*, 12.

[74] Charlotte Wiedeman, "The Martyrs of the Revolution. Religion in the Arab Spring", In: *Qantara* 23.08.2011, URL: http://en.qantara.de/The-Martyrs-of-the-Revolution/17005c174 90i1p219/ (retrieved 19.05.2012).

sation vs. fundamentalism that had governed so much of political discourse in the Middle East and elsewhere" as Charles Hirschkind noticed. They could build on a process of joint activism of secular leftist organisations and Islamist ones in the recent years.[75] On a personal level, most of the protagonists of the first hour would certainly describe themselves as Muslims and a number of them explicitly related to Islamic references. It was, for example, rarely reported in Western media that Asmāʾ Makhfūẓ, a founding member of the Movement of the 6th of April, an awardee of the Sakharov Prize for Freedom of Thought by the European Parliament (along with Bū ʿAzīzī and others), quoted the Koran in her famous YouTube video that prompted thousands to join the first major protest on January 25 in Tahrir Square with the verse: "It is because God would never change His favour that He conferred on a people until they changed what was within themselves" (8:55).[76]

The framing of the uprisings as a movement that began in a secular nature and was later "hijacked" by Islamist organisations is related to the preconception of Islam and democracy being at odds and the perception of Islam being a "political religion", which reduces Islam to Islamism (or political Islam) as represented by the Muslim Brotherhood and fails to acknowledge that individual Muslims may see their political activism in accordance with requirements they find in their religion.

The opposed reactions to the two martyr models of the suicide bomber and the self-immolator are telling with regard to the mechanisms with which the "secular West" upholds its paradigms in embracing the one martyr and rejecting the other. Instead of arranging the actors – and with them the martyrs – according to a paradigm that puts the religious in opposition to the secular, the examples of these martyr-figures can be taken as an invitation to rethink this opposition. In fact, the role of martyrs reveals that religious and secular aspects are difficult to differentiate. As the examples have shown, the martyr undermines the antagonism of the sacred and profane, the division between religion and politics, and the demarcation of modern and pre-modern, all of which belong to the binary oppositions which organise modern secular discourse.

---

[75] Charles Hirschkind, "The road to Tahrir. Uprising in Egypt", *The immanent frame. Secularism, religion, and the public sphere* 9 February 2011, URL: http://blogs.ssrc.org/tif/2011/02/09/the-road-to-tahrir/ (retrieved 31.05.2012).

[76] Whereas Islamic references are often omitted, Islamist references are even more difficult to find. An example is the representation of Tawakkul Karmān, who won the Peace Nobel Price in 2011. It was hardly ever related in Western media that she is a member of the Muslim Brotherhood. The irony that Tawakkul Karmān and Asmāʾ Makhfūẓ, who both wear the Islamic head-covering, were awarded in Europe, where at the same time in several nations restrictions against Islamic dress codes were discussed and introduced in the name of freedom and women's rights, is also rarely mentioned.

Picture Credits

[Dehghani]

Fig. 1:   media.photobucket.com

[Neuwirth]

Fig. 1:   Eric Butel, "Martyre et sainteté dans la literature de guerre Iran-
                     Irak (1980-1988)", in: *Saints et héros du Moyen-Orient contempo-
                     rain*, ed. by C. Mayeur-Jaouen, Paris 2003, 301-318.
Fig. 2   Elias Sanbar, *Les Palestiniens: La photographie d'une terre et de son
                     peuple de 1839 à nos jours*, Paris 2004.

[Palizban]

Fig. 1, 2, and 4: Photos by Meysam Karimpour and Foad Khaknejad

[Bombardier]

Fig. 1-4:   Postcard published by the artistic centre of the Islamic Propa-
                     ganda Organisation

[Horsch]

Fig. 1 and 2:   Al-Sahab, "Winds of Paradise", source: archive.org
Fig. 3:   "Shaheed in Chechenya", source: youtube.com
Fig. 4:   Inspire, fall 1431/2010, 69.

[Franke]

Fig. 1:   Poster provided by Lisa Franke

[Horsch]

Fig. 1:   Friedrich-Ebert-Stiftung, www.fes.de (Photo: Joel Sames)
Fig. 2:   Ganzeer
Fig. 3:   Tim O'Brien, drawger.com
Fig. 4:   Joseph Antenucci Becherer, *Pietro Perugino: Master of the Italian
                     Renaissance*. Rizzoli, New York 1997.

EX ORIENTE LUX
Rezeptionen und Exegesen
als Traditionskritik

ISSN 1863-9348

Herausgegeben von
Eli Bar-Chen – Almut Sh. Bruckstein – Navid Kermani
Angelika Neuwirth – Andreas Pflitsch – Martin Tamcke

Eine stets aktualisierte Liste der in dieser Reihe erscheinenden Titel finden Sie auf unserer Homepage http://www.ergon-verlag.de

Band 1
Amirpur, Katajun
Die Entpolitisierung des Islam
ʿAbdolkarim Sorūšs Denken und Wirkung
in der Islamischen Republik Iran
(vergriffen) 978-3-89913-267-0

Band 2
Sinai, Nicolai
Menschliche oder göttliche Weisheit?
Zum Gegensatz von philosophischem und
religiösem Lebensideal bei al-Ghazali und
Yehuda ha-Levi
2003. 115 S. Kt. € 26,00 978-3-89913-312-7

Band 3
Gumpert, Gregor
Lust an der Tora
Lektüren des ersten Psalms im
20. Jahrhundert
2004. 181 S. Kt. € 28,00 978-3-89913-331-8

Band 4
Hasselhoff, Görge K. – Fraisse, Otfried (Eds.)
Moses Maimonides (1138-1204)
His Religious, Scientific, and Philosophical
Wirkungsgeschichte in Different Cultural
Contexts
2004. 634 S. 4 S/w-Abb. Kt.
€ 68,00 978-3-89913-333-2

Band 5
Horsch, Silvia
Rationalität und Toleranz
Lessings Auseinandersetzung mit dem
Islam
2004. 136 S. Kt. € 19,00 978-3-89913-376-9

Band 6
Botros, Atef (Hrsg.)
Der Nahe Osten – Ein Teil Europas
Reflektionen zu Raum- und Kulturkonzep-
tionen im modernen Nahen Osten
2006. VIII/324 S. Kt.
€ 42,00 978-3-89913-476-6

Band 7
Bar-Chen, Eli
Weder Asiaten noch Orientalen
Internationale jüdische Organisationen
und die Europäisierung „rückständiger"
Juden
2005. 180 S. Kt. € 28,00 978-3-89913-477-3

Band 8
*Hartwig, Dirk – Homolka, Walter –
Marx, Michael J. – Neuwirth, Angelika (Hrsg.)*
„Im vollen Licht der Geschichte"
Die Wissenschaft des Judentums und die
Anfänge der kritischen Koranforschung
2008. 299 S. Kt. € 38,00 978-3-89913-478-0

Band 9
Kamil, Omar
Arabische Juden in Israel
Geschichte und Ideologie von Ben Gurion
bis Ovadia Yosef
2008. XII/345 S. Kt.
€ 45,00 978-3-89913-633-3

Band 10
Dressel, Diana
Bühne der Geschichte
Der Wandel lokaler Dramen in Palästina
und Israel
2010. 330 S. Kt.
€ 42,00 978-3-89913-749-1

ERGON VERLAG · WÜRZBURG

EX ORIENTE LUX
Rezeptionen und Exegesen
als Traditionskritik

ISSN 1863-9348

Herausgegeben von
Eli Bar-Chen – Almut Sh. Bruckstein – Navid Kermani
Angelika Neuwirth – Andreas Pflitsch – Martin Tamcke

Band 11
Horsch-Al Saad, Silvia
Tod im Kampf
Figurationen des Märtyrers in frühen
sunnitischen Schriften
2011. 292 S. 3 S/w-Abb. Kt.
€ 38,00 978-3-89913-841-2

Band 12
Pflitsch, Andreas
Zweierlei Barbarei
Überlegungen zur Kultur, Moderne und
Authentizität im Dreieck zwischen Europa,
Russland und arabischem Nahen Osten
2012. 309 S. 27 S/w-Abb. Kt.
€ 38,00 978-3-89913-685-2

Band 13
Jonker, Gerdien
Im Spiegelkabinett
Europäische Wahrnehmungen
von Muslimen, Heiden und Juden
(1700-2010)
2013. 194 S. 8 Abb. Fb.
€ 32,00 978-3-89913-962-4

Band 14
Dehghani, Sasha –Horsch, Silvia (Eds.)
Martyrdom in the Modern Middle East
2014. 225 S. 20 S/w-Abb. Kt.
€ 37,00 978-3-95650-030-5

ERGON VERLAG · WÜRZBURG